THE GLASSHOUSE

THE JOHN
GLASSHOUSE HIX

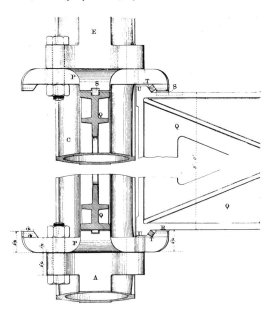

CONTENTS

INTRODUCTION

MY fascination with glasshouses first started in 1968 when I was teaching at Cambridge and my students brought my attention to some interesting historical material. I discovered that solar heating, using glass and natural methods of environmental control, had its origins in the seventeenth century when people had first wanted to nurture tropical plants brought home by explorers in cold climates. If the gardener could adapt to a sudden drop in temperature by moving closer to the fire, his plants could not. Consequently gardeners, through trial and error, and the application of innovative techniques, developed glasshouses in exquisite forms; the heating equipment that they advanced to protect the hard won exotics was far more sophisticated than that of any appliance in domestic use at that time.

I WAS haunted by the veracity of Reyner Banham's statement in *The Architecture of the Well-Tempered Environment*:

> *An intelligent commercial glasshouse operator judiciously metering temperature, moisture and carbon dioxide levels … has more environmental knowledge at his fingertips than most architects ever learn.*

THEN as now, I was concerned that most architects were overly focused on style and had abandoned the fundamental purpose of buildings – the natural control of climate – to others. This problem is not new for I found in the nineteenth century that architectural style and botanical needs were often in conflict. The simplistic hermetically sealed, but often highly styled structures of the late twentieth century, however, depend upon improvident machinery using excessive energy just to make them habitable.

THE raison d'être of every sheet of glass placed over a plant for shelter has always been the conversion of the sun's energy. Orangeries, conservatories and winter-gardens only became enriched and embellished in diverse and wonderful ways when we discovered that we could enjoy the sun's warmth under glass. This book should reveal to contemporary designers, architects, engineers and horticulturists that the thin-skinned structures of today have a fascinating legacy from which to learn. It charts the work of important innovators such as John Claudius Loudon, Joseph Paxton, Hector Horeau, Richard Turner, Charles McIntosh, Charles Rohault de Fleury, Friedrich Ludwig von Sckell and Alphonse Balat, and in North America Lord and Burnham, and reveals their influence on design in both the nineteenth and twentieth centuries.

THE glass visionaries, the Expressionists, most notably the writer Paul Scheerbart and the architect Bruno Taut, were inspired by the great nineteenth-century glasshouses. Their foresight was such that they were able to accurately predict the extensive application of glass in today's buildings. Any contemporary designer should be aware of the potent poetry of the real and imagined glass spaces which were conceived in that idealistic era.

John Hix
Tottenham, Ontario
January 1996

Hector Horeau compiled several of his glass structures into one watercolour of 1852, including a sectional perspective of his winter-garden in Lyon.

BEGINNINGS

I

THROUGHOUT its evolution the glasshouse has been propelled forwards by the desire to protect and nurture plants in a controlled environment. Even in the nineteenth century, its perfection as a building type depended on the experimentation of gardeners who aspired to overcome the technical problems of heating, ventilation, light and shade. The glasshouse's earliest history began long before it was glazed. Its first prototypes were the basic horticultural shelters of antiquity, which preceded the use of glass. Even in the sixteenth century when a renaissance of interest in botanical learning revived the idea of placing plants under cover, the greenhouse in its many permutations did not immediately include glass; a luxury that was generally limited to ecclesiastical buildings and the houses of the wealthy. It was not an obvious choice for what were, until the emergence of the orangery and the botanical glasshouse, little more than elaborate garden sheds.

THE fabrication of artificial climates for plants is first hinted at by writers in fifth-century BC Greece in references to the Gardens of Adonis; though Plato may only be describing a superior natural microclimate in the *Phaedo* when he says, 'a grain of seed, or the branch of a tree, placed into these gardens, acquires in

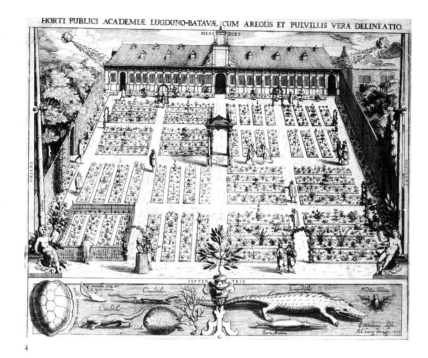

4

5

6

eight days a development which cannot be obtained in as many months in the open'. By the first century AD, Pliny the Elder, author of the *Natural History*, describes the use of a forcing-house similar to those of the eighteenth century, and Columella, who wrote on agriculture and gardening in his *De Re Rustica*, describes the growing of cucumbers in immense containers:

It is also possible, if it be worth the trouble, for wheels to be put on to the larger vessels so that they can be brought out with less labour. In any case, the vessels ought to be covered with slabs of transparent stone, so that in cold weather when the days are clear, they may be brought into the sun. By this method Tiberius Caesar was supplied with cucumbers during almost the whole year.[1]

This 'transparent stone', according to Seneca and Pliny, was *lapis specularis* (mica).[2] It was exceptionally transparent when split into thin sheets and often used for glazing.

THE hot water and flue systems of Roman houses could easily have been modified for the forcing of vegetables. In Pompeii, which was destroyed in 79 AD, archaeologists have identified *specularia* (stoves), complete with masonry tiers for plants and heating flues in the walls. Seneca had taken a sceptical view of this when he asked whether it was not 'contrary to nature to require a rose in winter and to use hot water to force from winter the later blooms of spring?'[3] Organized collections of plants first appeared during the fourteenth century, most notably in Salerno and Venice. In the sixteenth century they reappeared as botanical gardens throughout Europe, with the founding of universities at Padua (1533), Pisa (1544), Bologna (1568), Leipzig (1580), Leyden (1587) and Paris (1597); for it was not until the Renaissance that there was a methodical approach to the study of nature and, in particular, the growth of plants. In Padua, a wintering shed or *viridarium* was built for the more delicate species. It was no more than a masonry shed with a brazier to supply heat. The University of Leyden also had a plant-chamber in its botanical garden before its larger plant gallery was built in 1599.

4 Leyden University
Botanic Garden, 1610.
The winter gallery was
unfortunately sited on
the south of the garden,
facing north and received
little sun.
5 Orange Pyriforme, an
illustration from *Histoire
et Culture des Oranges*,
1872.
6 A wintering gallery
in Leyden University
Botanic Gardens.
7 The grotto orangery
in the Ducal Park at
Meiningen, built *c* 1800.
In the winter, wood and
glass components (see
bottom) formed a roof
and south front, and in
the summer they revealed
the open masonry grotto.
8 Machine for transporting
orange trees.

IN England, the sixteenth-century plant environments were also closely linked to commercial exploration and the expansion of international trade. The Eastern trade through Venice and Genoa brought many new plants into the gardens of the north Italian merchants and the new university botanical gardens where they could be seen by other European travellers. William Turner, who had spent much of his life in the botanical centres of Europe, was considered the first original botanical author in Britain. A Doctor of Physics at Oxford, Turner also oversaw the garden at Syon House, near London, and introduced from Italy and the East Indies many plants that required protection from the English winter.

RENAISSANCE gardeners inherited from antiquity myrtles, pomegranates, oleanders, citrus trees and jasmine. The lime, the lemon and particularly the orange, with its fragrant flowers and fruit, captured the enthusiasm of the aristocracy and their gardeners. In Italy, to the north of Naples, temporary wooden houses were constructed over the citrus trees to protect them from the cold or, alternatively, they were put into caves or stone buildings, light being considered unimportant during the plants' dormant winter months. In effect, two methods of protection had evolved in Europe: building temporary sheds over trees or moving potted trees indoors. At the Villa d'Este, Tivoli, movable trees were preferred, whereas at the Villa Pratolino in Tuscany wintering sheds were constructed over the citrus plantations. In France the preference for setting out boxed trees from orangeries was established as early as 1555 in the grounds of the châteaux at Anet, Fontainebleau and Versailles.

BETWEEN 1580 and 1588, during Elizabeth I's reign, many new plants were introduced into Britain by Sir Walter Raleigh and Thomas Cavendish. The first known orange seeds brought to England were purported to have been given to Sir Francis Carew by Raleigh. Carew was an enthusiastic procurer of citrus trees, which were planted in the ground at his estate in Beddington, Surrey. His grove was protected by a temporary wooden shelter, with

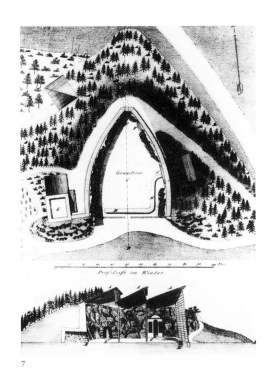

7

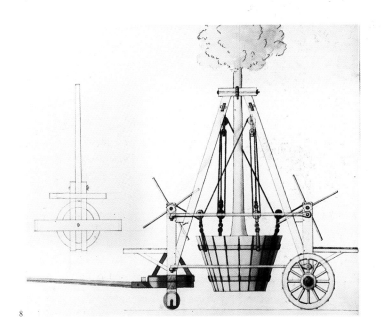

8

the main supporting columns left standing during the summer; it was similar to the design for Duke Francesco de Medici at the Villa Pratolino, but substituting a board roof for tiles. John Gibson's *A Short Account of Several Gardens near London* of 1691 describes it as 'the best orangery in England … the house wherein they are being above 200 feet long … and the gardener said he gathered at least 10,000 oranges last year'. John Evelyn, the diarist and inventor, said of his visit to the decaying Beddington House and grounds nine years later in 1700, '… and the first orange trees that had been seen in England, planted in the open ground, and secured in winter only by a tabernacle of stoves and boards removable in summer, that, standing 120 years, large and goodly trees, laden with fruit, were now in decay, as well as the grotto, fountains, cabinets …'[4] It was later reported that they were all killed in the harsh winter of 1739.

GIBSON also describes at Hampton Court Palace, 'a large green house divided into several rooms, and all of them with stoves under them, and fire to keep a continual heat. In these are no orange or lemon trees, or myrtles, or any greens but such tender foreign ones that need continual warmth.' It is said that the first pineapple to be grown in England was presented to Charles II by His Majesty's head gardener John Rose.

AT Kensington Palace there was no wintering place. Orange trees, lemon trees and myrtles had to be moved in winter to the Brompton Park greenhouses of the famous nurserymen London & Wise. However, an improvement was made in 1704 with the construction of the new orangery. Gibson went on to describe Brompton Park: 'they have a large greenhouse, the front all glass and board, the North side brick … their garden is chiefly a nursery for all sorts of plants of which they are very full'; and the work of a certain Dr Uvedale at Enfield, who 'is become master of the greatest and choicest collection of exotic greens that is perhaps anywhere in this land. His greens take up 6 or 7 houses or roomsteads.' Gibson was often critical, as he was of Sir Thomas Cooke's garden at Hackney: 'There are two greenhouses in it but the greens are not extraordinary for one of

10

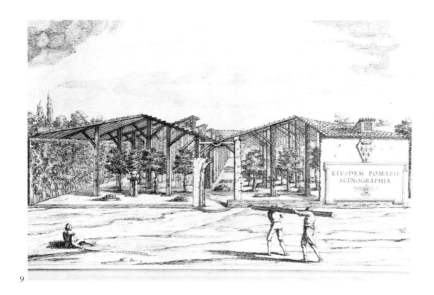

EIVSDEM POMARII SCENOGRAPHIA

9

11 *The Presentation of the first
pineapple to be grown in
England to Charles II by his
head-gardener John Rose*,
Henry Danckerts, *c* 1660.
12 *Bromelia Ananas, Ananas
Cultive*, Pierre Redouté
(1759–1840).

11

12

the roofs being made a receptacle for water, overcharged with weight, fell down last year upon the greens and made a great destruction away the trees and pots'; he said of Lord Falconbergh's Sutton Court: 'The greenhouse is very well made, but ill set … it is so placed that the sun shines not on the plants in winter, where they most need its beams, the dwelling house standing between the sun and it'; he wrote of Sir Robert Clayton's orangery at Morden, Surrey: 'He built a good greenhouse but set it so that the hills in winter keep the sun from it'; and when he visited John Evelyn's garden at Deptford, he wrote it off as 'a pretty little greenhouse with an indifferent stock in it'.

HENRY Compton, Bishop of London, was one of the most memorable figures in seventeenth-century gardening. An enthusiastic collector of foreign plants, he made Fulham Palace a destination for travelling botanists; Stephen Switzer claimed that Compton had 'a thousand species of exotick plants in his stoves and gardens'. According to Kenneth Lemmon in *The Golden Age of Plant Hunters*, Sir Hans Sloane mentions

in his preface to *The Natural History of Jamaica* that in the mid-1600s, James Harlow was sent to Jamaica by Sir Arthur Rawdon to bring back foreign plants for his garden at Moira in Ireland.[5] Many of Harlow's shipload of finds were distributed throughout the country, but none, according to Sloane, were better nurtured than by the Duchess of Beaufort, at Badminton, in her 'stoves and infirmaries'.

IN the mid-seventeenth century botanical knowledge was disseminated by personal letters between botanists, printed pamphlets and books, often with copperplate illustrations. In 1654 Sir Hugh Platt published practical advice and general reflections on forcing plants and greenhouse gardening under the title, *The Garden of Eden*: 'I hold it for a most delicate and pleasing thing to have a fair gallery, great chamber and other lodging that openeth fully upon the east or west, to be inwardly garnished with sweet Herbs and Flowers, yea and fruit if it were possible'. Gardening in roomsteads, as those curiously assembled stoves and greenhouses were called, often had overtones of profane

13 *Passion Flower*, W Curtis.

14–5 Portable wooden and permanent stone orangeries illustrated by Saloman de Caus in his *Hortus Palatinus*, 1620. De Caus designed these buildings for the Elector Palatine in Heidelberg.

13

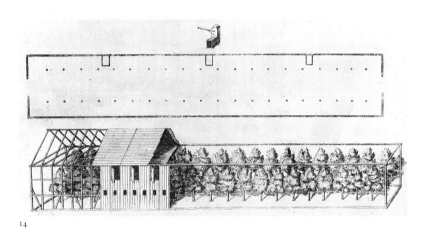

14

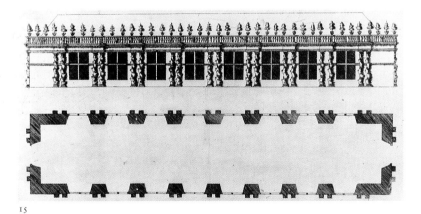

15

conjuring. Platt reveals this in his defence of Ripley, an alchemist 'who suffered death,' he says, 'as the secret report goeth for making a pear tree to fructify in winter … But it was the denial of his medicine and not the crime of conjuration which killed him.'

THE aristocracy developed a fervent interest in gardening and competed to employ the best gardeners, who very often made valuable contributions to botanical science by keeping small physic gardens for their private use to study and experiment with 'herbs and simples'. For them the dung bed and oiled paper or green-glass frame were sufficient to temper the climate. The main preoccupation of their fashionable patrons, however, remained the citrus fruit, valued for both its taste and its decorative qualities. The environmental demands were not great but the size of the citrus trees necessitated buildings of some magnitude. In his book, *Upon the Garden of Epicurus* of 1685, the diplomat and traveller, Sir William Temple wrote with pride of his own oranges and of his journeys to see other citrus trees. Temple would have seen ambitious projects on the Continent. In 1620 Salomon de Caus described his design for a portable wooden orangery for the Elector Palatine in Heidelberg; the building was to be 280 feet long:

It covers thirty small and four hundred medium-sized trees and is made of wood which is put up every year about Michaelmas and the orange trees are warmed by means of four furnaces all the winter, so that in the time of the great frosts one can walk in this orangery without feeling any cold … At Easter the framework is taken away, to leave the trees uncovered all summer.[6]

Born in Normandy, De Caus had designed the garden at the newly renovated Somerset House in London for James I and his wife, Anne of Denmark. He went on to Heidelberg to design the Hortus Palatinus, for James's daughter, who had married Frederick, the Elector Palatine. The success of his wooden structure there led Salomon de Caus to suggest an advanced orangery with permanent stone walls. It was only necessary to construct the roof and close the windows for the winter. This was an early example of what would become the permanent, roofed orangeries-cum-banqueting houses enjoyed by the aristocracy throughout the seventeenth, eighteenth and nineteenth centuries on the Continent and in England.

BEFORE De Caus had arrived in Heidelberg, Olivier de Serres, the skilful French garden authority, wrote in his *Le Theatre d' agriculture* of 1600 that the Heidelberg gardens were well known for their protected citrus fruits. Because he designed plant houses heated by charcoal braziers, with permanent thatched roofs, operable skylights and removable glass south walls, Serres's name is venerated with the French word *serre* meaning greenhouse.

LOUIS XIV of France loved oranges and his first orangery was designed by Louis le Vau in 1664, and his second, which can be seen today at Versailles, was designed by Jules Hardouin Mansart in 1685. It required a large excavation and extensive stonework to create a sunken protected microclimate in the orangery parterre, outside the lofty south-facing windows which

16

16 The interior of the Orangery at Versailles, Jules Hardouin Mansart, 1685.
17 An eighteenth-century Dutch forcing-frame. This had many sophisticated environmental devices including a flue-heated system.

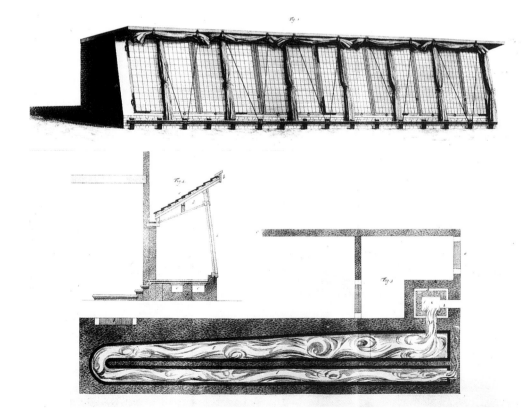

17

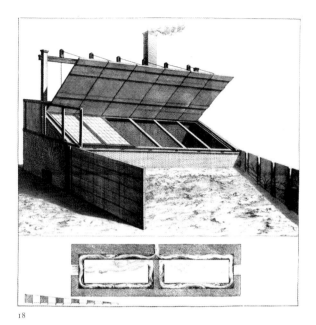

18

provide the capacious vault with light. The main central facade is 508 feet long and flanked by two galleries of 375 feet each. It has no heating system and relies on its orientation to the sun, the underground warmth from the earth surrounding the orange vaults and the microclimate created by the sunken south-oriented parterre. It was said that the Sun King laid out a ritual path for visitors, which would include the huge orangery, and had the citrus trees brought into the upper Hall of Mirrors for state occasions.

BY the end of the seventeenth century, the glasshouse or glazed greenhouse was starting to come into its own alongside the masonry-walled orangery. Though the line between the glasshouse and the orangery could often be blurred in practice, making it difficult to categorize particular buildings, the glasshouse tended to be purpose-built and independent of the demands of architectural style. Initially made from a structure of wooden planks, its most immediate descendants were the large European forcing-frames most common in Holland. The improvement in glass-making

18 A flue-heated Dutch forcing-frame, 1737. With its mechanically-operated cover panels and sliding wind-shield it is an early example of microclimate control.

19 Winter place in the garden of Pieter de Wolff, illustrated by Jan Commelyn in *Nederlantze Hesperides*, 1676.

19

20 The ancient Orto
Botanico, Pavia, started
in 1556. L Canonica later
built the iron and stone
glasshouse.
21 Engraving of the Orto
Botanico, Pavia, G A
Scopoli, *Deliciae Florae et
Faunae insubricae*, 1706.
22 Danby Gate, Oxford
Botanic Garden, 1773.
This illustration shows
how glasshouses grew up
on either side of the gate.

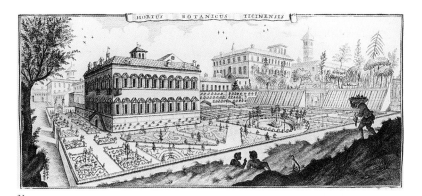

21

20

and the economic viability of glazing helped to facilitate the glasshouse's emergence. Whereas the houses at Leyden (1599) and Heidelberg (1620) would have had solid walls and latticed windows glazed with spun-disk panes, by 1720 the more innovative glasshouses would have had glazing throughout the south-facing wall and roof. By the second half of the eighteenth century, ideas on the latest structures and technologies were being disseminated by the international botanical and horticultural network. This helped to transform glasshouse building into a scientific art. Combined with the innovations of the industrial revolution, it enabled glasshouses to be constructed with even more extensive glazing and sophisticated heating systems across Europe and the Americas.

THE onset of the industrial revolution not only improved the standard of glass and its availability, it created a larger class of merchants and industrialists, who, in imitation of the aristocracy, displayed their wealth and status with the acquisition of land, country houses and gardens designed in the fashion of the day. As Lemmon

points out, 'a nation without riches cannot afford the luxury of plant hunting …', and that 'highly technical conservatory gardening skills allied to the desire for scientific knowledge of plants and a rich aristocracy with leisure and money to spare for purely non-mercenary interests in the natural sciences' were essential.[7] England enjoyed these ingredients and by the end of the seventeenth century the botanical search was on. Wealthy private collectors and institutions, like the Oxford Botanic Garden, funded plant and seed hunting expeditions around the world. The Oxford Physic Garden was established in 1632. Henry Danvers, the Earl of Danby gave five acres of ground, built a greenhouse and stoves and provided a house for the first gardener, Jacob Bobart. By 1648 there were nearly 1,600 species grown; Loggan's plan of the garden of 1675 shows the symmetrical layout, the elevation of the gates and the masonry conservatory. Thomas Baskerville remarked in his *Account of Oxford,* 1690: 'Amongst the several famous structures and curiosities wherewith the flourishing University

22

of Oxford is enriched, that of the Physic Garden deserves not the least place, being a matter of great use and ornament.' A 1773 print shows additional decorative glass ranges on each side of the Danby Gate, which allowed for the expansion of the collection. Experimentation with plant substances to relieve contemporary maladies, such as malaria, was carried out in this important early garden, as well as in the Apothecaries' Garden at Chelsea. John Ray's pioneering botanical studies at Cambridge and those in the Edinburgh Botanic Garden and the Westminster Physic Garden were also significant for the medicinal herbs which were grown. IN 1768 Joseph Banks privately financed what was to be his triumphant three-year long voyage in *The Endeavour* with Captain Cook. The plants and seeds collected from thoughout the New World, from as far away as the newly discovered Botany Bay, made extraordinary demands on the stoves, pits and greenhouses to cope with each species' subtle requirements. As President of the Royal Society, a position he was to enjoy to the end of his life, Banks encouraged the refinement of the glasshouses at Kew, as well as at his own residence, Spring Grove. Though he did no travelling in his later years, pineapples continued to be served at his table by proxy and he enjoyed the palms and exotics brought back to Kew by the botanical collectors financed by the Royal Society. The collection at Kew was growing; as early as the 1780s, with a mind to economic botany, Kew had begun to export camphor and mango trees to Jamaica. Banks had purchased the private herbarium of Philip Miller in 1774 and that of Carl Linnaeus's son in 1783. Later he was to organize the infamous and unsuccessful economic transport of breadfruit plants from the Pacific to the West Indies.

AN even earlier traveller, Sir Hans Sloane, knighted by George I on his return from the West Indies, wrote an important treatise on the botany of that area. He bought the Manor of Chelsea in 1712, near Sir Christopher Wren's Royal Hospital, and gave a freehold to the Worshipful Company of Apothecaries in 1722, on condition that they donate to the Royal Society fifty new plants a year for forty years. Under the hand of Philip Miller, hired by the

23

company in 1722, the Apothecaries' Garden at Chelsea at that time was probably unrivalled in its number of 'curious exoticks'.

MILLER was a professional gardener noted for his abilities in keeping foreign plants alive. The son of a Scottish market-gardener, he began his career as a florist in St George's Fields, where he combined an encyclopedic knowledge of plants with an extraordinary skill in growing them. His work was important, not from an ornamental point of view, as in Victorian times, but for the medicinal use of plants. It was a period when naturalists were making the first accurate descriptions and classifications of the natural world. Miller was able to give plants to Carl Linnaeus, the great Swedish naturalist, when he visited his famous Chelsea gardens in 1736.

THE gardens in Chelsea were only matched in scope and ambition by those at Leyden University, founded in 1587. In Leyden, and indeed Holland as a whole, the development of the glasshouse from the crude winter-shed was most apparent, as the building type was constantly experimented and elaborated on. In 1599 the University's Senate Curatores built one of the first wintering buildings there, a gallery that served as a conservatory, lecture room and ambulacrum, which replaced a previous plant-chamber. However, it was unfortunately sited on the south of the garden, facing north, and it received little sun: there was still much to be learned. Decorated with maps and Indian curios, it was filled with plants and animals. Before its completion, a letter to the Dutch East India Company transmitted a request from the burgomasters and curatores to allow a person going to the Indies to collect plants, seeds, spices, drugs and minerals to enrich the garden; for in the seventeenth century it was one of the duties of the Professor of Botany to build up the collection through expedition or exchange with the other botanic gardens emerging at this time. It was said that a merchantman never left a Dutch port without the captain being asked to procure seeds and plants from distant shores.

DURING this period, other Dutch wintering buildings (often called, 'Dutch stoves') were constructed to a plan similar to the gallery at Leyden. In his book *Nederlantze Hesperides* of

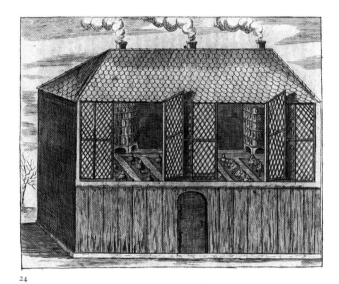

24

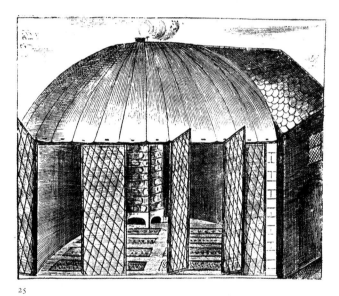

25

24–5 Hothouses as illustrated
in the 1696 and 1714
editions of *Neue Garten-
Lust*, by Heinrich Hesse.
The house in the earlier
edition, above, has small
casement windows; the
house in the later edition,
below, with its full-
length windows has
far more glazing.

26 Plan of the Apothecaries'
Garden, Chelsea, John
Haynes, 1751. This
engraving shows the
architectural
conservatory with its
glass wings built by
Philip Miller.

26

27 Leyden University
   Botanic Gardens, 1718.
28 Entrance to the
   Orangery, Cheverny,
   1701.

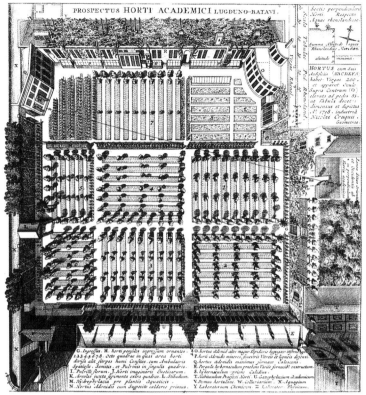

27

28

1676, Jan Commeleyn shows his own 'winter places' and those of Pieter de Wolff and Jan Roeters. These houses have brick floors, solid back walls and high double-casement windows with small glazed panes overlooking the garden. A high exposed-timber ceiling supports a storage loft under a shed roof. These lofts, used for the storing of tools, seeds and flower bulbs, also insulated the chambers below when filled with buckwheat chaff. Ornate cast-iron fireboxes on legs with dampered metal chimney flues were equidistant along the back masonry wall. It is probable that these freestanding stoves were stoked through the night with peat and charcoal and were considered efficient even for tropical plants. 'Stove' was the name used in England for a building suitable for tropical species.

PLANT houses of many sizes and types began to crowd around the Leyden Garden during the seventeenth century. From a description of the plants collected it is clear that by 1580–7 (under the directorship of Carolus Clusius) the garden had proper glasshouses, though they might have had only very small glass frames. During the

directorship of Herman Boerhaave, between 1709 and 1730, the garden was surrounded by numerous glass forcing-frames, large heated stove-houses with glass casement windows and an additional large gallery, this time with proper south orientation. The Leyden Garden had become, in essence, an environmental machine for nurturing and producing plants. Boerhaave, who was a physician and Professor of Medicine, Botany and Chemistry, used it as a laboratory, and his experiments are described in his voluminous correspondence. Under him, the botanical collection became one of the finest in the world.

BY the beginning of the eighteenth century the Dutch had already developed forcing-frames with sloped glass roofs, producing citrus fruits, pineapples and grapes. The sloped-fronted forcing-frame was engineered to manipulate the often difficult grey weather and cold temperatures. The back wall and floor were built of massive masonry, which absorbed the sun's rays and retained the warmth into the night. Hot air and smoke from the furnace followed a circuitous path in a flue to the top of the wall. The south wall was constructed entirely of glass set in hinged wooden frames, large enough to allow plants to be moved. Windows were opened in the summer for maximum ventilation and sun, but in the winter they were sealed against draughts and only opened on warm winter days. Oil paper in frames was often fixed under the glass to act as double-glazing. Canvas curtains could also be drawn over the windows, providing three layers of protection against the cold. Another mechanized frame had a series of wooden shutters hinged at the top to be lifted by pulleys and ropes, enabling the gardener to expose the glass on a sunny winter's day. Sliding wood panels, perpendicular to the house, protected it from the prevailing winds, but could also be pushed back for ventilation, an early example of mechanized climate control.

ALTHOUGH these devices may now appear crude, they produced admirable gardens such as those for George Clifford, which Carl Linnaeus described in the *Hortus Cliffortianus*, 1737. Clifford, a rich Anglo-Dutch financier and a director of the Dutch East India Company, was an enthusiastic horticulturist and zoologist. The gardens and private zoo at Hartekamp, his estate on the road to Leyden, were famous throughout Holland. Linnaeus took charge of the gardens, the hothouses, the fine library and the herbarium, which later made an invaluable contribution to his classification of all known plants. The gardens, Linnaeus tells us, were 'masterpieces of Nature aided by Art', with their 'shady walks, topiary, statues, fishponds, artificial mounds and mazes'. The zoo was 'full of tigers, apes, wild dogs, Indian deer and goats, peccaries, and African swine', with a variety of birds 'that made the garden echo and re-echo with their cries'. But most exciting were the 'houses of Adonis', the hothouses, which Linnaeus describes in his dedication to Clifford. They maintained cloves, poincianas and mangosteens; 'monstrous' plants from Africa, the mesembryanthemums, carrion-flowers and euphorbias; and plants from the New World like cacti, orchids, passion flowers, magnolias and tulip-trees. Clifford's collection obviously excited Linnaeus, who goes on to say, 'I desired

29

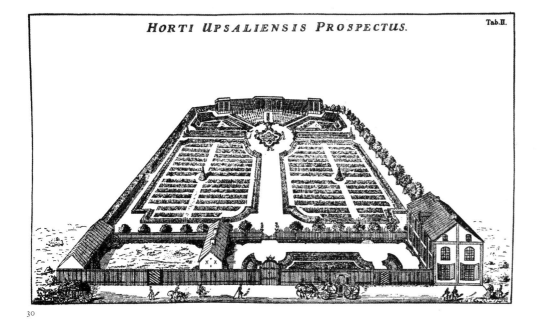

HORTI UPSALIENSIS PROSPECTUS.   Tab. II.

30

29 *Grapes*, J Le Moyne de Morgues, *c* 1568.
30 The Trädgard, Carl Linnaeus, *Hortus Uppsaliensis*, 1748. This garden was the Hortus Botanicus of Uppsala, Sweden, where Linnaeus was director. In the back of the garden is a wood-burning caldarium.

above all things that you might let the world have knowledge of so great a herbarium, and did not hesitate to lend you a hand.'

THE colonial age was a boon to botany, and many of the imported plants were useful to the economy. In 1789 *Hortus Kewensis* listed 5,500 exotic species at the Royal Botanic Gardens in Kew. Many individual enthusiasts, like the Duke of Devonshire, who had his estate at Chatsworth, also financed collectors around the world.

THE quest for light in the late seventeenth century caused gardeners not only to use more glass, but also to slope it to catch more sun. Though John Claudius Loudon (1783–1843) says that the Orangery at Wollaton Hall in Nottingham was one of the first to have a sloped glass roof, this innovation is not depicted in a painting of 1696 by Jan Sieberechts of the Wollaton grounds. In 1699, a Swiss fellow of the Royal Society, Nicolas Facio de Douiller, designed the first sloping walls, which he presented in *A Way to build Walls for Fruit Trees Whereby they Receive More Sunshine and Heat than Ordinary*.

Such developments anticipated the important observation of the founder of vegetable physiology Stephen Hales, in 1727: 'May not light, by freely entering the expanded surfaces of leaves and flowers contribute much to enabling principles of vegetation?'[8]

THE German book, Heinrich Hesse's *Neue Garten-Lust*, first published in 1696 and revised several times, offers a dramatic example of this developing awareness of light. In the first edition a house with lattice casement windows extending from the roof to halfway down the wall is shown, while in a later edition the glass area has increased and windows are covering the whole south-facing wall.

AT the Chelsea Apothecaries' Garden, Philip Miller began to understand the importance of sunlight and redesigned the greenhouse accordingly. The original greenhouse was built at Chelsea in 1680, some forty years before Miller started working there. From the outset, the ground floor of this house was used for plants with apartments above, as can be seen in all the illustrations in Miller's *The Gardener's Dictionary*

31

31 Masonry greenhouse, Norton Conyers, North Yorkshire, 1774.

32 Wooden glasshouse, Saltram, Devon, built for Theresa Parker, 1775. Despite the wooden structure and masonry back wall, the front wall was largely glazed.

32

33 Making crown-glass,
c 1800.

34 A flushed table of crown-
glass, as it was made
between 1826 and 1872
in St Helens, Lancashire.

33

34

of 1731. The plan shows an architectural house in the centre with a shed wing on each side. In 1731 the wings still had tiled roofs, but by 1751 they had 45-degree pitched glass roofs. The greenhouse had become the glasshouse. Miller described his reason for this change, 'The most tender exotic plants ought to have their glasses so situated as to receive the sun's rays in direct lines as great a part of the year as possible. For which reason the stoves which have upright glasses in front and sloping glasses over them, are justly preferred to any at present contrived.'

THOUGH the extent of glass in glasshouses increased greatly during the eighteenth century, the size of structures remained limited. These early glasshouses in botanical gardens and private estates were assembled from bull's-eye glass that was cut in small diamond panes. Made by the crown-glass method, the glass was blown and spun into a disk. The centre of this formed the bull's-eye and the rest was cut into flat panes. It was not until the development of the cylinder method during the nineteenth century,

in which the use of compressed air replaced the glassblower's lungs, that it became possible to produce longer cylinders and larger sheets of glass. Even into the first half of the nineteenth century the use of glass was confined by its expense. A highly skilled craft, manufacturing crown-glass required ten specialist glass-makers. The various techniques involved were closely guarded by family firms, who were able to slow down the transformation of glass production into an industrial process. Moreover, the various taxes on glass, including the window tax, which continued until the second half of the nineteenth century in England, maintained its luxury status.

THE landscape gardener Stephen Switzer also experimented with sloping glass and the glazed lean-to, which eventually became the standard form of the forcing-house. He had been an apprentice to London & Wise, the notable nurserymen and garden architects, who were presumed to have designed the glass-covered orangery and gardens at Wollaton Hall. Switzer describes in his book of 1724, *The Practical*

35 Glasshouses on the Pont des Arts, Paris, after 1803.

36 J C Loudon's sections through hothouses comparing the front glass angle at various latitudes (from left to right and top to bottom): Herman Boerhaave at Leyden, 1720; Carl Linnaeus at Uppsala, 1740; Michel Adanson, 1760; Adanson, 1760; Nicolas Facio de Douiller at Belvoir Castle, 1699; typical Dutch vinery *c* 1730; Thomas Knight's vinery; Thomas Knight's peach house; slope recommended by Philip Miller and Rev Wilkinson; M Thouin in the Jardin de Semis, Paris; Sir George Mackenzie's semi-dome, 1815; and Mr Braddick of the LHS for Mr Palmer, Kingston, Surrey.

35

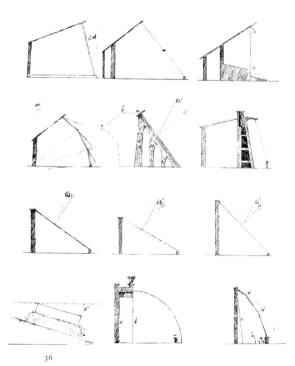

36

Fruit Gardener, a lean-to house with a 45-degree sloping glass front and brick back wall for the Duke of Rutland at Belvoir Castle. This early vinery was heated from behind by internal flues fed by small stoke holes. After this experiment, Switzer remarked that though the sun acted with more rigour on the 45-degree slope than on a perpendicular glass wall when it was in its solstice, it took an hour longer for the morning dew to evaporate from the slope. So what was gained at one time was lost at another. However orientation of the houses was more important to him, and he rightly advised that a south wall decline 20 degrees to the east to catch the early morning sun.

IN 1817 Loudon, one of the most important influences in nineteenth-century horticulture, reviewed various theories on the angle of forcing-frames to the sun. His *Remarks on the Construction of Hot-Houses* referred to a great variety of sources, including Herman Boerhaave, Carl Linnaeus, Michel Adanson and Nicolas Facio de Douiller. Their common goal was to maintain sun penetration perpendicular to the glass for a maximum period. Loudon claims that Boerhaave was the first to establish the principle for determining the slope of glass in 1732 in his *Elementa Chemiae*: an angle of 14½ degrees at 52½ degrees latitude north. Linnaeus, no doubt consulting the laws of Boerhaave, described his caldarium or dry stove constructed in Uppsala and the advantages of the slope that he fixed for the glass roof. In *Familles des Plantes*, 1763, the celebrated French botanist, Michel Adanson, countered all the angle studies by recommending perpendicular glass to avoid drops of condensation on the plants, but with sloping back walls or floors. He also gave rules, tables and diagrams to suit every latitude in the northern hemisphere.

BY the end of the eighteenth century foreign species had become so popular that it was possible to purchase greenhouse plants and even pineapples on the streets of London and Paris. The first nurseryman's glasshouses in Paris were built on the Pont des Arts, an iron pedestrian toll bridge spanning the Seine between the Louvre and the Académie, built after 1803.

24

IN France, Jean-François Boursault (1752–1842) is considered an early pioneer of horticulture. Throughout his life he maintained a passion for plants; he started his career as an actor, and later made his fortune clearing cesspools and selling the residue as fertilizer, thus he was aptly named Prince Merdiflore. His experiments on his property at Yerres revolved around a glass-covered trench (2 metres wide and 50 metres long) in which he grew his plants. Later a glasshouse was designed for him by the architect Jean Alavoine, who is better known for the July Column in the place de la Bastille in Paris. This glasshouse was 35 metres long and 4 metres high, and was divided by a vestibule in the centre. In 1805 he bought a property at the base of the then verdant hill, Montmartre, between the rue de Blanche and rue de Pigalle. There he organized an extensive garden surrounded by fine glasshouses filled with citrus trees, camellias, roses and tropical plants, mainly from the Americas, China and Japan. Boursault continued correspondence with British botanists and made several trips to Britain to acquire plants for his collection.

ACROSS the Atlantic in North America, glasshouses came relatively late. The earliest reference in Canada appears in an advertisement for the lease of Beaver Hall, the Montreal home of Joseph Frobisher, a partner in the Northwest Company. Dated 1810, in the *Montreal Gazette*, it describes a hothouse among the property's attractions. Frobisher began assembling the Beaver Hall estate in 1792 and the glasshouse would have been built later. According to the well-known Canadian architectural historian Steven Otto, Montreal was then a horticultural hot spot.[9] Its Horticultural Society was founded in 1811, only seven years after the Horticultural Society in London, seven years before the society in New York and twenty years before its equivalent in Paris.

IN New York City, David Hosack established the Elgin Botanic Garden in 1801, when he purchased twenty acres of south-sloping vacant land, three miles from the centre of the town; today it is the site of the Rockefeller Center. Hosack, a young and energetic Scottish doctor

37

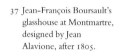

37 Jean-François Boursault's glasshouse at Montmartre, designed by Jean Alavione, after 1805.
38 Elgin Botanic Garden, New York, David Hosack, completed 1803.

38

named the garden after his home town. His masonry conservatory had two glass wings and was finished in 1803. In 1811, after trading for collections from around the world, he published the *Hortus Elginensis,* which contains the details of nearly two thousand species. New York State became the owner that year and gave control to the College of Physicians and Surgeons, which managed it poorly, and in 1825 Columbia University took it over. A plaque commemorating the Elgin Botanic Garden and dedicated to David Hosack, remains at the Rockefeller Center, embedded in the planter dividing the walkway leading to Fifth Avenue.

THOMAS Jefferson's greenhouse at Monticello, Virginia, was begun in 1806 as a south-facing extension to the house. Jefferson had planned a detached greenhouse, but it was never built. His intention was to have fragrant and decorative plants and, of course, citrus trees. These he nurtured with varied success; because he was often away and attending affairs of state, many of his plants perished for lack of attention.

BY the end of the eighteenth century diverse collections of plants from throughout the world, originally chosen for their medicinal and commercial prospects, had been established in extensive gardens. The collections of plant hunter Francis Masson from the Cape and David Nelson from Polynesia, China and as far as the Aleutian Islands filled Kew's glasshouses and surrounding gardens. There were large collections in Russia, Europe and in the private gardens of the king and other nobility in England.

CORRESPONDENCE about seeds, plants and nurturing methods proliferated among gardeners. The glasshouse as a scientific environment was moulded by hundreds of empirical observations. The shape and construction of 'plant roomsteads', were not the only topics to occupy these new scientists: ventilation, heating, light, shade, humidity and plant transportation were constant concerns. Plant loss at sea was a major problem. As a precursor to the famous Victorian Wardian case (a glass container used for housing delicate ferns and similar plants, named after its inventor Dr Nathaniel Bagshaw Ward),

39 Thomas Jefferson's
greenhouse at
Monticello, Virginia,
1806.

39

26

40 Orangery, Pythouse,
Wiltshire. This is a
typical architectural
conservatory of the early
nineteenth century, built
in stone and glass.

41 Lindley's design for a
portable greenhouse,
*Transactions of the Royal
Horticultural Society*, 1822.

40

Dr John Lindley, Assistant Secretary of the Horticultural Society's garden at Chiswick presented his solution in a paper to the society in 1822, *Instructions for Packing living Plants in Foreign Countries, especially within the Tropics; and Directions for their Treatment during the Voyage to Europe*. Exacting specifications were given for the best plant cabin called a 'portable greenhouse' and for boxes to protect the plants at sea. The sloping glass roof could be opened in good weather, but closed and covered with unrolled tarpaulin for protection from sea spray and cold. IT has been estimated by Kenneth Lemmon that during George III's reign and up to his death in 1820, though thousands of exotics were lost in transport, nearly seven thousand plant species were 'introduced' to England, putting formidable demands on the science of the glasshouse.[10] However, it was to take a revolution in industry and the arrival of a new Liberal Age, with a voracious appetite for engineering and science, for the larger and more sophisticated structures to be built and the great glasshouse era, the nineteenth century, to emerge.

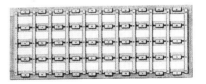

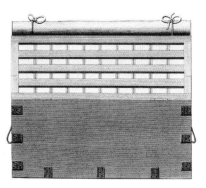

41

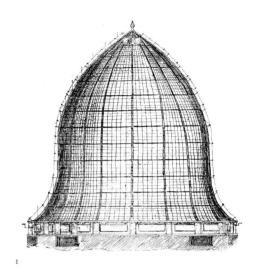

THIS LIBERAL
AND IMPROVING AGE

II

BY the dawn of the nineteenth century a culture of scientific fascination had matured throughout Britain and Europe. Gardeners had acquired a new rational and empirical approach in their quest to create larger glasshouses for bigger species. These could let in a greater amount of light and be more efficient in their environmental controls. The eighteenth-century colonial legacy had brought the wealth, plants and patrons; and the newly emerging industries provided materials and technology. The most revolutionary innovation was made by John Claudius Loudon, the famous horticultural encyclopedist, when he invented the iron sash bar. Previously the wooden frames of palm houses or other greenhouses, which enclosed humid, tropical climates, had a limited life. Wood and glass houses also required substantial structural members and glazing bars that encroached on interior space and blocked light. In contrast, iron-filigree structures took the glasshouse into a new realm in terms of their capacity for light and large open spans.

IT was not only the specialists who were enthused by the possibilities of scientific learning. World travel was in its infancy, and individuals and institutions were collecting animals, insects, curios and plants: the natural world

28

4

was being systematically recorded. Though war was often raging, knowledge was so revered that a scientific paper could be presented in the adversary's capital city by leave of passage. The author Patrick O'Brian, in his series of nautical novels, illustrates this fervour with his mythical character Dr Stephen Maturin, who travels the New World as a surgeon on a man-of-war, gathering and recording at every spare moment.

LATE Victorian writers were to refer to this period as having a 'mania' for the glasshouse. This fanaticism spread internationally. Already in 1810, Walter Nicol wrote that 'a garden is not now reckoned complete without a greenhouse, or conservatory with flued walls and with frames and lights'.[1] Such a conservatory was built in 1803–5 by Napoleon Bonaparte's wife, Josèphine de Beauharnais. It was located in the surrounding park of the seventeenth-century Château Malmaison, with adjoining farms on a bend in the Seine, six miles from the outskirts of present-day Paris. She had purchased the estate in 1799, three years after her marriage, while Bonaparte was in Egypt. During the Peace of

Amiens (signed in 1802 and lasting fourteen months) François de Meneval, Bonaparte's secretary, translated Josèphine's correspondence with European and English botanists and nurserymen with whom she traded new and rare plants for the collection she was forming, which, along with her roses, was to become one of the finest in Europe.

THE major experimenters in glasshouse design, the professional gardeners, developed artificial climates with rigorous empiricism. They presented their innovations in newly founded forums: horticultural societies, periodicals and gardening books. John Claudius Loudon, in his introduction to *Remarks on the Construction of Hot-Houses* of 1817, described the new era of interest that infused London's horticultural and botanical societies; members included 'men of rank and influence', scientists and keen gardeners, who gave 'a degree of éclat and salutary consequence to the study'. Loudon was taken with the spirit of 'this liberal and improving age', and he enthused about his own field of glass horticulture, which now enabled people to 'exhibit spring and summer in the midst of winter … to give man so proud a command over Nature'. Kenneth Lemmon has said of the 1830s and the advent of the portable Wardian case, which revolutionized the transport of plants, that 'the gardeners of England had advanced in their techniques of propagation, in the structure of their propagating houses and covered gardens generally, so that it could be truthfully said they could grow almost anything from anywhere – once they had received it in a viable state'.[2]

ANOTHER man of the age was Thomas Knight, elected President of the London Horticultural Society in 1811. In his inaugural address he discussed a subject that was to occupy his fellow members for years to come – the construction of glasshouses. He blamed the members for the 'generally very defective' construction of forcing-houses, for, he said, 'not a single building of this kind has yet been erected in which the greatest possible quantity of space has been obtained, and of light and heat admitted, proportionate to the capital expended'. A perfectionist, he had

presented a paper in 1808 on the subtle and specific art of angling the glass of a forcing-house. He calculated that an angle of 34 degrees at a latitude of 52 degrees would produce a highly flavoured, rather than an early crop of grapes. He was convinced that control of the environment under glass was capable of producing 'a peach … ripened in greater perfection in St Petersburg, in a house properly adapted to the latitude of that place, than in the open air at Rome or Naples'. Clearly Knight was bringing the art of horticulture into the realm of science. In this spirit he challenged his colleagues when he told them in his inaugural address that 'the proper application of glass where artificial heat is not employed, is certainly very ill understood'.

IN a bold attempt at hothouse improvement Sir George Mackenzie sent a paper to Sir Joseph Banks, 'On the form which the glass of a forcing-house ought to have in order to receive the greatest possible quantity of rays from the sun.' In 1815 he read it to the London Horticultural Society and instructed its members to 'make the surface of your green house roof parallel to the

5

4–5 Colour lithographs of the exterior and interior of Josèphine de Beauharnais's Conservatory at Malmaison by Garneray, 1803–5.

6 Quarter-sphere
hothouse, elevation, plan
and section, Sir George
Mackenzie, *Transactions
of the Horticultural Society
of London*, 11, 1817.

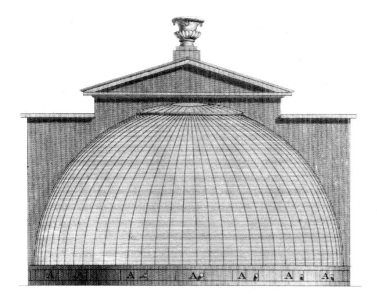

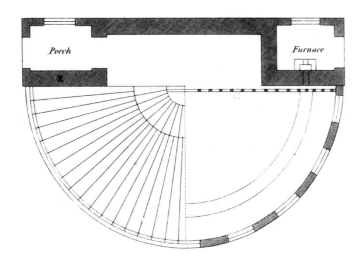

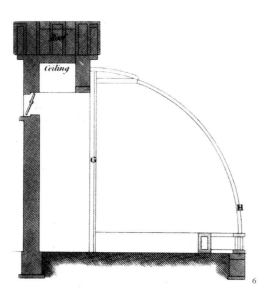

6

vaulted surface of the heavens, or to the plane of the sun's orbit'.[3] This was the first proposed curvilinear glass roof for horticulture. The letter and drawing described an elegant iron and glass quarter-sphere backed by a brick wall on the north. The radius of the dome was set at 15 feet, 'as anything less would be too confined and anything greater would render necessary an inconvenient height'. A vertical trellis for grapes was placed along the back wall. Mackenzie suggested that his semi-dome 'could be made in two movable parts to open in the manner of an observatory dome so as to expose the whole of the plants in the interior to the direct influence of the sun'. Loudon, though impressed by the beauty of Mackenzie's semi-dome, attacked its deficiencies. He objected to the distance from the glass skin to the trellis, and suggested the trellis should follow the curve of the vault. He noted that when the sunlight was perpendicular at any one point, it would not be perpendicular to the rest of the surface. He thought that Mackenzie's house was too high, relative to its length and width, there were too many bars at the top of the dome and its flatness would collect condensation, which would drip and injure the plants. He proposed an alternative design with improvements to answer his own complaints. Its 'acuminated apex', as Loudon called it, would not collect condensation and the 'spread out' base would provide a special place for small plants close to the glass.[4] Loudon's proposal had practical application because many of the desired species, particularly the palms, which were beginning to arrive from the New World grew to great heights. Loudon was obviously impressed by Mackenzie's curved iron design: 'Its appearance is most elegant, and it admits of a happy combination of lightness with strength in the construction; it may be considered, with the improvements of which it is susceptible, as a most valuable acquisition to the horticultural architecture of this country.'[5] He had earlier suggested that iron could not be adopted for a forcing-house without considerable disadvantages and could only be used in houses for maturing fruits. However, in a short time he became an avid proponent of iron construction and in 1816 he invented a wrought-iron bar that could be heated and then drawn through a mould to a desired curvature. This Loudon sash bar, which replaced curved bars made of several short pieces, opened a new era in curvilinear glass construction. Outward-curving bars formed strong arches and, when supported by cast-iron columns, could span large areas.

IN his *Remarks on the Construction of Hot-Houses*, Loudon also described an elegant improvement to the common lean-to, which he called his 'forcing-house for general purposes'. Based upon the semi-dome ideas of Michel Adanson and George Mackenzie he added 'ridge and furrow' glazing to the skin. This simply meant long bands of peaked glass roofing which, as Loudon said, could catch the 'two daily meridians of the sun'. With this pleated skin, the sun's rays would be caught perpendicular earlier in the morning and held later in the afternoon. The articulated skin also accumulated the condensation which flowed down the astragals (the iron bars holding the glass, also designed to collect and carry the water away). Loudon was later to propose a horizontal ridge-and-furrow system over vast areas, an idea that influenced the ridge-and-furrow experiments of Sir Joseph Paxton (1801–65) at Chatsworth and eventually led to his Crystal Palace design.

LOUDON'S glazed environments embodied concepts as sophisticated as the engineered plant-chambers of today. There was a louvre system connected to ropes to open the glass, and this could be connected to the automatic thermostat which James Kewley patented in 1816. Canvas blinds retained the heat, 'air valves' top and bottom replaced the stale damp air, and there was an automatic rain machine.

LOUDON saw the commercial possibilities of his inventions. He formed an arrangement with the construction company W & D Bailey, and advertised to custom-design and build glasshouses throughout the British Isles. He hired a former apprentice to act as the rural architect and sales representative for Ireland, Wales and Scotland, while Loudon himself covered the London area. Loudon built a remarkable prototype, it is assumed with the help of the Baileys, at his country home in Bayswater, one mile west of what was then London. The prototype, which spanned Bayswater Brook, used thirteen types of sash bars, seven types of glazing plus

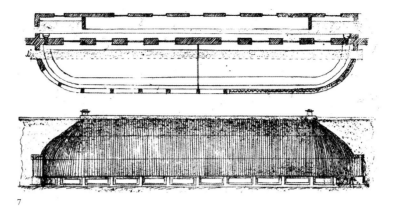

7

8

9

7 Forcing-house designed by J C Loudon with first ridge-and-furrow glazing to improve sun penetration, from *Remarks on the Construction of Hot-Houses*, 1817.

8 Loudon's demonstration that ridge-and-furrow glazing (top left) catches the morning and afternoon sun better than flat glazing (top right), *Remarks on the Construction of Hot-Houses*, 1817. The bottom sketch shows a larger ridge and furrow, not unlike that later used by Joseph Paxton.

9 Design sections through forcing-houses by Loudon, *Remarks on the Construction of Hot-Houses*, 1817. These sections maximize insulation and the storage of heat in massive back walls.

special paper and even corrugated iron to demonstrate the potential for covered markets, schools, theatres and churches. He said that his new glass and iron buildings could be designed in almost any shape with 'every conceivable variety of glass surface, without in the least interfering with the objects of culture'.

ALTHOUGH not an adept businessman, Loudon had a flair for writing and salesmanship. In his *Remarks on the Construction of Hot-Houses*, he compared the prices of various materials and thought his iron construction was better than even 'the best constructed wood houses at Kew, Kensington Gardens, and Chiswick'. His most convincing argument was his bar graph comparing the amount of light blocked by wood- and by iron-framed glasshouses. He said the dark area represented the lack of light and therefore 'insipidity and tartness', while the white was equated with 'aroma and flavours'. Could any gardener or green-thumbed patron have resisted this graphic argument?

LOUDON refuted major objections to iron, such as claims that the expansion and contraction of the metal causes glass to break, that iron loses heat by conduction, that it rusts and that it attracts electricity (lightning). He answered that most expansion and contraction occurred with brass and copper, not iron; that the house could be covered with canvas to prevent heat loss and that the bars could be lined with wood for insulation. To prevent rust the bars should be heated red-hot, then coated with coal tar or paint: tin, lead or pewter. As to lightning, he observed that even foundries, built completely of iron, had existed for fifteen years without any electrical damage. Loudon's arguments had to be decisive because, at that time, the new iron glazing bars were much more expensive than wood.

HE envisaged a new style of architecture that 'may be beautiful without exhibiting any of the orders of Grecian or of Gothic' design. This Loudon wrote as a challenge to architects: 'may not therefore glass roofs be rendered expressive of ideas of a higher and more appropriate kind, than those which are suggested by mere sheds, or a glazed arcade'.

THE alliance between Loudon and the Baileys

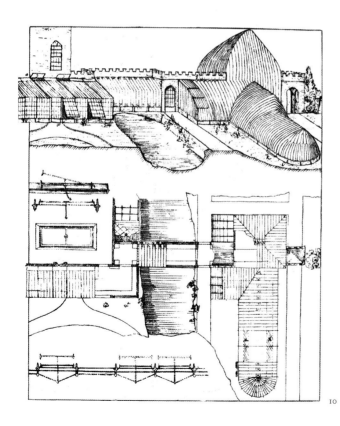

10

11

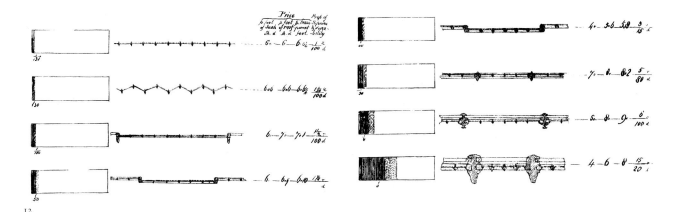

12 A comparison by J C
Loudon of light blocked
by various glazing
techniques, to prove the
superiority of iron bars
over wood with the
sweetness of the peach,
*Remarks on the
Construction of Hot-
Houses*, 1817.

13 Isometric view of
Loudon's double-
detached villa, Porchester
Terrace, London, *The
Suburban Gardener and
Villa Companion*, 1838.

14 The Loddiges's nursery,
Hackney, which was in
business between 1771
and 1854, comprised
a variety of glasshouses,
including a palm house
and a double camellia
house.

12

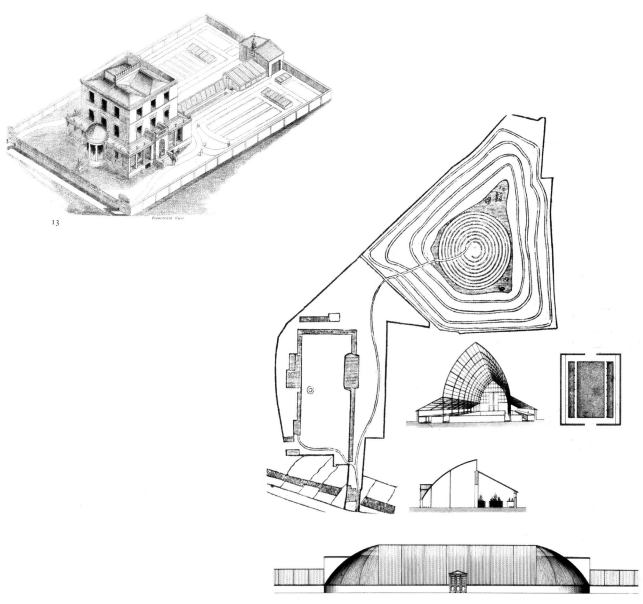

13

14

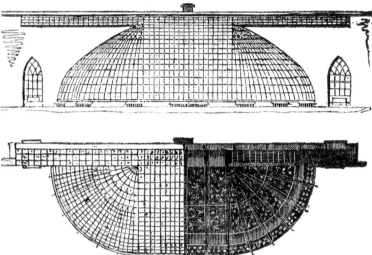

15

16

produced the most elegant curvilinear glass and iron shells in Britain. Loudon explained how this alliance had come about in his first issue of the *An Encyclopaedia of Gardening* of 1822. He had invented the curvilinear iron sash bar in 1816, and he presented it to the Horticultural Society in May of that year. By 1818 he had, presumably with the Baileys, completed the prototypes at his Bayswater home. That year he transferred to W & D Bailey the rights to the bar, while maintaining a design relationship with them that remains undefined. The Baileys erected curvilinear houses designed by Loudon at the Loddiges's nursery in Hackney, in the garden of Mr S Chilver in Finchley and for Lord St Vincent, a retired First Lord of the Admiralty, at Rochetts in Essex. It is not clear, but it can be presumed that this relationship went on for many years, making Loudon the true father of curvilinear iron and glass architecture. It is most probable that Loudon did not enjoy the same profits as the Baileys, who appeared to have eventually worked without his advice, design royalties being difficult to collect.

HOWEVER, Loudon was a more prolific writer than designer and his voluminous published work is filled with creative and original ideas relating to villas and gardens. By the time of his death in 1843 he had written thirty books. These included well-known works like *An Encyclopaedia of Gardening* (1822), *An Encyclopaedia of Plants* (1829), *An Encyclopaedia of Cottage, Farm, and Villa Architecture and Furniture* (1833) and *An Encyclopaedia of Trees and Shrubs* (1842) to name but a few.

THE glasshouses that W & D Bailey built in the 1820s with Loudon's glazing bar were numerous, elegant and sometimes very large. One of the finest was a pine pit and vinery constructed for Mr V Stukey at Langport, Somerset, in 1817. Another was exported to a site near Antwerp. Built for Mr M Caters de Wolfe, it had two elegant curvilinear hothouses on each side of the older masonry orangery. Loudon reports in 1826 that a 'rich collection of the choicest exotics was procured [by Caters de Wolfe] from the Hackney [Loddiges's] Nursery'.

THE Hackney Botanic Nursery was a series of

hothouses around a square filled with pits and frames. A commercial operation, the nursery was started in 1771 by the German gardener, Conrad Loddiges. Among the lean-to hothouses were, according to Loudon, the world's largest palm house (an 80-foot-long structure), and a double camellia house roofed in copper sashes by Timmins of Birmingham on one side of the masonry wall, and on the other side a curvilinear glass roof 120 feet long designed by Loudon and made by the Baileys. There was a 1000-foot-long walk through the connected glasshouses and steam heating with automatic rain equipment for the palms. Joseph Paxton bought all of the exotic plants in 1854 on the closure of the nursery and moved them to the Crystal Palace at Sydenham.

IN 1833, while working on the designs for the Jardin des Plantes in Paris, Charles Rohault de Fleury visited Loudon at his new home in Porchester Terrace and the Loddiges's glass gardens. He studied the nursery's steam heating and the iron construction, for Loudon was the champion of iron as a new material in the

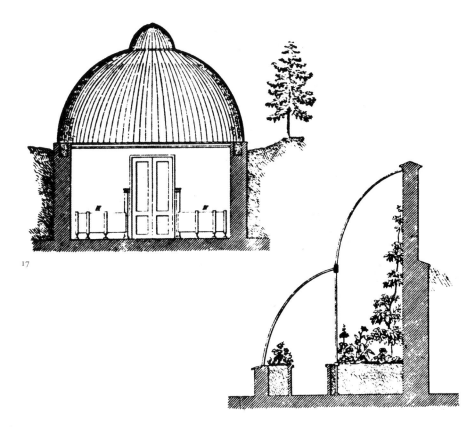

17

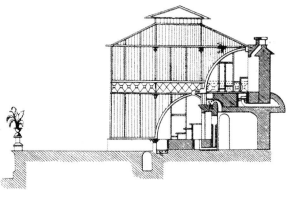

18

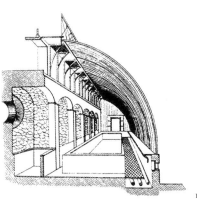

19

17 The curvilinear glasshouse in Regent's Park seen by Charles Rohault de Fleury on his visit to England, *Allgemeines Deutsche Bauzeitung*, 1837.

18 Berlin Royal Botanic Palm House, Karl Friedrich Schinkel, 1821. In contrast to British iron and glass examples, Schinkel's wooden structure succumbed quickly to rot and was replaced after only nine years.

19 Sections through the Jardin des Plantes, Paris, Charles Rohault de Fleury, 1833.

building of greenhouses. Rohault also visited the curvilinear glasshouses of Mr Cottam and the Baileys, the Horticultural Society's garden at Chiswick, and a group of glasshouses in Regent's Park called the Coliseum, which served as an early form of winter-garden with an exhibit hall. Rohault found two of these Regent's Park glasshouses interesting. One had masonry walls sunk into the ground and a dome-shaped glass roof and the other, which was 46 feet long and 25 feet high, formed a walkway along a masonry wall and was made from two curved half-vaults. These appear to have influenced his design for the Jardin des Plantes, though the drop in the site may have been a deciding factor. Rohault was later to write, 'The main advantage of the use of curved iron rebated ribs for glass houses [is] … high uniformity in the incidence of the sun's rays.'[6]

ONE of the most significant forerunners of the great conservatories at Chatsworth, Chiswick and Kew was the detached conservatory of 1827 built for Mrs Beaumont at Bretton Hall, Yorkshire. The structure was 100 feet in diameter, 60 feet high and constructed with wrought-iron sash bars on the Loudon principle. From these grand dimensions, it is easy to understand why Loudon was not impressed by the much lower dome at the Surrey Zoological Gardens, also 100 feet in diameter, but built three years later.

LOUDON gives an extensive description of Bretton Hall in *An Encyclopaedia of Cottage, Farm and Villa Architecture and Furniture*. This building, which would be a wonder today, seems to have had a brief ill-fated history involving Loudon's partners, the Baileys:

there were no rafters or principal ribs for strengthening the roof besides the common wrought-iron sash-bar … This caused some anxiety, for when the ironwork was put up, before it was glazed, the slightest wind put the whole of it in motion from the base to the summit … As soon as the glass was put in, however, it was found to become perfectly firm and strong, nor did the slightest accident, from any cause, happen to it from the time it was completed in 1827, till, on the death of Mrs. Beaumont, in 1832, it was sold by auction and taken down.

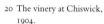

20 The vinery at Chiswick, 1904.

20

38

21–3 Section, elevation
and plan, glass and iron
curvilinear conservatory,
Bretton Hall, Yorkshire,
built by W & D Bailey,
and illustrated in J C
Loudon, *An Encyclopaedia
of Cottage, Farm and Villa
Architecture and Furniture*,
1832–3.

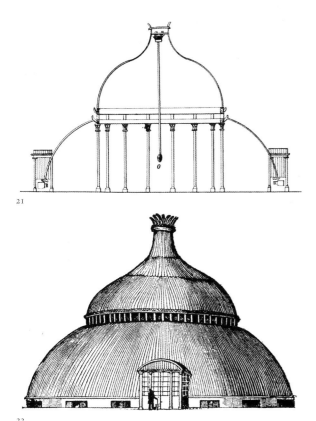

ACCORDING to Loudon, pieces from Bretton Hall conservatory were used on various patchwork greenhouses throughout the country. It is not clear what role Loudon had in this grand curvilinear design. In his 1853 *The Book of the Garden*, the master gardener at the Dalkeith estate in Edinburgh, Charles McIntosh, says that the Bretton Hall Conservatory was designed and erected by the Baileys. It is entirely possible that over an eleven-year period, which began with Loudon's invention of the first bar, they had developed a design-build confidence of their own. A large model of Mrs Beaumont's short-lived conservatory made its way much later to Frogmore Gardens, where it was presented to the Princess Royal by D & E Bailey, W & D's successors, who were installing the new heating equipment there. It was their intention that it should be converted into a Wardian case for the Princess.

BESIDES the curvilinear conservatory that they partially built for the Horticultural Society at Chiswick, D & E Bailey constructed the Pantheon Bazaar Conservatory and Aviary in Oxford Street, London, in 1834. This led from a Great Marlborough Street entrance into the Pantheon Bazaar designed by Sydney Smirke, on the site of the old Pantheon (now occupied by Marks & Spencer Ltd). Inside the conservatory were tropical birds and fish in bowls, along with papier-mâché ornaments and sculpture. The Baileys most probably also built the triple-domed conservatory at Dallam Tower, Milnthorpe, Kendal, in the Lake District, and the delightful Palm House at Bicton Gardens, near Budleigh Salterton, in Devon, both of which still stand.

THE date of the Bicton Gardens Palm House is questionable. Nikolaus Pevsner considers that it was built between 1820 and 1825.[7] However, Loudon made a trip to Lord Rolle's Bicton estate just before his death in 1843 and makes no mention of the curvilinear construction in an extensive description in *The Gardener's Magazine*. This might have been an oversight caused by professional envy, as Stephan Koppelkamm claims the Palm House is represented on a 1838 map.[8] Whatever the date, the Palm House is a late and beautiful descendant of Loudon's early designs. The detail of the elegant ironwork is reminiscent of other Bailey constructions, for example, that in the Loddiges's Camellia House at Hackney or the Vinery at Langport. This unique design, which halves the number of glazing bars at the top of the dome, stems from Loudon's early *Sketches of Curvilinear Hot-Houses* of 1818. The ventilator at the ridge is exactly like the ventilator on the curvilinear conservatory at Chiswick, built in 1840 by D & E Bailey. The assemblage of small pieces of lapped glass, like fish scales, held in thin iron glazing bars with minimal interior structure is one of the most daring examples of composite shell construction, in which the glass also can be said to be structural. It demonstrates Loudon's unparalleled influence on glass construction.

THOUGH many of the glasshouses that are extant today owe their longevity to Loudon's iron sash-bar principle, the changeover from wood to iron was not an immediate one. The debate between the merits of each material for sash bars and beams continued into the middle of the nineteenth century. One disadvantage of iron-framed glasshouses was the condensation caused by iron's high thermal conductivity. This was counteracted to some degree by cladding the sash bars with wood, providing double-glazing and drainage channels for the condensation. Joseph Paxton was one of the main proponents of wooden sash bars. He used them in the crystal palaces at Hyde Park and Sydenham over structures that combined the use of iron and wood.

RATIONAL construction methods alone cannot explain the ascendancy of the glasshouse in the nineteenth century. The horticulturists and gardening enthusiasts, such as Loudon and Paxton, who immersed themselves in every aspect of a structure's design, also concerned themselves with light, ventilation, heating and watering systems. For finely tuned environmental controls were as essential as a building's actual structure and enclosure in creating the accurate replication of a constant and foreign climate for growing plants.

24 Interior of the Pantheon Bazaar Conservatory and Aviary, Oxford Street, London, D & E Bailey, 1834.

24

25

26

25–7 The Palm House, Bicton
Gardens, Devon, built
by W & D Bailey, 1820.

27

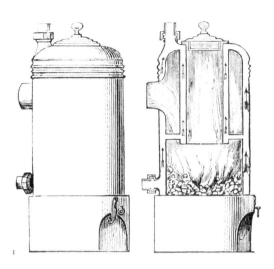

THE ARTIFICIAL CLIMATE

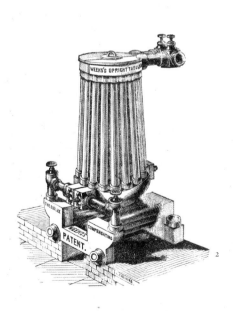

III

THE dramatic dimensions and beauty of glasshouses make it easy to lose sight of their basic purpose as enclosures that recreate the temperature and atmosphere of a plant's native habitat. The phrase 'artificial climate' was first coined by John Claudius Loudon and represents the positive, even arrogant, confidence in technology that was prevalent in the nineteenth century. Today, in an architectural context, it refers to no more than a tempering of the ambient environment that allows for our varied activities. In the nineteenth century, however, it evoked the idyllic milieu of the New World and recently discovered tropical lands, in contrast to the cold and unpleasant climate of northern Europe and the British Isles. The content of glasshouses reflected the period's romanticism, they were often filled with the artefacts, legends and botanical wonders of lands that few could visit, but all could dream about. Vast efforts were marshalled to imitate oriental styles in garden pavilions (the most ostentatious being the Prince Regent's Royal Pavilion at Brighton of 1815–22, designed by John Nash) and the conservatories of the colonizers. In his *Remarks on the Construction of Hot-Houses* of 1817 Loudon even looked forward to a time 'when such artificial climates will not only

Preceding pages
1 George Stephenson's
  double-cylinder boiler,
  an early example of a
  water-jacketed boiler
  illustrated in Charles
  McIntosh, *The Book of
  the Garden*, 1853.
2 Weeks's Upright Tubular
  Boiler, exhibited by
  Weeks & Co at the
  Great Exhibition in 1851.
3 The humid atmosphere
  of the Palm House,
  Royal Botanic Gardens,
  Kew, Decimus Burton
  and Richard Turner,
  1844–8.

4

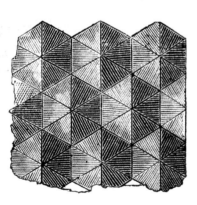

5

be stocked with appropriate birds, fishes and harmless animals, but with examples of the human species from the different countries imitated, habited in their particular costumes and who may serve as gardeners or curators of the different productions'. He was also able to recognize the practical potential of heating glass structures in his *An Encyclopaedia of Gardening*: 'In Northern countries, civilized man could not exist without glass; and if coal is not discovered in these countries, say, in Russia, the most economical mode of procuring a proper temperature will be by at once covering whole towns with immense teguments of glass, and heating by steam or otherwise, the enclosed air common to all inhabitants.' He illustrated a ridge-and-furrow and polyprosopic glass roof designed to cover vast areas of land and went on to say: 'Indeed, there is hardly any limit to the extent to which this sort of light (ridge and furrow) roof might not be carried; several acres, even a whole country residence.' He made provision for artificial rain, steam heat and vents, controlled by Kewley's automatons, and a roof

as high as 150 feet, to admit 'the tallest oriental trees, and the undisturbed flight of appropriate birds among their branches'. Later Loudon suggested beginning at 25 feet, and raising the roof by adding to the columns as the plants grew. In this controlled environment Loudon suggests that: 'A variety of oriental birds and monkeys and other animals might be introduced; and in ponds, a stream made to run by machinery, and also in salt lakes – fishes, polypl, corals, and other productions of fresh or sea-water might be cultivated or kept.'

LOUDON's faith in the ability to create grand artificial climates was sustained by a legacy of experiments in environmental control. These began in the sixteenth century with the practical challenge of recreating indigenous climates for exotic plants imported into Europe. In 1721 the Professor of Botany at Cambridge, Richard Bradley, was the first to describe the relationship of plants to their environment. Bradley said in his *A Philosophical Account of the Works of Nature* of 1724: 'As every animal has its climate and food natural to it, so has every plant an

4 Oxford Botanic Garden, 1773.

5 Ridge-and-furrow and polyprosopic glass roof for covering vast areas of land with an artificial climate, J C Loudon's *An Encyclopaedia of Gardening* 1822.

6 Greenhouse illustrated by John Evelyn in *Kalendarium Hortense*, 1691. In the top figure the cold air at the bottom of the house is drawn down the floor extract duct (see bottom) to the furnace. Evelyn suggested that the south wall be enclosed with glass windows, for 'the light itself, next to air, is of wonderful importance'.

exposure, temper of air, and soil, proper to nourish and maintain it in a right state of health.' HORTICULTURISTS became the first heating and ventilation experts. The successes and failures of experiments were discussed in the letters of gardeners and travellers who reported on their visits to other European countries. By the beginning of the nineteenth century men like Dr James Anderson, Walter Nicol, John Abercrombie and Loudon were compiling this information in encyclopedias of gardening and dissertations on hothouse design.

ONE of the earliest forms of heating, the smudge pot, is still used in the citrus groves of Florida when frost is expected. An open fire or brazier, it was used for orange trees as far back as the sixteenth century. Insulated by wood enclosures or masonry, which has a good thermal storage capacity, the slow-burning peat fires could maintain the plants in a smoke-filled room during cold and frosty nights. Refuelling these fires required considerable labour in noxious, unpleasant environments. An offshoot, but certainly not an improvement to these crude fires was used at the Oxford Botanic Garden until the end of the eighteenth century. This method relied on an iron wagon filled with burning charcoal; an idea attributed to Jacob Bobart, a German who was the first Keeper of the Garden in 1632. On a severe night the wagon was drawn back and forth through the houses. Scorching and asphyxiation from the open fires must have been commonplace, as Richard Bradley noted in his *New Improvements of Planting and Gardening* of 1718, while warning of a graver hazard: 'several men have been choked by them and sparks from them have set fire to the house'.

THE most basic indirect heating system took the form of a vault under a house with a fire at one end and a flue channelling smoke through to the other. John Evelyn, the eminent natural philosopher, diarist and garden enthusiast, saw an underground vault in 1685 at the Chelsea Apothecaries' Garden, which protected 'the tree bearing the Jesuit's bark [Quinine] which had done such cures in quartans [a form of malaria]'. Evelyn was much impressed with the 'very ingenious … subterranean heat, conveyed by a stove under the conservatory, which was all vaulted with brick'; the system was so good that

'he leaves the doors and windows open in the hardest frost, secluding only snow, etc'.[1] Evelyn designed his own hot-air furnace, having consulted Christopher Wren and Robert Hooke, fellow members of the Royal Society. This was for his 'new conservatory or green house', presented in his *Kalendarium Hortense or, The Gardener's Almanac* of 1691. He criticized 'ordinary iron stoves' and 'subterranean caliducts', and their effect on the exotic plants, which he described in almost human terms.

HE believed that the trouble came from the, 'dry heat emitted from the common stoves, pans of charcoal, and other included heaters, which continually preyed upon, wasted and vitiated the stagnant and pent-in air, without any due and wholesome succession of a more vital and fresh supply'. His 'contrivance, whereby to remedy this inconvenience' is one of the earliest known hot-air circulation systems. Though doubtless very inefficient, the system works on the principle that hot air rising in the chimney draws internal air through the floor duct and back to the fire. This creates a negative pressure in the house that in turn draws fresh air through the three heated intake pipes. The temperature was probably controlled by the extract system, for over the opening hung a thermometer, certainly one of the earliest.[2] In 1694 Sir Dudley Cullum of Hawstead, Suffolk, reported in the Royal Society's *Philosophical Transactions* the success of a house that he had built and heated on Evelyn's principles.

IMPROVEMENTS were inevitable, and by the end of the seventeenth century the iron stove was common in the 'winter-places' of the wealthy in Holland and Germany. These were often referred to as the stove. Inside the 'stove' a freestanding, sometimes ornate cast-iron box with a metal stack passing through the roof was fired throughout cold winter nights. The peat or charcoal fire, when combined with a highly insulated attic and shuttered windows, kept most of the house above freezing. The heat, however, was unevenly distributed: plants near the iron boxes were scorched and dried, while the others succumbed to frost and damp. In his caldarium at Uppsala, Carl Linnaeus used a portable stove, which could be moved to various locations to lower the relative humidity

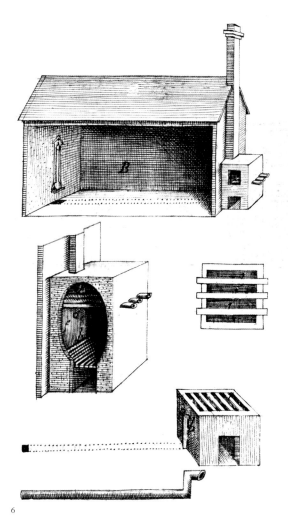

6

when severe weather did not permit opening the sashes. Later, with the introduction of the Dutch glazed-tile masonry stove and its German equivalents, masonry mass provided an even heat throughout the night.

NOT all heating systems were by necessity sophisticated. Philip Miller, in *The Gardener's Dictionary*, described a more primitive but none the less workable method of heating adopted at the Apothecaries' Garden in Chelsea; as he stated, 'without which the English could not enjoy so many products of the warmer climates'. The hotbed was simply a shallow trench filled with dung, covered with earth and enclosed in a glass frame. By stirring and adding bark, the heat from this controlled oxidation could last for two to three months; the tan-bark hotbed was preferred for all tender exotics and fruits that required warmth for several months. Miller's bark stove also had flues through the tan bark and it was divided into various chambers, the furthest from the furnace being the coolest.

BY the eighteenth century flues, which were in floors and back walls or exposed within the house, were, in the main, the most common form of glasshouse heating. Gardeners, however, still had to stoke numerous small furnaces through the night during severe weather. Flues drew with difficulty and temperature control was often impossible. There was a constant struggle to increase their length within the floor or back wall, and still have them draw. Because they were so inefficient, flue systems consumed great quantities of coal or peat and when the walls of the flues cracked, noxious fumes and smoke escaped into the house. Loudon designed a flue that he presented to the nursery of Dickson & Shade in Edinburgh. At the age of twenty-two, the inventive and enterprising Loudon made models of flue and hothouse systems and sold them for one to three guineas. His improvements dealt mainly with fuel consumption, slowing down the flue gases, insulating the house at night, creating an artificial breeze, and tempering the ventilation from outside.

THE flue system was able to support impressive botanical establishments such as the glass gardens built at St Petersburg's Imperial Botanic

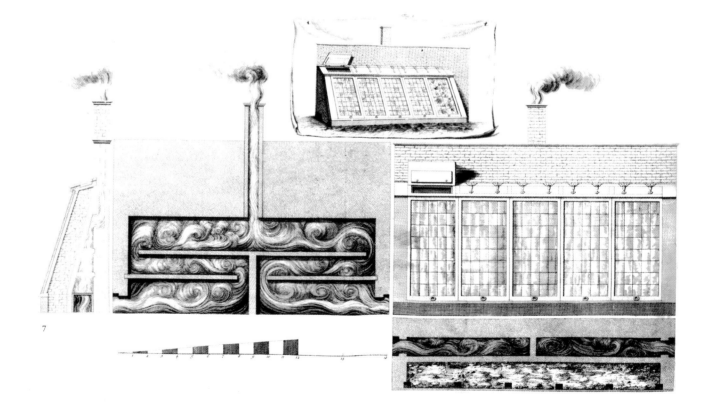

7

Gardens on the Apothecaries' Island in the Neva River, during Alexander I's reign (1801–25), from where plants were distributed all over the Empire. As the name of the island suggests, medical botany was practised on a large part of the grounds. In 1828 the glasshouses provided hospitals with 4,560 lbs of *aconitum napellus* leaves (monk's hood, a narcotic and analgesic). By 1829 the gardens, according to Loudon, contained eighty thousand plants and eleven thousand species.

THERE were three major glasshouses, each 700 feet long and 20 to 30 feet wide, connected by double-glazed covered corridors. These corridors were filled with decorative greenhouse plants and provided space for promenading. The three major ranges had sloped glass facing south, and were backed by masonry sheds. Two ranges were divided into five compartments for hardier plants with birch-log furnaces in niches every 12 to 15 feet. The middle range was divided into seven chambers with furnace niches every 9 to 12 feet, providing more heat for the delicate tropicals.

8, 9 Loudon's early smoke flue with partitions and his system of insulation, as shown in *A Short Treatise on Improvements recently made in Hot-Houses*, 1805. Air was replenished in the chambers by means of bellows or a box-like air pump. Coarse woollen curtains were drawn down for insulation at night.

10 The interconnected glasshouses of the Imperial Botanic Garden, St Petersburg, located on the Apothecaries' Island, in the Neva River, described by J C Loudon in his *An Encyclopedia of Gardening*, 1835. These included three major glass ranges, each of 700 feet, facing south.

8

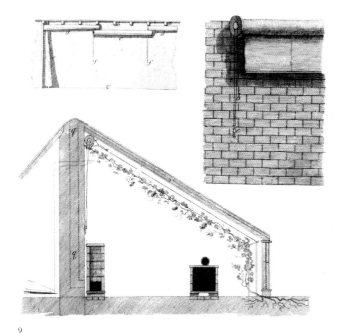

9

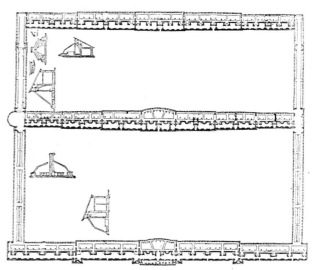

10

11 Longitudinal and transverse sections through vinery and pinehouse depicted by J C Loudon in *A Short Treatise on several improvements recently made in Hot-Houses*, 1805. The space around the flues was filled with water to produce moist heat that would rise up through the rubble base.

12 A section through a European glasshouse, as illustrated in J C Loudon, *An Encyclopaedia of Gardening*, 1822. This features the curved wood reflectors found in northern European glasshouses.

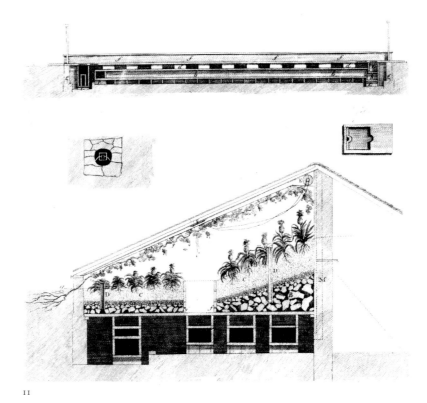

11

12

GLASSHOUSES in Russia were, by necessity, narrower than in warmer countries and were always backed by galleries, corridors or walls, to combat the ferocious winter winds. At St Petersburg, the back sheds functioned as insulation and also as temperate chambers supplying air to the glasshouses. An army of men kept the hundreds of furnaces stoked. During severe weather they were filled with logs at twelve-hour intervals, one of the refuelling times was between 1 and 2 am so that the highest flue temperature coincided with the coldest hours of the night, when it could easily have been −30°F. This system resembled Loudon's except that the flues were constructed of thick brickwork, providing a massive heat magazine with slow transferral into the surrounding air. The central building was 40 feet high and had an upper suite from which the royal family could look down on the plants. According to Loudon there were also apartments within this range for the Director, Dr Fisher, an English botanist; his two chief gardeners, a Dane and a Frenchman; two secretaries, a Frenchman and a Russian; and a botanical painter from Germany. The total complex of conservatories, greenhouses, stoves and glazed corridors formed a rectangle of glass 500 by 700 feet; the houses measured 3,624 feet, nearly three-quarters of a mile long, supposedly the largest in the world at that time.[3] The lean-to houses were formed from glass and wood sashes either sloped to the parapet or half gambrel to provide more volume for larger plants. These sashes were sealed with pitch and moss to keep out the severe winter cold. The poor quality of glass available in Russia at that time meant that it was of varying thickness, consequently it broke easily during frosts. It also contained bubbles and inequalities that concentrated the sun's rays, blistering the plants. Huge curved-wood reflectors, backed with hay and cotton insulation, were attached to the back wall of the houses. These were rubbed smooth and painted white and their reflection produced astonishing growth, according to Loudon, and kept the plants from bending toward the windows.

STEAM heat heralded a new era in environmental control. Though the potential of steam had

48

13 North's New-Invented
   Portable Engine, 1802.
14 The Heating Machinery
   at the Loddiges's nursery,
   Hackney, drawn by
   George Loddiges, 1818.

been foreseen in the seventeenth century by Sir Hugh Platt, an observer of husbandry and gardening, in his book *The Garden of Eden* of 1654, it was not until the end of the eighteenth century that it was possible to apply steam in any way. A Mr Wakefield of Liverpool is purported to be the first to use steam for forcing in 1788, and in 1791 a Mr Hoyle of Halifax secured a patent for steam heating hothouses and other buildings.[4] Hoyle's system actually returned the condensed steam back to the boiler for recirculation. The turning point came in 1789 when Matthew Boulton, the partner of James Watt, heated a room and a bath in his house with steam. In 1793 the gardener to the Earl of Derby saturated his tan bark and dung pits with steam. In 1807 the horticultural architect John Hay of Edinburgh discharged steam daily into beds of stones that retained the heat through the night.

IN 1805 Loudon had no use for steam heat, which he considered 'is not only unnecessary but an immense expense'.[5] Yet in his *Remarks on the Construction of Hot-Houses* of 1817, he was praising it for its capacity to carry heat over long distances at an even temperature, its cleanliness over the old flue system, and its saving in fuel and labour. Loudon's original reservations had pertained to early steam devices, like North's engine, which boiled water openly in the houses and caused condensation on glass and plants. This basic method had no perceivable advantage over pouring water on hot flues.

BY 1817 steam was being contained in vaults and pipes, and used to heat gravel or to bubble through water tanks below the plant beds. The royal gardens at Kensington and Hampton Court had steam machines devised by an ironmonger and brazier-maker, a Mr Fraser. Loudon describes the 1000-foot run of glass buildings at the Loddiges's nursery in Hackney as having a modern steam apparatus with a gravity-fed cistern, safety valves and mercury-filled pressure gauges. Distributed over half a mile of 4-inch cast-iron pipes, it maintained a winter temperature of 80–90°F.

LOUDON's fertile imagination forecast the use of central steam-boilers as an all-purpose power source for small country estates: heating the

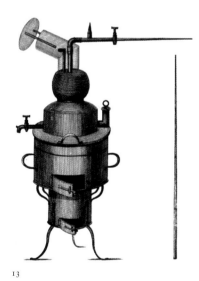

13

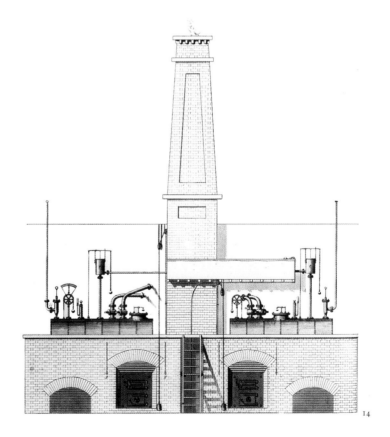

14

15 Steam-heated vinery and
    pine pit, James Brown,
    *Transactions of the
    Horticultural Society,*
    II, 1818.

THE GLASSHOUSE

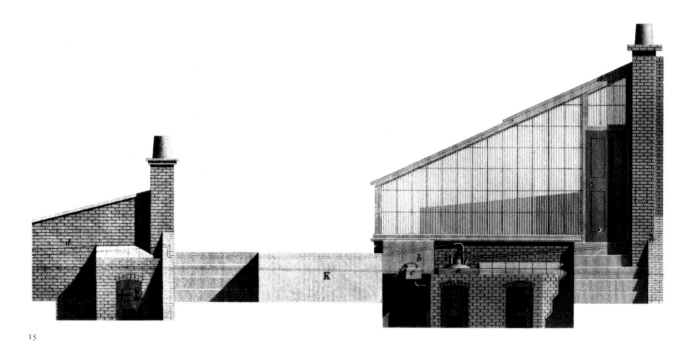

15

glasshouses, stables, a mansion, baths, laundries, malt kilns, cattle and poultry houses, while providing power for the fire engine, mill, threshing machine, turnip and straw cutter, in addition to pumping water to elevated reservoirs, which would supply water-closets and 'water cocks'.

THE early volumes of the *Transactions of the Horticultural Society of London* provide beautifully illustrated examples of steam heating.[6] James Brown, gardener to Richard Shawe in Dulwich presented in 1817 his steam apparatus for forcing pineapples in a pit and for a vinery. Gardeners, however, remained undecided between using the old flue systems and the new steam heating. Most steam houses were simply converted flue houses. Brown's twenty-four gallon boiler was cistern-fed and equipped with that necessary device, the safety valve: the earlier boilers had been the cause of fatal accidents as they were more likely to explode.

IN 1819 a pineapple and grape forcing-house was built by Martin Miller Call for the Imperial Gardens in St Petersburg. Although a flue system was retained along the front wall, the 100-foot-long tan-bark house was heated primarily by steam. Heat transfer was simple. A cistern-fed boiler developed steam at 3 lb per square inch and forced the vapour into a horizontal pipe suspended over two 50-foot water tanks made of caulked timber. Vertical pipes bubbled the steam into the water at 6-foot intervals. The boiler maintained the tank water at 100°F and the tan bark into which the potted pines were plunged at 88°F to 100°F.

THE following year Joseph Hayward presented to the Horticultural Society a sophisticated heating system based upon a steam unit invented by Hague, an engineer from Spitalfields. Introduced into a factory run by Hayward in 1819, its patented system distributed heat by radiation and convection and returned the condensate to the boiler, saving fuel and water. Coupled with normal radiation, the convection system introduced outside air into the house, in a way similar to twentieth-century methods. A closed system, it required complex metering and safety devices, including an air cock at the end of the return pipe, a goose-neck steam gauge at the head of

16, 17 End section and ground
plan of the steam pits
in the Imperial Gardens
of the Taurida Palace,
St Petersburg,
*Transactions of the
Horticultural Society,*
IV, 1822.

18, 19 Section and plan
of Hague's Steam
Apparatus, system
applied to a hothouse
by Joseph Hayward,
1819, illustrated in
*Transactions of the
Horticultural Society,*
IV, 1822.

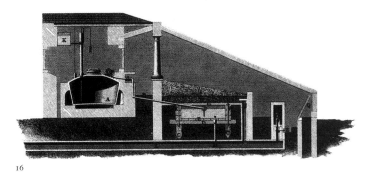

16

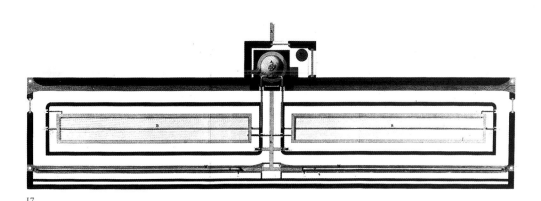

17

the rising main, a water gauge and a safety valve at the top of the cauldron.

A GREAT variety of steam systems continued to be developed into the 1830s. Henry Stothert, for instance, a civil engineer from Bath who built steam systems in southwest England, is notable not only for the number of systems he designed, but also for their efficiency. A major problem with exposed pipes was their inability to retain heat, so that boilers had to be fired constantly. Stothert's innovation combined the advantages of steam as a conductor of heat, and water and stone as retainers. This was first tried in a forcing-house belonging to a Mr Sturges near Bath, and later adopted in an iron conservatory belonging to the Marquis of Aylesbury at Tottenham Park. In England today many homes are heated with off-peak, electric storage heaters, which are simply a stack of bricks absorbing cheap electricity at night and radiating it during the day. Stothert's steam storage heater was based on the same principle, except that a perforated pipe distributed steam into a sealed stone chamber filled with rubble, and the condensate was drained off.

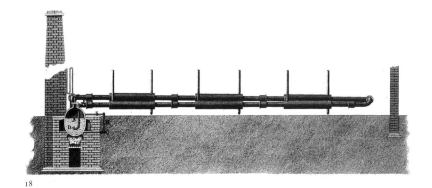

18

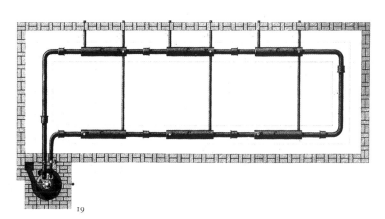

19

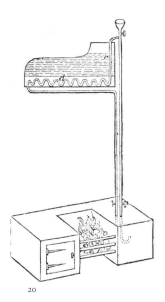

20

Steam cocks at the top of the chamber could be opened for extra humidity and the pipe had more perforations towards the end of its run for an even distribution of heat.

DESPITE the interest it generated, steam heating was short-lived. By the end of the 1830s nearly every gardener was discussing the merits of hot water. Steam distribution systems could be extended for long distances from a central point, but the fires had to be stoked constantly to keep the water boiling. The cauldron took several hours to come to the boil, it needed constant attendance and there was always the threat of an explosion. Inventors, therefore, tried to find better ways to distribute heat and to maintain an even temperature.

THE first hothouse to be heated with water was designed by the Marquis de Chabannes at Sundridge Park, Kent, in 1816. By 1818 the Marquis had written a pamphlet, *On Conducting Air by Ventilation and Regulating the Temperature in Dwellings, with a Description of the Application of the Principles as Established in Convent Garden Theatre, and Lloyd's Subscription Rooms*. It was illustrated

with a diagram of a hothouse heated by a water-jacketed boiler. It fed hot water to radiant pipes below the earth bed and the returning water entered at the bottom of the boiler to be recirculated. The most interesting plate, however, showed a complete hot-water system for the home. A kitchen fireplace boiler supplied hot water to a bath on the same level and to cast-iron heating urns on the three floors above.

WILLIAM ATKINSON was therefore mistaken in thinking that he was the first to plan a hot-water system at the Bacon estate, Aberamen, Glamorganshire, in 1822. The boiler in Atkinson's scheme was simply a cauldron that could heat the chambers of the glasshouse throughout the night with one well-stoked fire. Water began to circulate as soon as the fire was lit. Hot water rose and flowed in the top tube through the house and into a cast-iron reservoir. When it cooled it flowed back to the boiler to be recirculated again. The water never turned to steam, and the level could be replenished by lifting the wooden lid of the boiler. The system must have been extremely efficient, for heat came from the

20 Thomas Fowler's Thermosiphon, heating a bath, depicted in J C Loudon's *The Gardener's Magazine*, V, 1829.

21 Henry Stothert's methods of heating by steam, *Transactions of the Horticultural Society*, I, 2, 1835.

22 Section through the Marquis de Chabannes's patent *calorfière fumivore*, fireplace and boiler, adapted to two or more hotbeds, in 1818; as shown in *The Gardener's Magazine*, IV, 1828.

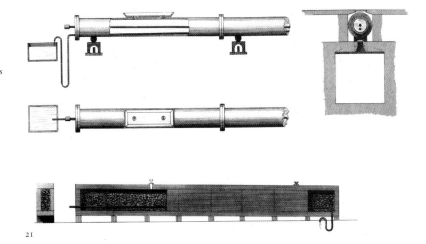

21

22

23, 24 Section and plan of
W Atkinson's hot-water
system applied to a
hothouse in the gardens
of Anthony Bacon,
Aberamen, Glamorgan-
shire, 1822, as depicted
in *Transactions of the
Horticultural Society*
VII, 1830.

25 The Marquis de
Chabannes's hot-water
system for a house, based
on his pamphlet of 1818.

23

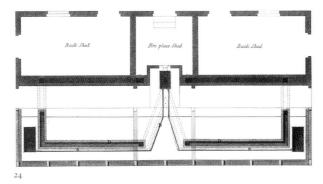

24

hot water as well as the smoke and gases from the fireplace, which circulated along the front wall, then to the back wall and out of the chimneys.

CHABANNES'S system was more sophisticated than Atkinson's. It pre-empted a similar invention by the engineer Thomas Tredgold by a decade and Alexander Cruickshank's water-jacketed boilers by eighteen years. Like modern critics, Loudon criticized an architect for not keeping up with the latest technical innovations: 'We are not surprised that Mr. Atkinson should not have heard of what Chabannes had done; for we have learned … that when some of the Bank of England directors proposed to heat a part of their establishment by hot water, their architect [Sir John Soane], had not heard of such a mode of heating.'[7]

THOUGH Thomas Tredgold had developed a steam-heating method at Syon House, he was also an advocate of hot-water heating. He read a paper on the subject to the London Horticultural Society in August 1828. This described how Atkinson's device worked and presented some important hydrodynamic principles and statistics: the specific heat of various liquids, the coefficients of friction and expansion, and the formulae for heat retention and boiler size in relation to the area of horticultural glass. The art of heating had finally developed into a science, based on principles established in 1701 when Sir Isaac Newton had presented the laws of heating and cooling to the Philosophical Society.

HOT water circulated by siphonage was invented separately by Thomas Fowler and James Kewley. Kewley used the method at Colvill's nursery in 1826 and later at the Oxford Botanic Garden, and Fowler acquired a patent for the siphon in 1829. While previous systems, except that of Chabannes, required that the boiler and the distribution pipes be at the same level, the siphon permitted a supply of water above and below the boiler. Fowler published a pamphlet on his thermosiphon, which could heat a bath on the upper floors from a boiler in the kitchen. It created a complete circuit of water from the boiler to the water-jacketed bath and back to the boiler again. The descending water drew the hot water to the bath in a

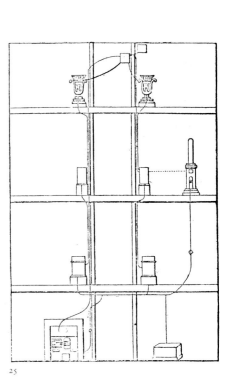

25

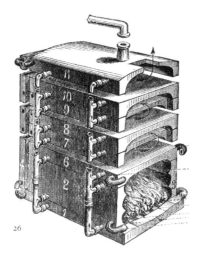

26

27

continuous circuit. Fowler provided a simple diagram. The side of the pipe system that was curved, and therefore longer, cooled the water first, which flowed back to the boiler while the hot water was siphoned up.

DURING the 1830s A M Perkins developed high-pressure, hot-water distribution by hermetically sealing the entire system and adding an additional tube that allowed expansion of the water as high-pressure steam. The system did not require a boiler, but several loops of half-inch pipe were embedded in a masonry core around the fire. The average heat of the pipes was 350°F which developed a pressure of 135 lb per square inch. Though used mainly in factories and dwellings, the system was also found in hothouses like those of John Hornsley Palmer, a bank director from Parson's Green, Fulham, and John Nash's extant architectural conservatory at Kew Gardens, reconstructed by Sir Jeffry Wyatville in 1836 when the system was added.

THE Chabannes boiler of 1816 was presented in a paper to the Horticultural Society in 1834 by Alexander Cruickshank, who described the boiler as that which a 'friend in France' used to heat his study. The cylindrical boiler, needing no masonry enclosure, was completely surrounded by a water-jacket similar to those on the high-pressure steam-engines being developed for the railway. Cruickshank described other boilers that, along with George Stephenson's double-cylinder boilers, were forerunners of modern hot-water systems.

BY the mid-nineteenth century, dozens of iron-mongers, iron founders, engineers and glasshouse merchants had entered the new hot-water heating trade with their 'ideal' boiler and distribution systems. In his *The Book of the Garden* of 1853, Charles McIntosh appears to have described and illustrated nearly every one of them. Weeks & Co of Kings Road, Chelsea, who produced just one of his choices, had also displayed their upright tubular boiler at the Great Exhibition in 1851.

THOUGH glasshouse heating systems did not reach North America until the latter part of the nineteenth century, when they did an extensive commercial market was realized. Frederick A Lord, a carpenter and amateur greenhouse builder, established his American glasshouse

company in 1856. By the 1870s he was building large forcing-houses and glass ranges for estates in upstate New York, concentrated along the Hudson River, near his plant in Irvington. In 1873 Lord and his son-in-law, William Burnham, put their first boiler on the market. This was a cast-iron sectional, probably similar to those used in England at the time, but the first in the United States. The boiler had very little direct heating surface and could not have heated a greenhouse through a very cold New York winter night. Lord & Burnham's second attempt to design a boiler was in 1878. Giving up the 'sectional' model because of leaks, they marketed a very expensive, but highly efficient, brass-tube heat exchanger inside a cast-iron case. The brass tubes, however, burned out because of the electrolytic action of brass, cast-iron and water. In the 1880s the company reverted to a cast-iron water-jacketed boiler, which they sold in hundreds to florists and private gardeners. But by the 1900s, because of the shipping and installation difficulties of the huge and heavy one-piece boiler, a new 'sectional' replaced the standard. This was similar to the sectional boiler of Hitchings & Co who merged with Lord & Burnham in 1905.

IN the 1880s Hitchings & Co had developed the 'camel back' cast-iron boiler with a corrugated firebox and circuitous channels for extracting heat from the hot-flue gases. The boiler was virtually identical to Cruickshank's model of 1834 and the water was distributed by siphon action previously demonstrated by Kewley in 1828. To meet the growing market of the middle-class gardeners who had more modest greenhouses, Hitchings & Co also patented a domestic water-jacketed siphonic heater, which was required to be in a basement below the glasshouse.

THE close of the nineteenth century was the end of an epoch in which gardeners and horticulturists had taken the lead in environmental controls; more sensitive heating systems had been developed for plants than for domestic use. The success of glasshouse heating systems meant that their manufacture had become a commercial venture, beyond the realm of the gardener. Needing far less intensive labour and care than their early prototypes, they represented the first step towards the goal of a self-sufficient, automatic garden.

26 English cast-iron boiler in sections, *The Floral World and Garden Guide*, 1871. Because of its weight it had to be made in sections for shipping.

27 Modest domestic hot-water boiler on the thermosiphon principle, offered by Hitchings and Co of New York, in their catalogue *Greenhouse Heating and Ventilating Apparatus*, 1889.

28 Section of the architectural conservatory at Kew Gardens by John Nash, later renovated by Jeffry Wyatville, c1836, heated by A M Perkins's high-pressure hot-water system.

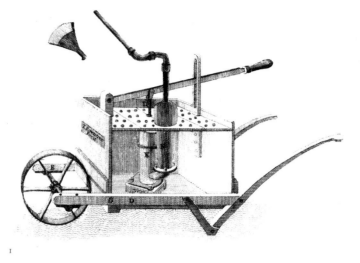

THE AUTOMATIC
GARDEN

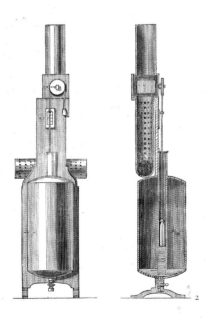

IV

TO recreate a plant's natural environment in glasshouses required constant attendance to regulate temperature, light, rainwater and the circulation of fresh air. Consequently gardeners strove to make their glasshouses automatic. However, it was only in the nineteenth century, when innovation became the result of studied empiricism rather than trial and error, that automation, or rather the accommodation and smooth running of every aspect of an artificial climate, became a realistic goal.

IN his *A Short Treatise on several improvements recently made in Hot-Houses* of 1805, Loudon was one of the first plant environmentalists to note the need for both ventilation – the changing of the air in a hothouse – and air movement inside it. Ventilation was no problem in the summer when sashes could be removed or the glass skin opened like venetian blinds (skilfully demonstrated in his designs in *Remarks on the Construction of Hot-Houses*, 1817). When the houses were sealed in the winter, however, the problem of introducing cold outside air into the damp, stuffy plant-chamber presented itself. Loudon suggested that air be blown in from sheds behind the plant-chambers with bellows or his own box-like pump. It was, however, the movement of air that

Preceding pages
1 Barrow water-engine
  from the early nineteenth
  century, C McDonald,
  Gardener's Dictionary,
  vol II, 1807.
2 George Mugliston's
  temperature controlled
  apparatus for ventilating
  hot-houses, *Transactions
  of the Horticultural Society*,
  V, 1824.
3 Interior of the Palm
  House, Royal Botanic
  Gardens, Edinburgh,
  R Mathienson, 1858.

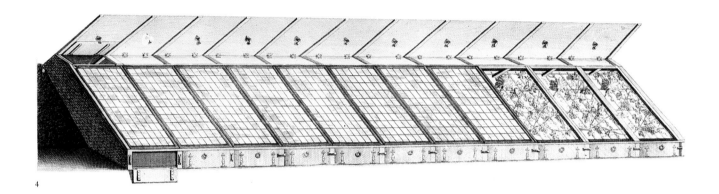

4

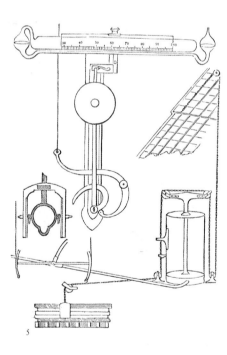

5

Loudon found was essential and difficult to reproduce. He had observed that hothouse plants, even when they received adequate air, heat and light, grew weak and spindly. It was only on their exposure to the breeze in summer that they developed bushy and vigorous shoots. In his 1805 treatise he emphasizes man's success in imitating nature, up to a point:

In hothouses, nature has been imitated, more or less perfectly in most things. Heat is produced from the furnaces and flues. Light is admitted through the glass; rain is supplied from the syringe or watering-pot; dew is rarefied by pouring water upon the flues or by steam apparatus and fresh air is admitted at pleasure. There is still something missing. What makes up the want of those refreshing and genial breezes, which fan and invigorate the real nature?

LOUDON adapted a common winnowing machine, which was hand powered and hung from the rafters, to generate 'the breeze'. He modelled one on the roasting jack: the fan was powered by descending weights and positioned in a box on wheels to be towed to any place in the glasshouse. A mechanism caused it to revolve, fanning air in all directions. His other apparatus was a proper windmill or fan, powered by a key-wound spring.

IN his *A Description of a Patent Hot-House* of 1803, James Anderson was certainly one of the first people to describe a solar-heat sink for heating and ventilation. He proposed that air chambers under or adjoining the greenhouse be filled with the 'superfluous' air, which would then be heated by the sun during the day and 'sucked' into the house at night with a winnowing machine in a cylinder. This was a very early example of passive solar heating, which was so popular in the 1970s.

IN the early 1800s forced ventilation was adopted in factories, hospitals and homes. In 1811, Mr Strutt from Derby provided a type of natural ventilation for his house and the Derby Infirmary. He connected a funnel-mouthed pipe to a wind vane and dug it underground some 100 yards from his house. The constant temperature of the ground cooled the air in summer and tempered it in the winter. It was a forerunner of today's earth-source heat pumps.

IN 1812, Benford Deacon patented one of the first forced, warm-air furnaces, which was the system used to heat the Old Bailey and a greenhouse in Streatham.[1] A description of the patent shows it to be very similar to fan-coil units used in the twentieth century. A fan fixed in a semicylindrical chamber in the basement drew in outside air and forced it through a tube-filled chamber. The tubes were charged with steam or hot water in the winter. In the summer, the air was drawn from a cool cellar and the tubes filled with cold water. Having no electricity, the fan was powered by a descending weight machine and the air was distributed (as also proposed by Loudon) in canvas tubes; polyethylene tubes are used in a similar way to distribute tempered air in greenhouses today.

LOUDON thought that Deacon's hot-air system, combined with automatic control, would produce a perfect artificial environment and be important in 'pneumatic medicine'; by which he meant a 'hothouse for invalids' that a Dr Kentish established in 1813 near Clifton. Throughout the nineteenth century a number of similar proposals were made, including Joseph Paxton's 'Crystal Sanitarium' in 1851. It is safe to say, however, that even today the English do not like forced warm-air heating, perhaps because it is dry and ruins antique furniture, which is attuned to a damp ambient environment.

IT was James Kewley's innovative system that really stirred Loudon's imagination and convinced him that a perfect artificial environment was feasible. This thermostatic device could, when coupled with a hopper-fed steam-boiler, a bell system and various types of ventilators, control the climate 'without the labour of man'.[2] Loudon named Kewley's regulating thermometer the 'automaton gardener', for to him it was a horticultural robot.[3] He was constantly suggesting the attachment of Kewley's device to his proposed 'polyprosopic' roofs, with the roof glass in ridge and furrow, and octagonal or hexagonal pyramids. The top edges of these roofs were to be hinged, creating venetian louvres attached to rods. Chains and pulleys were actuated when the 'automaton gardener' reacted to temperature changes and

harsh weather. The system was a precocious forerunner of today's horticultural glasshouse vents and curtains regulated by thermostats, photo cells, solenoids and motors.

KEWLEY took out a patent for the thermometer in 1816 when he moved from Douglas, Isle of Man, to London and installed a prototype in his rooms on the New Kent Road. The 'automaton' was on display at W & D Bailey's premises in Holborn and later Kewley applied it to a hothouse in Colvill's nursery in the Kings Road, Chelsea, during the summer of 1819. The machine was shown to Royal Society President, Sir Joseph Banks, and to the Horticultural Society, but Thomas Knight, the President, and the other members thought 'such a machine was not wanted in gardening'.[4]

IN a patent for his 1803 glasshouse Dr James Anderson described a hermetically sealed 'oblong bladder', which expanded with an increase in temperature and opened the hinged sashes. He also suggested that metals with a high coefficient of expansion, like brass, lead or mercury, be connected to vertical rods to lift the roof vents. Two papers describing similar self-acting ventilators on the expansion principle were read to the Horticultural Society on 6 April 1824. Horticulturist John Williams's 'self-acting ventilator for hothouses' was placed in the sun on the back wall of the house. The expansion and contraction of air in a sealed tank actuated a column of water that forced a cylinder to open or close two 'registers', one high on the back wall for the escape of hot air and the other near the floor for the admission of cold air. The other self-regulator, designed by another horticulturist, George Mugliston, from Repton in Derbyshire, was intended to protect his vinery from excessive heat during the night if the fires had been over-stoked in expectation of frost. A copper air chamber was painted black to absorb the radiant heat of the flues. A glass float (a corked bottle) was attached to a balancing weight by a cord that passed over the wheel connected to the 'air valve'. As the air expanded, the water column and the bottle rose, opening the 'air valve' in a tube connected to an intake on the roof.

STALE, still air in tightly constructed iron and glasshouses, like that of the Royal Horticultural

4 Dutch forcing-frame with movable ventilation flaps, Pieter de la Court van de Voort, *Landhuren, Lusthaven, Plantagien*, 1737. The back panel held the hinged flap and acted as a sun reflector and wind protector.

5 James Kewleys's Automaton Gardener, patented in 1816 and illustrated in J C Loudon, *An Encyclopaedia of Gardening*, 1822.

6 John Williams's self-acting ventilator for hothouses of 1824, reproduced in *Transactions of the Horticultural Society*, VI, 1826.

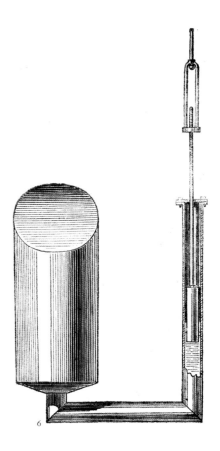

6

7 Section through The
Grange Conservatory,
Hampshire, built by
Thomas Clark for Lord
Ashburton, 1825.

8 Interior of the Camellia
House, Wollaton Hall,
Nottingham, constructed
by Thomas Clark, 1823.
This photograph shows
the columns which also
act as rainwater pipes.

Society's conservatory at Chiswick, nurtured inadequate plant specimens because of ventilation deficiencies. Even the President, Thomas Knight, obviously did not have sufficient regard for ventilation. In 1822 he presented a design for an improved curvilinear hothouse with only small openings top and bottom for ventilation. However, by the 1840s the art of ventilation was well developed in glazed kitchen-gardens like those of Frogmore, Windsor, and Dalkeith. BY 1846 Dr John Lindley, first editor of Joseph Paxton's magazine, *Gardener's Chronicle*, distinguished ventilation (letting external air into a forcing-house) from aeration (keeping the atmosphere in motion with fresh air currents). Realizing that the mechanical effects of motion strengthened the plants and helped sap to rise, Lindley also hinted at the need for carbon dioxide for plant growth and the fact that a plant cools itself by transpiration.

ANOTHER essential factor in a plant's healthy growth is the exact amount of the right kind of water. Rainwater is better for plants than well water. Rain has good pH characteristics and contains fewer unwanted minerals and oxides; plants have evolved and adapted genetically to rain. It was therefore normal to collect rainwater from glasshouse roofs and transfer it to large cisterns below. The water was often piped to these cisterns through structural columns, as at The Grange Conservatory in Hampshire, the Wollaton Hall Camellia House and Paxton's Great Conservatory at Chatsworth. Constructing rainwater pipes as structural columns was easy for iron founders like Matthew Boulton and James Watt, who were already making pipes to convey steam and water for steam-engines and hollow structural columns for factories and markets. They had only to integrate cast-iron structural gutters with cast-iron columns and drain water through them.

THE Grecian-style Conservatory at The Grange, built in 1825 by manufacturer Thomas Clark, led directly into the new ladies' apartments and dining room, which had recently been added to by the architect Charles Robert Cockerell (1788–1863), the original house having been designed by Inigo Jones (1573–1652).

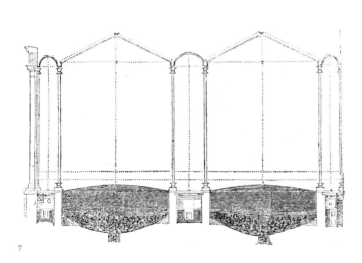

7

8

9 Section of half the
Great Conservatory
at Chatsworth, Joseph
Paxton, 1834–8. This
section shows how the
columns connect to an
underground drainage
system.
10 Detail of hollow rain-
water columns at The
Grange Conservatory.
11 Interior of The Grange
Conservatory.

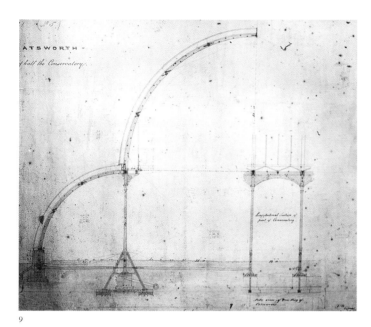

9

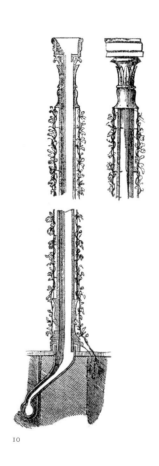

10

The glasshouse section shows curved iron roofs over the walkways and glass pyramids spanning the two planting beds between. The curved covers were of double-iron skins 'enclosing a body of air to prevent the escape of heat'. Iron walkway gratings were positioned at the top of the curved covers for maintenance. Rainwater flowed from cast-iron gutters down through the supporting cast-iron columns into a large tank under the portico. The water was then brought to plants by a 'forcing pump'. The house was heated by a combination of Sylvester's hot-air stove and steam in chambers under the floor, which entered the house through small plant-stands in the window recesses. Charles McIntosh, in *The Book of the Garden* of 1853, pointed out a missed opportunity suggesting that half the columns could have drained the roof, while the others should have been filled with hot water for heating. The glasshouse protected all sorts of delicacies, including oranges and lemons, Chinese magnolias, proteas, camellias and gardenias, indicating that it was a cool or temperate house.

11

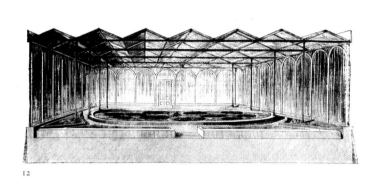

12

13

14

12, 13 Section and exterior
of the Victoria Regia
House, Chatsworth,
Joseph Paxton, 1850,
as illustrated in *The
Gardener's Chronicle*,
31 August 1850.

14 The Victoria Regia
water-lily with Queen
Victoria's autograph.
This illustration was
the frontispiece to a
catalogue for the Royal
Horticultural Society's
exhibition in South
Kensington, 1862.

THE importance of transporting water for civilization meant that the science of hydraulics emerged relatively early. In the eighteenth and nineteenth centuries field and well-pumps were adapted by gardeners. Their watering kits included various hand-held pump-syringes and larger contraptions like the barrow watering-engine. This portable pump was invaluable in the glasshouse; its spray of 40 to 50 feet watered the plants easily and helped put out any fire started by a faulty heating system. Some pumps had their own water tanks, as well as hose attachments for drawing rainwater from the cisterns below.

TODAY'S watering and hydroponic systems (in which species are grown in gravel and watered with dissolved plant food) have their antecedents in the early nineteenth century. Hothouse steaming-engines produced moisture for tropical exotics, a close imitation of the tropical jungle. But often the condensed moisture was injurious to the delicate plants, and the damp atmosphere produced mildew and fungi. Loddiges's nursery developed a rainmaking system for their 60-foot palm house at Hackney,

which the Horticultural Society awarded a medal by in 1817. Water was pumped to a tank above the house and connected to a series of half-inch lead pipes suspended below the ridge and roof at intervals of 6 to 8 feet. These rain pipes, controlled by a stopcock, were pierced with fine needles every 2 inches, and even closer at the end of the run, to equalize the 'fine stream that, in descending is broken and falls on the plants, in a manner resembling a gentle summer shower'.[5] Loudon was very impressed by the Loddiges's rainmaker and enthusiastically suggested it for all artificial climates. He installed it in the experimental square-domed glass prototype at his Bayswater house.

THE emergence of the aquatic house in the 1840s introduced a new climatic challenge for glasshouse designers – maintaining and controlling water temperature. The aquatic house was not without its precedents. There had been earlier glasshouses in Britain solely for water plants. One was built by G Tod for the Marquess of Blandford at White Knights, near Reading, and was described in his *Plans, Elevations and Sections* of Hot-Houses, Greenhouses ... an Aquarium, Conservatories etc. It had a small gable roof, a hot-air flue around the periphery of the house and two flues that heated a lead-lined tank. Loudon, with his incredible imagination and foresight, had described, though never built, 'a proper aquarium for plants'. It ought, he said, to resemble the natural habitat of aquatic plants, even the turbulence of the temperate waters. Loudon's 'aquarium', presented in *An Encyclopaedia of Gardening* of 1822 was circular and contained two ponds, one on the periphery for plants that grew in stagnant water and a central pond for river plants (see fig 23). The glass roof was shaped low over the edge of the outer pond for the shorter aquatics and high in the middle for taller plants. The vault below the central pond contained a furnace and a 'wind-up-jack' descending weight machine, which needed winding twice a day and powered a turntable that kept the river plants in perpetual motion. Plants that thrived in rapid streams were to be near the edge of the large circular platform, and those that required 'less agitation', towards its centre.

IT was the challenge of nurturing the blooms of the queen of the aquarium, the Victoria Regia water-lily, however, that inspired the aquatic house's popularity. The Victoria Regia had been known to early botanical travellers, though it was not until 1837 that Sir Robert Schomburgk, exploring British Guiana for the Geographical Society, brought back the first specimens and drawings of the plant that stirred the imagination of Victorian collectors. Seeds were planted at Kew Gardens in 1846. However, the sensitive plants did not prosper. In spite of this initial failure, by the 1850s proper pond houses could be found at Chatsworth, Syon House, the Royal Botanic Society at Regent's Park, the Veitch's nursery at Exeter, Sheffield Botanic Gardens and Dalkeith estate. In 1852 the master of iron and glass construction, Richard Turner, built the Victoria Regia House at Kew, which stands today beside his magnificent palm house.

IT was Paxton who made the breakthrough and built the first successful giant water-lily house. In 1849 he constructed a heated tank in a

15

16

15 *Protea speciosa, Perigonia pistillum* by Leopold Trattinick, *Thesaurus Botanicus*, 1819.
16 The Victoria Regia in bloom at Chatsworth for the first time, *Illustrated London News*, 17 November 1849. The leaves were sufficiently strong to support the weight of a child.

17, 18 Interior and exterior of
the Victoria Regia
House, Kew, Richard
Turner, 1852.

17

18

19 Victoria Regia House,
    Chatsworth, with staff,
    c 1870.
20 Greenhouse at
    Somerleyton, Suffolk,
    Joseph Paxton, 1850.

19

curved-roofed glasshouse at Chatsworth. In it, he put in a giant water-lily seedling with leaves less than 6 inches in diameter, which he had procured from Sir William Hooker, Kew's Director. The plant was so small that it arrived in a 13½-inch-square box and was set in the soil of the 12-foot-square tank on 10 August 1849. By the end of September the largest leaf measured 3½ feet in diameter and the tank size had to be doubled. These were Midas years for Paxton: the lily bloomed on 8 November 1849 and a week later he presented the first English bloom and a leaf to Queen Victoria and Prince Albert at Windsor Castle. The lily tank had been temporarily set up in the elliptical-roofed glass 'stove' of 20 by 60 feet, built on Paxton's ridge-and-furrow principles in 1836 to demonstrate wood-laminated construction as a prototype of the Chatsworth Great Conservatory. However, it was too narrow for the Victoria Regia's astonishing growth habits. The construction of a new house was imminent. In the spring of 1850 the New Victoria Regia House was ready to nurture the ever-expanding prize,

which that year produced a total of 112 flowers and 140 leaves.

THE speed of building the new flat-roofed, ridge-and-furrow Victoria Regia House may surprise us today. In fact, Paxton had developed his ridge-and-furrow model ten years earlier in a design for a flat-roofed conservatory on Lord Burlington's estate. Later, he added a ridge-and-furrow glasshouse to Adam Washington's mansion at Darley Dale near Matlock and he built the extant ridge-and-furrow roofed greenhouse at Somerleyton. At Chatsworth, Paxton commanded a large force of men and had direct contact with glass manufacturers and iron founders. He had already constructed his sash-bar machine, later to be used for the Crystal Palace, and could order pipes and boilers from many companies, which were more than pleased to sell to Joseph Paxton, a ditinguished gardener whose patron was the eminent Duke of Devonshire.

PAXTON's acute understanding of the lily's environmental needs were superbly realized in the new house. A Burbidge & Healy boiler

20

21

22

23

supplied hot water to a series of cast-iron pipes around the external walls, and a Sylvester's Hot Air Furnace heated the cavities around the tanks. The pathways above had boards with quarter-inch gaps between them, allowing the heat into the house. In the 16-foot lower section of the tank itself were several four-inch pipes under the earth mound, warming the roots. The cold-water supply, which powered the water wheels for mixing, could be adjusted to maintain the water temperature at 83–5°F, an extremely fine tolerance. Lower ventilation, drawn through openings between the masonry piers and roof vents, provided through ventilation, keeping the air temperature between 80° and 90°F throughout the year.

ENTHUSIASM for the giant water-lily spread internationally. First flowering at Chatsworth in 1849, then at Kew in the following year and in Amsterdam in 1859, the Victoria Regia burst forth at Leyden in 1872, where nearly thirty thousand people came to marvel. Alphonse Balat, for whom the Art Nouveau architect Victor Horta later worked, designed a Victoria

66

24 The Victoria Regia
House, Leyden, 1870.
25 The Vinery, Hampton
Court, first built in the
seventeenth century and
extended in the
nineteenth century. The
vine it houses was planted
in 1769 by Capability
Brown.

24

25

Regia House in 1854 for the Royal Society of Zoology and Horticulture in the Jardin Zoologique, later known as the 'Parc Leopold', in Brussels. Elegant curved-iron trusses radiated from the corners of the octagonal plan and culminated in a large ironwork crown. Another house built in 1870 for the Victoria Regia in Leyden University's famous garden imitated the shape of Loudon's aquatic glasshouse, conceived nearly fifty years before. It was a beautiful, delicate glass and iron construction, which, like Balat's house, was distinguished by an iron crown. In 1882, a ten-sided house depicting the archetypal shape of the water-lily houses in botanical gardens throughout Europe was built in the Berlin-Schöneberg Royal Botanical Gardens.

IF the aquatic house broadened the climatic considerations that a gardener had to take into account, the idea of the automatic garden was epitomized by the horticultural greenhouse in the kitchen-garden. Harvesting produce out of season, however, was regarded by many in the nineteenth century as an artificial practice. The architects' aesthetician, John Ruskin, believed that every climate gave its vegetables to living creatures at the right time and called 'glasshouse forcing' a vile and gluttonous modern habit. Ruskin's negative views were perhaps a response to the many urban glasshouses constructed for the production of fruits and vegetables in the early part of the nineteenth century, such as Forsyth's rational and undecorated prototype design. By the 1850s, many large estates in the surrounding countryside had vast horticultural glass ranges, producing vegetables, fruits and flowers. These were usually at the north end of walled gardens, which could be huge. Even the garden walls were often heated to provide agreeable microclimates for the fruit trees espaliered along them. Descriptions of these gardens reveal sophisticated heating, ventilation and humidifying equipment in the great glass ranges. These first integrated environmental systems allowed the head gardener to supply a prodigious variety of produce for the Christmas table, including cucumbers, strawberries, pineapples and grapes.

AS late as the 1830s, the supply of fresh fruit and vegetables to the British royal table was poor in quantity and quality. The royal gardens, nearly a dozen in number, each with various kinds of glass structures, totalled about fifty acres, but because they were at separate sites miles apart and badly managed, the fruit and vegetables were produced at considerable expense. A Garden Inquiry Committee (Paxton, Lindley and Watson, appointed in 1838) recommended selling the kitchen-garden glass at Kensington Palace and demolishing the kitchen-gardens at Cumberland Lodge, Cranbourne Lodge, Windsor Castle, Buckingham Palace, Osborne House and later at Hampton Court. A new modern kitchen-garden was proposed at Windsor. In 1844 it was established within the brick walls of a thirty-one-acre site, where it was close to the royal residence. The £45,000 investment built a range of glass envelopes with specific environments producing fruits, vegetables, mushrooms, decorative plants and flowers for Queen Victoria and her family. Starting at the main east gate and porter's lodge, a visitor would

pass a stove and greenhouse, a pineapple stove, an apricot and plum house, a late vinery, a peach house and an early vinery. These houses were all over 50 feet long, with the exception of the late vinery which was over 100 feet, and were connected by glass corridors. Arriving at the central dwelling, the series then repeats itself symmetrically on the other side. Behind the main range were smaller vineries and the cucumber, melon, French bean and pineapple pits, filled with manure or compost and heated with hot water. Asparagus beds in the northeast corner were forced by hot water that also heated the two cherry houses in the centre. Directly behind the main range were various lean-to sheds used for washing vegetables and pots, as storerooms, seed and tool rooms, mushroom houses, and rooms for the foreman and a few of the workmen.

THE dwelling house in the centre of the main range had two apartments for the Queen's use. It also provided lodging for the head gardener who commanded about 150 gardeners, assistants and apprentices. Kitchen-gardening was a refined and an extremely time-consuming art. Each

26

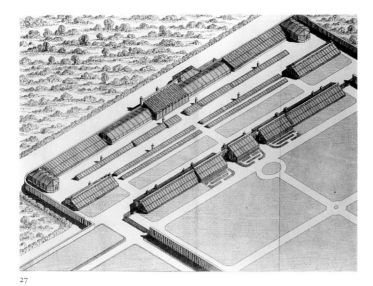

27

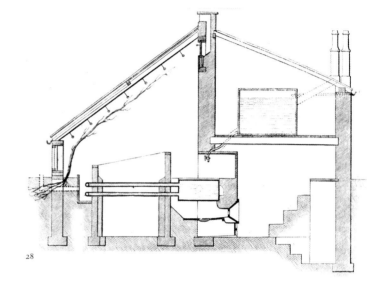

28

fruit on the pear tree was tied in a separate muslin bag to ward off wasps and bees. When the peach houses were opened to the September sun, an apprentice spent his days running back and forth with a swatter to keep the insects away. Cucumbers were grown in long glass tubes so as to be perfectly straight for the royal table.

THE Frogmore kitchen-garden glasshouses were later rebuilt and added to by glasshouse contractors Mackenzie & Moncur, who used 44,000 cubic feet of teak, 156,000 square feet of glass and 11 miles of heating pipe. Acclaimed as the largest private range in the world, it had: fourteen vineries, eight peach houses, three fig houses, two palm houses, six orchid houses, two show houses in the style of the conservatory at Malmaison, two carnation houses, two flowering-plant houses, a tropical house, a laelia house, two propagating houses, two stove houses, two crypripedium houses, two Dendrobium, a begonia house, two cyclamen houses, two geranium houses, three azalea houses, a fernery, two amaryllis houses, four cucumber houses, four melon houses, two tomato houses, two eucharis

houses, two imantophellum houses, two pelargonium houses, a rose house, gardeners' quarters, cottages, a back office, stables, car sheds and workshops.

THE *Book of the Garden* by Charles McIntosh, head gardener at Dalkeith estate, describes, among other examples, the Dalkeith kitchen-gardens, one of the most superb in Britain. Before McIntosh designed the forcing-houses there he visited gardens all over Scotland and England, including those at Frogmore. Methods of water supply, heating and ventilation were meshed together at Dalkeith to form a highly integrated environmental system; and the twenty acres of enclosed gardens were certainly as ambitious as the Queen's at Windsor. Very little of the glass remains, but all of the sheds and walls still stood in 1968 when the author visited them for the first edition of this book. They create a melancholy echo when compared to the grand illustrations in McIntosh's book. The four parallel glass ranges were placed on the north side of the garden enclosed within hollow brick walls, 12 feet high and 20 inches wide. These

27 Glass ranges at Dalkeith, near Edinburgh, designed and built by Charles McIntosh, and illustrated in his *The Book of the Garden*, 1853. Each glasshouse had a particular shape depending on the specific requirements of the produce inside.

28 Section through Charles McIntosh's vinery and pine pit at Dalkeith, *The Book of the Garden*, 1853. This house was a remarkably efficient environmental machine: the furnace flue cut diagonally to the chimney warming the backroom and the water cistern, it also topped up the boiler and was used for watering the plants. In the winter, air passed underground before entering the house as a direct cold blast would damage the vine.

29 Ground plan and
perspective of Poltalloch
kitchen-garden,
Argyllshire, Charles
McIntosh, *Book of the
Garden*, 1853. The
perspective shows
openings for the intake of
air at the bottom along
the low plateau wall.

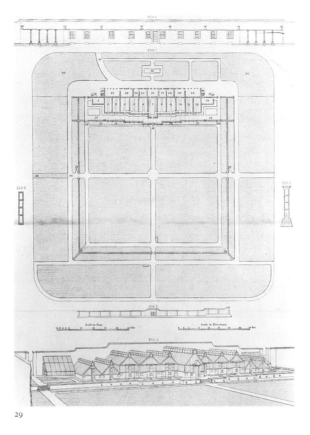

29

29 Ground plan and perspective of Poltalloch kitchen-garden, Argyllshire, Charles McIntosh, *Book of the Garden*, 1853. The perspective shows openings for the intake of air at the bottom along the low plateau wall.

were heated with four-inch hot-water pipes, providing an improved microclimate for the espaliered fruit trees. From a cellar behind the camellia house, three boilers heated the entire range. Each house had its own cistern for rain-water supply, McIntosh calculated that the 5,866 square yards of roof, exclusive of the pits, produced 739,116 gallons of water per annum: it rains a good deal in Scotland. This was piped into a huge tank in the orchid house, individual iron cisterns storing 1,000 cubic feet each, and the main reservoir in the front range cellar storing over 2,000 cubic feet. Liquid manure was produced in a tank filled with pigeon drop-pings, guano, ashes and sewage from the lavato-ries in the gardener's house; a forerunner of hydroponics, this fed the plants.

MCINTOSH designed his most sophisticated glass range in a kitchen-garden at Poltalloch, on the west coast of Argyllshire for Neil Malcolm. The dimensions show the enormous commit-ment made in producing fruits and vegetables on the estate. The walls around this immense garden (300 by 300 feet, approximately two

American football fields) were heated by hot water, as at Dalkeith. Behind the 19-foot-high north wall were the usual storerooms, work-rooms, furnaces and apartments for the work-men. To the south of this sun-reflecting wall were eleven gable-roofed glasshouses and two lean-tos, providing the exact environment for pears, peaches, apricots, pineapples, grapes, melons, cucumbers and tropical plants. Cutting an architectural section through each house would show varying combinations of water tanks and heated ventilation devices, depending on the requirements of each species grown. The cucumber house and the melon house with their myriad pipes and vents serve to demon-strate the degree to which McIntosh tempered the climate. Both houses, which were of the same construction, were heated by one boiler at the back of the wall that separated them. The pipes, which supplied the heating below the earth beds, had vents that allowed the heat to pass into the house when the temperature became too great. The house was warmed by a single pipe that ran along the top of the side walls. Air was drawn through large grilles in the front of the house and hot air escaped through the lantern along the ridge. During the Scottish winter, it was necessary to temper the outside air by drawing it through fired-clay ducts that ran underground and projected through the plinth on which the glasshouses were constructed above the garden.

MCINTOSH'S most ingenious application of the cast-iron gutter and machined-wood glazing bars was in an 1841 design to cover the kitchen-garden at Dalkeith with a structure that is the harbinger of commercial glasshouses today. He took as his model the new railway termini, particularly the North Midlands Trijunct sheds at Derby, designed by Francis Thompson and Robert Stephenson and built between 1838 and 1841. The garden of 220 by 240 feet was to be enclosed with a wide-span ridge-and-furrow roof construction, later used in Paxton's Crystal Palace and envisioned by Loudon so many years before. McIntosh believed that this type of construction could be extended over a hundred acres or more.

GLASSHOUSES had to contend with the range of temperatures outdoors and create variable conditions inside. Victorian kitchen-gardens were expected to produce, out of season, a great range of flowers, fruit and vegetables, which all had different climatic requirements. McIntosh solved this problem in his prophetic structure with an extensive system of portable glass partitions running on iron rails. These, combined with fixed partitions, enclosed diverse areas and allowed for varied temperatures. The wood and glass skin was to be supported by a wrought-iron and cast-iron truss and a beam formed from a cast-iron gutter and an iron 'suspension' rod. This structural module of 20 by 40 feet rested on round 'architectural' cast-iron columns that transferred the gutter water to cisterns below the floor. Each interior column was supported by a slab spanning a small reservoir of rainwater. A pump and a hose could draw out this water to spray the plants and fill the heating vases. The superfluous water in the reservoirs was piped to a central cistern for the boilers. The sliding wall sashes below the peripheral gutters were on

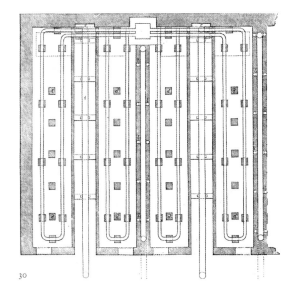

30

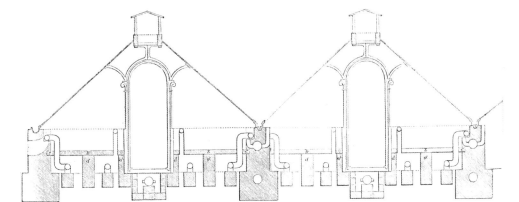

31

30, 31 Plan and section of the cucumber and melon houses at Poltalloch, Charles McIntosh, *The Book of the Garden*, 1853.

32 Design for a glass-
covered garden
at Dalkeith, Charles
McIntosh, *The Book of the
Garden*, 1853.

33 The kitchen-garden at
Glenbervie House,
Kincardineshire,
protected by the range of
glasshouses, constructed
by Moncrieffs of
Edinburgh.

'gun barrel' rollers, one sash slid behind the other, or the sash could be removed. A ventilating lantern along the ridge provided further summer ventilation. Winter ventilation was drawn by ducts from the outer wall of the platform on which the building was constructed.

THE most interesting part of McIntosh's prophetic glazed environment was the hot-water heating. A large circular vault was constructed under the very centre of the house. The building was divided into four heating zones, and boilers fed hot water in pipes to each zone. Besides radiation from the pipes themselves, ornamental cast-iron vases were positioned along them in each quadrant. The vases were shaped in such a way that convection currents of water rose up the middle and the cooler water descended to the return pipe. The lids were tight fitting, providing a steam-proof dry atmosphere; a humid atmosphere was created by removing the lids. In summer, the lids were removed and the vases filled with ornamental flowers in pots. Flues transferred smoke and gases from the twelve boilers to a horizontal flue

ending at a chimney hidden in the woods. This main flue ran parallel to a service tunnel of 7 by 7 feet leading from the vault to a door. Coal and air for combustion were to have been brought through the tunnel and ash taken away, so that it was used in a similar way to the one at the Great Conservatory, Chatsworth. McIntosh's design was well ahead of its time. The large-scale ridge-and-furrow roofs and his environmental equipment resemble in detail production glasshouses as we know them today. In horticultural areas, such as those in Holland, their presence still dominates the landscape.

ARTIFICIAL, automatic environments were refined throughout the nineteenth century, mainly for the protection and nurturing of plants and the production of fruit. This gradual scientific improvement, often by trial and costly error, also laid the groundwork for the environmental control of other building types. It made possible a parallel glasshouse development, the private conservatory, where contemporary commentators observed that the plants often enjoyed a healthier environment than their own.

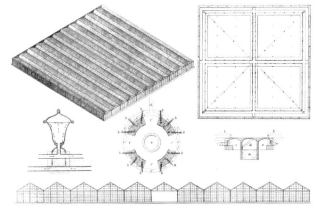

32

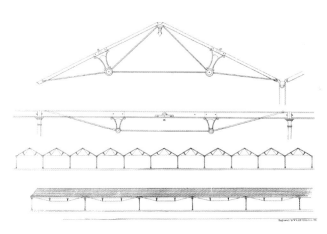

33

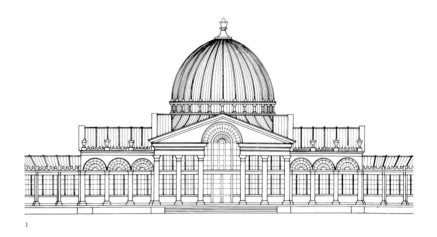

THE GRAND PRIVATE
CONSERVATORY

V

DURING Queen Victoria's reign as industrial cities discharged smoke and consumed human labour prodigiously, the private conservatory, as Loudon had already declared in the 1820s, remained 'not indeed one of the first necessities, but one which is felt to be appropriate and highly desirable and which mankind recognizes as a mark of elegance and refined enjoyment'. From the distance of the twentieth century, Walter Benjamin, the German intellectual, observed in his book *Paris, Capital of the Nineteenth Century*:

> *For the private citizen, for the first time the living-space became distinguished from the place of work … From this sprang the phatasmagorias of the interior … The collector dreamed that he was in a world which was not only far off in distance but also in time. From this epoch spring the arcades and the interiors, the exhibition halls and the dioramas.*
> *They are residues of a dream world.*[1]

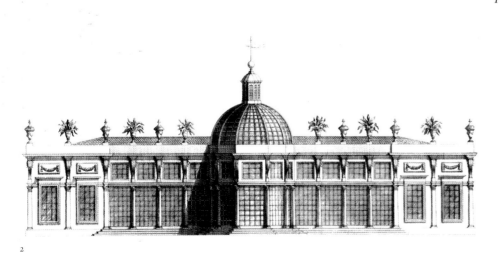

IN Britain the private conservatory adjoined to the house evolved from the exotic botanist's hothouse, though it had its most direct descendants in the detached orangery and architectural conservatory. Often used

Preceding pages
1 Elevation of central
  pavilion of the
  conservatory at
  Syon House, Middlesex,
  Charles Fowler, 1827.
2 Architectural
  conservatory by Richard
  Bradley, *New Improve-
  ments of Planting and
  Gardening*, 1717–8.
3 Interior of the
  conservatory, Syon
  House.

4

5

in the upper echelons of society for large-scale entertainment, it was also a place of relaxation and recreation close to the familial home. Though the conservatory reached the United States later, its appeal and function for the Americans was much the same as for the British. On the Continent, however, the private conservatory was subject to the decadence of the twilight years of the aristocracy, presenting for them a means of refuge and escapism. Set in extensive grounds, often on a grand-scale as part of a whole complex of buildings, glasshouses reflected the whims and fantasies of their owners in the diversity of their architectural styles. For European society at large, however, where people were on the whole more outward looking than their English contemporaries, the private conservatory did not enjoy the same popularity. Dignified gentlemen and elegant ladies of the middle classes preferred to promenade in public rather than stay at home. The consequence was the construction of winter-gardens in Berlin, Brussels, Karlsruhe, Paris, Vienna, Stuttgart and St Petersburg.

THE late seventeenth and early eighteenth centuries had seen the garden as the setting for the banqueting hall and summer supper-house. The hall gave the garden more accessibility, while the garden gave the hall isolation from the mundane world. The hall doubled as a winter storage place for the citrus trees, myrtles as well as other exotic plants, transforming its function with the change of seasons, Thomas Langford noted this in his work *Plain and Full Instructions to raise all Sorts of Fruit-Trees* of 1681: 'Greenhouses are of late built as ornaments to gardens, as summer and banqueting houses were formerly, as well as for a conservatory for tender plants, and when the curiosities in the summer time are dispersed in their proper places in the garden, the house being accommodated for that purpose, may serve for an entertaining room.' Christopher Wren, with the help of Nicholas Hawksmoor and John Vanbrugh, designed the beautiful Orangery at Kensington Palace for Queen Anne in 1704, intended as a winter promenade and summer supper-house.[2]

76

INITIALLY, during the eighteenth and early nineteenth centuries, garden orangeries and wintering places were turned into glasshouses simply by replacing the slate or tile roof with glass. The early architectural conservatories were so-called because their pilasters, cornices and friezes followed the formalist styles and attitudes of the day. Architectural styles were generally opposed by botanists and gardeners who wanted conservatories to serve the environment and the genera of plants more directly. It was only with the later appreciation of the importance of light that the roofs of the architectural conservatory were built of glass.

AN example of a building that never successfully served its botanical function, even once it was adapted, is the Orangery in Kew Gardens. Built for Augusta, the Dowager Princess of Wales, and designed by Sir William Chambers in *c* 1760, it originally only had windows in the south elevation. Even with additional ones on the east and west, the building did not provide enough light for the orange trees. Plants from New Zealand and Australia were tried and fared

no better. During the 1850s, the Director of Kew, Sir William Hooker, had a new temperate house built for these plants, which was completed in 1862. Brent Elliot explains that there was a well-understood distinction between a gardener's conservatory, which provided maximum light, and an architect's conservatory in which social use and harmony of style were more important than the needs of the plants.[3] The Kew Orangery is now a restaurant.

AN earlier design, however, balanced aesthetic and botanical considerations. In 1718 Richard Bradley presented a decorative greenhouse that 'conformed to the "Rules of Architecture", and at the same time considered the welfare of the plants'.[4] A glass dome was proposed over the most tender plants 'to receive more of the sun's warmth'. The Corinthian columns were as thin as possible to maximize insulation. The walls were covered with white Dutch tiles reflecting the light to the orange, lemon and myrtle trees inside. Bradley measured the success of such a house by the health of the plants in winter and its usefulness for entertaining in summer.

4 Orangery at Wye House, Mills River Neck, Maryland, Virginia, constructed 1750s.

5 *The Luncheon in the Conservatory*, Louise Abbema, 1877. This painting shows the social function of conservatories, which was still fashionable in the late nineteenth century.

6 The Orangery, Kensington Palace, Christopher Wren, Nicholas Hawksmoor and John Vanbrugh, 1704.

6

7–9 The Orangery, Belton
House, Lincolnshire,
Jeffry Wyatville, 1820.

THE GLASSHOUSE

7

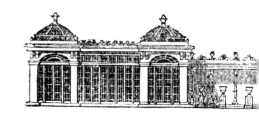

8

9

10

11

12

IN the North American colonies one of the first architectural conservatories was constructed during the 1750s at Wye House, in Mills River Neck, Maryland, only to be renovated and extended in 1784 when Elizabeth Tayloe Lloyd and her husband Edward built a new house after their marriage. Elizabeth Tayloe's family lived at Mount Airy, Virginia, where they enjoyed an orangery, and it is presumed that this structure (only parts of the walls remain) was influential in the new Wye design. An interesting detail of this stone and stuccoed brick conservatory are the wood voussoirs over the windows, which are painted to mimic stone. However, it also functioned well as an artificial climate, for a contemporary letter praises the healing powers of a lemon carried eighteen miles from the conservatory on horseback.

A COMPROMISE between the architect and the gardener is illustrated in a later structure that was erected in the 1820s at the villa of M Caters de Wolfe, near Antwerp, by the London firm of W & D Bailey. Two hothouses, curved to maximize the sun's effects, framed the architect's

conservatory. Architectural conservatories can still be found throughout England and Europe. The one at Belton House, Grantham, designed by Jeffry Wyatville in 1820 is typical of Wyatville and of the period: mainly stone, free-standing in the landscape or the garden, with a solid or glass roof.[5]

ACCORDING to Edward Diestelkamp, an expert in English glass gardens, Wyatville's early nineteenth-century conservatories, built for the wealthy aristocracy, display a mastery of elegance and natural lighting; to this end, he reduced the stone elements to a minimum and used iron for internal columns and roof structure.[6] Among his many achievements are the camellia houses at Bretton Hall (1812) and Woburn Abbey (1822); the conservatories at Longleat House (1814), Ashridge Park (1815), Belton House (1820), Wollaton Hall (1923); the Orangery at Chatsworth (1826); and the large 290-foot-long Botanical House at Woburn Abbey built for the sixth Duke of Bedford (1836).

THE Conservatory at Wollaton Hall was built by Clark & Jones. It is shown in a watercolour

10–11 Interiors of the Grand Conservatory at Alton Towers, Robert Abraham, 1827.

12 Elevation of the Grand Conservatory, Alton Towers.

13 The Grand Conservatory,
Alton Towers,
Staffordshire, Robert
Abraham, 1827.
14 Interior view of the
central dome of the
Grand Conservatory,
Alton Towers.
15 The cast iron and glass
domes covering the
Grand Conservatory
at Alton Towers.

13

14

sketch in their 1822 order book, but it has elements similar to the Camellia House at Bretton Hall by Wyatville. However, the order book does not mention Wyatville, who had been the architect for the renovations of the main house at Wollaton from the beginning of the century. It is not clear what contribution he made to the conservatory, but most certainly he would have been consulted. As cast and wrought metal were relatively new materials for buildings, the architect would have been dependent on the design, manufacturing and fabricating skills of the producers, who, in turn, until they became specialized, would look to the architect for the grand concept.

IN 1814 the fifteenth Earl of Shrewsbury started building Alton Towers in Staffordshire. He employed hundreds of labourers and artisans to build the house and a vast garden in a valley, which contained a pagoda, a Greek temple, caves, waterfalls, 'a cottage for a blind harper', moss-houses, an imitation of Stonehenge, Indian temples and conservatories. Shrewsbury was one of a small breed of nineteenth-century

eccentrics seeking the elusive Garden of Eden with his vast fortune. He commissioned architect, Robert Abraham, to build a small Greek-style architectural conservatory with a glass roof and a grand one with seven gilded-glass domes. This conservatory, still standing today, was built on the same large scale as the conservatory designed by the architect Charles Fowler for the Duke of Northumberland at Syon House, across the Thames from Kew Gardens. This magnificent symmetrical structure was the first large glass conservatory of its kind in 1827. Fowler placed a bell-shaped glass rotunda over the central hall and curved the plan to enclose a south-facing garden. Set on a base of Bath stone and glass, the cast-iron columns support the glass, which was originally secured with gunmetal glazing bars. The glass bell-dome resembles Loudon's 'acuminated apex' dome with 'spread out base'. The dome, high above the other roofs, allows heated air to rise into it, probably causing heating problems and expense – a not uncommon nemesis of the architectural conservatory.

16

ANOTHER glasshouse which stands in the Royal Botanic Gardens, Kew, is the architectural conservatory designed by John Nash, originally built adjoining Buckingham Palace. Three identical conservatories were built at the same time at each corner of the Palace, one was converted into a chapel, one remained as a conservatory and the third was transported in 1836 to Kew, where it was reconstructed by Sir Jeffry Wyatville as additional space for the palm collection and given a new Perkins's high-pressure water boiler. Although seemingly made of masonry, it has cast-iron trusses on cast-iron columns supporting the glass roof, which incidently was too low for palms. Its lines are similar to those of the conservatory at Barnsley Park, Gloucestershire, also said to be designed by John Nash in 1807.

THE great conservatories of the 1830s to the 1850s, being devoted to plants requiring warm temperatures and high humidity, were still often placed some distance from the country residence. As a result, they evoked the distance to a foreign climate and solved a major problem of

16 The central hall and glass-shaped rotunda of the conservatory at Syon House, Middlesex, Charles Fowler, 1827.

17 Circular conservatory at Dalkeith, Edinburgh, William Burn, before 1840.

18 Architectural conservatory at Kew, originally designed for Buckingham Palace by John Nash and reconstructed by Jeffry Wyatville in 1836.

19 Architectural conservatory, Barnsley Park, Gloucestershire, built for Sir John Musgrave by John Nash, 1807. This Ionic temple has long windows in its side wall which, as shown here, can be opened in the summer.

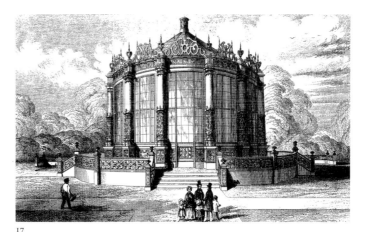

17

18

19

20 Chimney of the circular
conservatory, Dalkeith,
Edinburgh, before 1840.
21 Fern House, Ashridge,
Matthew Digby Wyatt,
1864.

attached conservatories causing damp in the residence. The Scottish architect, William Burn, designed a highly decorative white-sand-stone freestanding conservatory for the Duchess of Buccleuch at Dalkeith estate, which was built before the arrival of the famous gardener Charles McIntosh in 1840, who later criticized it in his books. Heavy, thick trusses from a central chimney supported the glass and wooden framed roof of the conservatory. These trusses, in keeping with the aesthetics of the building, blocked out the light. The raised platform housed boilers, which were considered the first in Scotland. It must have been an impressive sight with smoke disgorging from the centre chimney. The soot and stain obscured so much light from entering through the glass that it was abandoned as a plant-chamber.

IT is difficult today to view these buildings with a nineteenth-century aesthetic sensibility. Glasshouses that are now appreciated for their functional elegance (like the Crystal Palace) were not then recognized for their architectural qualities. Even though Matthew Digby Wyatt

had sat on the building committee of the 1851 Crystal Palace, advising Paxton how to decorate it, and had worked with I K Brunel in 1853–4, producing an inventive and sympathetic decoration for Paddington station, he chose to use historic masonry in his conservatories. He produced a neo-Greek architectural fern house for the Earl of Brownlow in 1864 and, even later, another stone conservatory at Castle Ashby, Northamptonshire, at the height of the glass and iron mania. Even Sir Joseph Paxton, in his role of 'architect', used masonry and tried nearly every style imaginable. The pragmatic lines of the Crystal Palace that we find so appealing obviously were seen then as a compromise, lacking style and refinement.

MRS Beaumont's conservatory at Bretton Hall, built entirely of glass and iron was, in 1827, one of the first curvilinear houses to stand as a transparent object in the garden. In contrast to the architectural conservatory, this environmental chamber, under the influence of Loudon, took its shape from the horticulturists' criteria using improved types of iron and glass.

21

20

22

23

THE rapid rise in popularity of the conservatory was described by Humphry Repton, the noted landscape designer. In his *Observations on the Theory and Practice of Landscape Gardening* of 1803, he proposes that the greenhouse resembles a nurseryman's stove, which would make it suitable for the flower garden, but not as an annex of the main house. By 1816, however, Repton was humming a different tune. In his new book, *Fragments on the Theory and Practice of Landscape Gardening*, he advocates connecting the house and conservatory to alleviate the 'parlour's formal gloom'. He illustrates this with a delightful pair of before-and-after drawings, a technique used throughout his beautiful books. After all, even the poet William Cowper wrote, 'who loves a garden loves a greenhouse too'.[7]

REPTON'S 'Fragment XXV, A Plan Explained to a Lady' of 1816 describes the conversion of an existing mansion into a residence of recreation and pleasure by integrating it with gardens and attached glasshouses.[8] The plan reveals his understanding of the influence of climate and sun. Few windows face north, which is 'sunless,

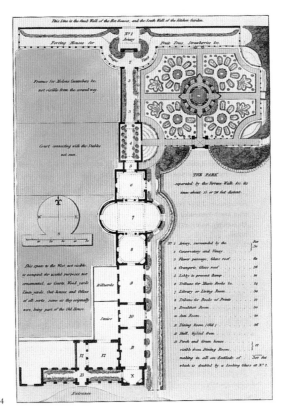

24

22–3 Drawings contrasting the parlour's 'formal gloom' with the delights that come from an attached conservatory, Humphry Repton, *Fragments on the Theory and Practice of Landscape Gardening*, 1816.

24 Plan for improving a mansion by the addition of gardens and greenhouses, Humphry Repton, 'A Plan Explained to a Lady', *Fragment XXV*, 1816.

25 The Indian Villa at Sezincote, Gloucestershire, Samuel Pepys Cockerell, 1806, etching by J Martin. The design was influenced by Humphry Repton.

26 Interior of the attached conservatory at the Indian Villa, Sezincote.

25

26

cold, gloomy', or west with its 'stormy rains and winds'. He preferred orientation and window placement to the south, which is 'hot, genial, cheerful', and the east that 'requires shelter in the spring'. There is an entry porch-cum-greenhouse, a lobby to prevent damp reaching the music room from the orangery, a flower passage, a conservatory, forcing-houses for fruit trees and strawberries, and a vinery.

REPTON gave advice on Indianizing the gardens and the new villa designed by Samuel Pepys Cockerell for his brother-in-law Sir Charles Cockerell, a retired Indian nabob, at Sezincote, Gloucestershire. The house was finished in 1806 and the attached oriental conservatory was one of two important glazed examples of the Indian style to be built in England, the other being the royal stables and glass-roofed riding house designed by William Porden for the Prince of Wales at Brighton. Repton was summoned to Brighton to give his opinion on the style of architecture for the Pavilion, which the Prince Regent wanted to remodel. He found the stables 'a stupendous and magnificent building', and proposed Indian-style alterations, which influenced the remodelling by John Nash. In 1808 Repton produced beautifully illustrated designs for the Brighton Pavilion, commissioned by the Prince, in which he presented a new idea in garden architecture, aspiring to make the garden, 'enriched with productions of every clime', unaffected by seasonal change. He proposed surrounding it with a glazed corridor or 'flower passage'. This continuous conservatory would link the main pavilion with the stables, a greenhouse, hothouses, an aviary, a pheasantry and an orangery. With its glazed panels removed, it could also become a summer kiosk.

AS the popularity of the conservatory grew, the debate between gardeners and architects intensified. The gardener's complaint was simple: too much effort was put into the architecture to the detriment of the environment. Robert Marnock (1800–89), Curator of the Royal Botanic Gardens at Regent's Park, succinctly summed up the position of the gardener in *The Gardener's Journal*:

87

27 Exterior of the end
pavilion of the Indian
Villa, Sezincote,
Gloucestershire, Samuel
Pepys Cockerell, 1806.

28 The flower passage
proposed to enclose the
Prince of Wales's garden
at Brighton, Humphry
Repton, *Designs for the
Pavilion at Brighton*, 1808.
The passage, which
would have been
connected to the new
pavilion would have
created a perpetual
garden.

27

*instead of spending £5,000 or £10,000 to cover
a few square yards of ground with a mass of
expensive but useless masonry, we would say,
spend it in a manner adapted only to the growth
of plants; and on this principle £10,000 would
cover an acre of ground, or any quantity in the
same proportion.*

MARNOCK must have been impressed by
Paxton's design for the Great Conservatory at
Chatsworth, conceived with the help of
Decimus Burton and built between 1836 and
1840. It cost the Duke of Devonshire £33,000;
some 123 feet wide and 277 feet long, with an
arched roof 67 feet high, it enclosed three-quarters of an acre. The conservatory was only part
of the enormous spectacle of waterworks, landscape and exotics, which Paxton's patron had
built with his enormous wealth. The total landscape design transcended horticultural considerations. Visitors passed the stepped waterfall,
through the palms, ferns, rhododendrons, bam-
boo and artificial rock works to a platform
overlooking the great glass structure. Inside

28

the immense double doors, everything was subordinated to the spectators' escape into fantasy. The eight hot-water boilers that fed the seven miles of four-inch pipe were discreetly hidden in vaults. A tunnel was laid ingeniously, with a tramway to supply coal and remove ashes. The smoke passed through a tunnel and a chimney into the surrounding woods. At the height of the Great Conservatory's fame it was filled with the most glorious plants from the Duke's vast collection from around the world, tropical birds flew among the palms, gold and silver fish swam in the pools below, and there were displays of large crystals and rock ores. The centre aisle was designed to allow visitors to glide through in an open coach, as did the Queen with her consort and the royal entourage in December 1843, the Conservatory being illuminated by twelve thousand lamps along the ribs. No expense was spared for this royal visit.

THE frame of the immense conservatory was made entirely of wood with the exception of the cast-iron columns that supported the laminated wood arches and doubled as rainwater pipes. The roof was a curvilinear ridge-and-furrow design. Paxton had previously described, in his *Magazine of Botany* of 1834, experiments with the ridge-and-furrow skin on a pine house in 1833 and on a greenhouse against a brick wall in 1834, to explain why he favoured wood glazing bars over metal. These prototypes, and another elliptical ridge-and-furrow hothouse of 26 by 60 feet, gave Paxton confidence to use the system on the Great Conservatory at Chatsworth and, eventually, on the 1851 Crystal Palace.

PAXTON saved thousands of man hours with his sash-cutting machine, which shaped grooves in the forty miles of glazing bar that enclosed the Chatsworth Stove. It is not clear how he managed to paint and glaze this glass mound, but he undoubtedly used a block and tackle, a less sophisticated form of the glazing platform that was later employed at the Crystal Palace. He designed the Conservatory with a cast-iron gallery around the main space, which enabled visitors to see all the exotics from above and provided the gardeners with a platform for watering.

29

29 Greenhouse at Chatsworth, Joseph Paxton, 1834. It was built as an experiment in ridge-and-furrow roof construction and a prelude to the Great Conservatory.
30 The Great Conservatory, Chatsworth, Joseph Paxton, 1836.

30

31 The Glass Wall at
Chatsworth, Joseph
Paxton, 1848.
32 The Great Conservatory,
Chatsworth, in the
process of being glazed.

31

BEFORE the Great Conservatory was finished, Paxton was working on a large conservatory for Edward Davies Davenport at Capesthorne Hall, Cheshire. According to George F Chadwick, the building must have been designed before Paxton went on Grand Tour with the Duke in October 1838.[9] This conservatory, which formed an addition to the mansion was not curvilinear like the Great Conservatory. The framework of laminated-wood arches (based on experiments at Chatsworth), forming the main space and side aisles, was curved like those of the Great Conservatory. However, the ridge-and-furrow skin was slightly pitched giving the appearance of being rectangular. Paxton was later to draw a blotting-paper sketch of the Crystal Palace, which recalled this form of construction.

PAXTON built other conservatories with the ridge-and-furrow skin, before and after the Crystal Palace, including a small flat-roofed conservatory attached to Darley House, near Chatsworth. Critics of the Crystal Palace claimed that the ridge and furrow would collapse and cause vast damage to the exhibition below. In his defence, Paxton requested and received a testimonial letter from Adam Washington, who was living at Darley House, and read it to the Society of Arts in November 1850, while the exhibition building was under construction. The cunning Paxton knew how to rebuke his critics. This, combined with exuberance and a unique talent, resulted in a fantastic and productive career, from garden apprentice to knighthood; with, of course, the help of one of the richest men in England, the sixth Duke of Devonshire.

THOUGH the construction of the conservatory wall was not unique to Paxton and could be found in many walled gardens in one form or another, his Great Conservatory wall at Chatsworth is, like most of the building, very large and dramatic, being some 330 feet long. The original ridge-and-furrow roof construction is also similar to the extant glass walls at Burton Closes, near Bakewell and at Somerleyton.

IN Loudon's *The Suburban Gardener & Villa Companion* of 1838, in which he described,

32

33 A drawing of an attached
conservatory and aviary,
Twickenham Park,
J B Papworth.

34 The ideal suburban
property, 'A villa of three
acres and a half … with a
first rate house' complete
with a south-facing
conservatory, design
from J C Loudon, *The
Suburban Gardener and
Villa Companion*, 1838.

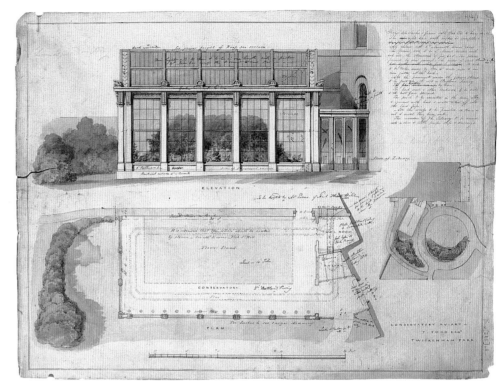

33

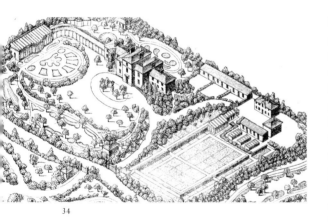

34

lauded and often criticized designs sent to him, a conservatory of some description was almost always included. Although it is not clear whether Loudon coined the word suburban, it is certain that his definition of the term was grander than the one we have today. He meant his book to be aimed at those living or wanting to live on property outside cities of at least half an acre. Suburban today more often means a plot of 20 by 80 feet. It is interesting to note some other features of his ideal suburban property. They include: a self-sustaining homestead, 'A Villa of three Acres and a Half, on a level Surface, with a First-rate House', which should provide the main source of food and enjoyment; a lodge entrance, stables, a coach-house – a source of dung for the frames and forcing-houses – a gardener's room and sheds; and a yew hedge that would protect the walled kitchen-garden, poultry-court and brew house from the wind, and hide it from the house. At the north end of the house is the drawing room, which leads to the south-facing conservatory by a covered way. Behind the covered way sits the aviary and house for fancy fowl. In front of the conservatory is the flower garden with a path that leads to a 'piece of water' with a seat and a small summer-house. Loudon remarked that this design was suitable for a person having an income of between £1,500 and £2,000 a year, a considerable sum.

FOR the more prosperous citizen, an attached conservatory had become a necessity. Usually adjacent to the drawing room, it was first considered mainly for feminine use as at The Grange, Hampshire, where it was situated opposite the lady's chambers by C R Cockerell (see pp 60–61). As Benjamin Disraeli had his heroine's father state in his novel *Henrietta Temple* of 1837: 'I built the conservatory, to be sure. Henrietta could not live without a conservatory'; in response, another character, Ferdinand pronounced, 'Miss Temple is quite right, it is impossible to live without a conservatory.' The Papworth Collection at the Royal Institute of British Architects has a number of drawings of these attached conservatories, most of which have a small aviary between

35 The Orangery, Port
   Eliot, Cornwall, built
   for Lord Eliot.
36 The Saracenic and
   Gothic conservatory
   at Enville Hall,
   Staffordshire, designed
   and constructed by the
   horticultural builders
   Gray and Ormson of
   Danvers Street, Chelsea,
   for the Earl of Stamford
   and Warrington, *c* 1854.

the conservatory and the drawing room. J B Papworth designed them for London clientele who wished to display their taste in the new gardening art even in the city. Throughout London's Belgravia, the remnants of attached conservatories still exist, though lead roofs have often replaced the glass.

A DETAILED example is presented in Charles McIntosh's *The Book of the Garden* of 1853. The conservatory, designed by Mackenzie and Matthews, is an addition to a house in Scotland. Besides providing a plant environment and a fountain off the drawing room, the boiler below heated a bathroom and the bath water, and so upgraded the gentleman's amenities to a nineteenth-century 'service module'. Two sliding doors, one of glass and the other of wood, separated the conservatory from the house. The owner could look out at the verdant world through the glass or close off the view completely when servants were watering the plants, or open the doors to let in the 'odoriferous aroma … which could incite even a valetudinarian to quit his couch and take a stroll

amongst them', as McIntosh observed. In order not to see the servant watering the plants, McIntosh suggested that a flower stage with a trap door and stair replace the fountain for the stealthful entrance and egress of those 'little' men. The Wilhelmstrasse Orangery at the Palais Prinz Albrecht in Berlin, designed by architect Karl Friedrich Schinkel in 1832, was just such an adjunct to a house. It was built on the south main floor of the palace directly off the apartments of the Prince. A small conservatory only 18 feet wide and about 120 feet long, it ended in a semicircular room, raised to form a terrace and reached by steps from the garden.

BY 1871, Robert Kerr's *The Gentleman's House* takes for granted the necessity of a conservatory. No longer is it seen as a simple extension of the dwelling, but an integral part of the upper classes' way of life. One of his illustrations is the plan of Somerleyton Hall, Suffolk. Its wintergarden, of 100 by 100 feet, nurtured a rare collection of plants interspersed with sculpture, rock work, shell work, fountains and pillars, in masses of creepers and runners. This large

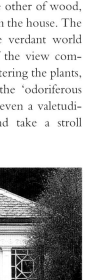

35

36

glass garden had most of the entertaining rooms centred on it. These Victorian house plans read more like recreation centres than the mundane houses of today.

THE *Floral World* was one of many periodicals on the art of horticulture available to the new middle-class conservatory owner in the later nineteenth century. In the magazine, the editor, Shirley Hibberd, described the value of conservatories for civilized living.

CONSERVATORIES were obvious places to hold parties, but many parties were held just to show off the conservatory. In August 1842 the *Illustrated London News* reported a summer-evening garden fête at Holland House: 'The gardens, orangery, conservatory and part of the pleasure ground with tiny lamps of all hues, shedding their sparkling lights in every direction among the trees, and the gay parterres, illumined the floral beauties everywhere. The room set apart for dancing was at the end of the orangery, forming the termination of a long conservatory.' At Wollaton Hall gooseberries were a speciality served with great ceremony.

At some dinners in the conservatory a fruit tree stood behind each chair so that guests could pick the fruit. Where there was one bountiful tree, the dinner table was arranged so that the hostess could sit in front of it and distribute the fruit. In a bad year, fruit might be purchased and tied to the tree. Underlying the gaiety of this new recreation was a social rivalry in successful growing and unique exotic acquisition.

WILLIAM Cobbett, a writer concerned about industrialization, suggested a unique moral contribution of conservatories for changing society. He states in *The English Gardener* of 1829:

It is the moral effects naturally attending a green house that I set most value upon. There must be amusement in every family. Children observe and follow their parents in almost everything. How much better during the long and dreary winter for daughters and even sons to assist their mother in a green house than to be seated with her at cards or in the blubberings over a stupid novel or at any other amusement than can possibly be conceived!

37

38

39

41

40

DURING the 1870s and 1880s, the attached conservatory was frequently combined with a games room, smoking balcony or music room. An example is the attached conservatory and billiard room constructed by Weeks & Co at Theydon Grove, Epping. The billiard table rested on brass rails embedded in the floor so that it could be pushed away for dancing and concerts. At one end was the smoking gallery, fitted with an organ, the whole overlooking the conservatory and its fountain through large plate-glass windows.

THE desire for a sizeable garden and for the conservatory that they required was beyond the means of many, and so miniature glasshouses in windows became the rage. They were based on the hermetically sealed Wardian case by Dr Nathaniel Ward, which was successfully used to transport plants in the 1830s, most prominently by the plant hunter John Gibson for Paxton at Chatsworth.

ROOFS in congested urban areas have always attracted the eye of the visionary. As land is scarce and expensive, they provide the ideal location for a sun terrace. In London, several roof-top conservatories were built or suggested during the nineteenth century. This was rather courageous, since pollution from coal heating was infamous and glass was certainly difficult to maintain. The architect Charles Fowler built the conservatory at Syon House and Hungerford Market Hall in 1827, and in the same year the roof-top conservatories on the upper terrace of the New Covent Garden Market in London for the sixth Duke of Bedford. Two conservatories were built on the terrace above the east entrance colonnade of Russell Street. In the centre, between the conservatories, was a highly polished Devonshire-marble fountain fed by tanks in the market roof supplied by an artesian well.

W BRIDGES Adams, a major proponent of iron and glass construction and an urban visionary of the nineteenth century, proposed stripping off the existing roofs of London terraces and replacing them with roof gardens, in an article in *The Gardener's Chronicle and Agriculture Gazette* of 14 June 1860:

37 The Wardian case and winter-garden, *Rustic Ornament,* 1857.
38 Conservatory and billiard room, Theydon Grove, Epping, Weeks and Co, as illustrated in *The Gardener's Chronicle,* 1880.
39 A summer garden fête at Holland House, *Illustrated London News,* August 1852.
40 The roof-top conservatories at Covent Garden Market, built for the sixth Duke of Bedford.
41 Illustration to an article by W Bridges Adams proposing roof gardens for London, *The Gardener's Chronicle and Agriculture Gazette,* 1860.

42

42 Rooftop winter-garden,
Residenz, Munich,
constructed by August
von Voit and Karl von
Effner for Ludwig II,
1867.

43 The rooftop conservatory
of Barr and Sugden, King
Street, Covent Garden,
The Garden, April 1875.

43

*Gardens of this kind would be as in the East,
the resort of the family in fine weather and in bad
weather a warm greenhouse on the roof would be
a more pleasant thing than a dark parlour. Scarcely
anything could be conceived more beautiful than the
enormous expanse of London roofs covered with
shrubs and flowers. And it would be a perfectly
practicable thing so to construct the greenhouses
that they might be opened or closed at pleasure.*

He appeals straightforwardly to fashion and
snobbery:

*Every housekeeper might possess his own bit of
Crystal Palace, his own fountains, his own flower
baskets, watered not by hand, but by art without
labour, so that the lady of the house, by a process as
easy as ringing a bell would effect this object. Think
too of the wine parties, supper parties and open air
dinners that might take place with the upper crust
of London restored to its proprietors.*

D T FISH, editor of *Cassell's Popular Gardening*,
proselytized the benefits of the house-top

94

44 Conservatory at
   Cherkley Court, *The
   Gardener's Chronicle*, 1885.
45 Conservatory at Lessness,
   Messenger & Co, *The
   Gardener's Chronicle*, 1886.
46 Winter-garden at
   Willaston, Harrogate,
   The Gardener's Magazine,
   1910.

45

44

conservatory for all: 'Glass, through being so long and so heavily taxed, is still by many of the working classes considered a luxury beyond their reach. On the contrary, it is now among the cheapest of all roofing materials, taking into account its durability being virtually indestructible, unless in the case of accidents.' He was not deterred by obstacles: 'From the almost universal prevalence of sloping opaque roof, of course such structures have hitherto been rare. But they exist in sufficient numbers to prove the practicability of growing plants, flowers and even fruit, to perfection in crowded cities.'[10]

THE premises of Barr & Sugden, plantsellers in King Street, Covent Garden, were designed in 1875 by the architects Spalding and Knight. The whole facade was a showcase for plants. In order to comply with the Duke of Bedford's lease and concern for leaks, a flat lead roof was built under the floor of the roof-top conservatory. However, it was not the first roof-top conservatory to be erected in London. The horticultural builder W H Lascelles had also built one above his offices at Bunhill Row, Finsbury.

THE most celebrated and exotic winter-gardens to be built high above the street were those of the Bavarian kings Maximilian II and Ludwig II in Munich. In 1867, under the direction of architects August von Voit and Karl von Effner, Ludwig's romantic fantasy was constructed as a glass and iron barrel vault over his existing residence. According to Stephan Koppelkamm, it took four years to build and outfit – the utmost effort being made to reconstruct the ambience of Nepal in a natural-style garden.[11] The setting was enhanced by a painted background of the Himalayas, exotic birds flying among tropical trees, a waterfall, a brook and Lilliputian lake, an oriental pavilion, kiosks, silk marquees and a fisherman's reed hut. A stair from Ludwig's residence below enabled him to quickly ascend to the side of the pool, which was large enough for rowing a boat. Except for his servants few were allowed to see it before its demolition in 1887 after his death.

JUST as the popularity of the wood glazing bar dwindled with the advent of curvilinear iron in the early nineteenth century and then was

46

revived in the middle of the century, the arrangement of plants in glasshouses fluctuated as fashions changed. Earlier in the century plant genera were sought to complete grand and comprehensive collections. Many of these plants from the New World, the Cape and Botany Bay were not attractive with no spectacular flowers or leaves. They were placed in pots and tubs or on rigid staging. Loudon was an early critic of this. He advocated assembling collections for their colour and attractiveness and planting them in natural beds. By the 1840s flowering tropical and subtropical shrubs and vines, which created colour and beauty in the conservatory, became popular, however, they were still arranged in pots. It was not until the late 1850s that planting in beds became widely practised. Later in the 1860s, 1870s and 1880s concerted ingenuity rendered an impression of natural settings using the appropriate rock out-croppings, waterfalls, huts, curios and birds. By the Edwardian period, however, many conservatories became social rooms filled with strategically placed wicker and garden furniture. The plants were relegated to being a mere backdrop placed along the walls. Palms and ferns were again confined in tubs as they had been in the early part of the previous century.

IN 1843, at Penllergare in Wales, a conservatory designed for Dillwyn Llewellyn was one of the first 'planted in admirable disorder' like a tropical forest. The idea was suggested by the explorer Schomburgk's description of the Berbice and Essequibo Falls in Guyana.[12] An artificial falls of heated water splashed over rocks and into an aquarium in the middle of the conservatory. An island of rock was covered with ferns, orchids and lycopodiales. Tropical species floated on blocks of wood or hung in baskets, all growing in wild profusion, imitating their native world.

THE natural or picturesque style of garden design, or *jardin Anglais* as it was known on the Continent, found its way into the original design of the Jardin d'Hiver in Paris. It was further popularized in the 1850s, 1860s and 1870s by such proponents as H Noel Humphreys and Edouard André. Noel Humphreys was an

47 The Fernery, Tatton Park, Cheshire, attributed to Joseph Paxton, 1859. Fern houses became popular in the 1850s and 1860s in England.

48 Conservatory at Hohenheim Park, Stuttgart, designed by Prince Karl Eugen of Hohenheim, 1789. This was probably the first iron-frame hothouse in Germany.

47

artist and writer, who contributed to Loudon's magazine as a young man and in later years to William Robinson's *The Garden,* and André was a French writer on gardens. These authors promoted the turn away from rigid geometry and the planting of individual specimens. Every effort was made to hide the iron structure and the enclosing glass roof and walls in order to recreate the natural exotic habitats of tropical Brazil, Africa or India. The path to a typical enclosed 'tropical forest' would wind through the 'valleys of rocks' covered with yuccas and other exotic plants, which could withstand the English climate. A curved rock-work tunnel hid the conservatory door in its darkness. Once mysteriously inside, the visitor found the ground irregularly banked against the enclosing walls. Larger thickly branched trees, ferns and climbing vines stood as a macabre backdrop to this verdant stage set. Some of the props were dead tree-trunks held with iron stakes just above the ground to prevent them from decomposing in the moist and dripping atmosphere; or rockeries, bubbling with tepid water, robed in moss and ferns, which formed around the pools filled with bright tropical fish. Streams flowed between fragments of rock and boulders; above the fine-gravel path and natural-stone benches, the giant ferns, palms and climbing Passiflora hid the roof with their dense foliage. Imported chrysalides matured into exotic butterflies that fluttered about the tropical flora.

IN nineteenth-century Continental Europe, the glasshouse thrived in brief times of peace. The aristocracy, who were increasingly threatened by changes brought on by the French Revolution of 1789 and the growth of the newly emerging middle classes, retreated to their estates, in which they were able to invest their surplus income and frustrated desire for the lost world outside. According to Georg Kohlmaier and Barna von Sartory in *Houses of Glass,* Prince Karl Eugen of Hohenheim near Stuttgart, who built the first iron conservatory in Germany in 1789, was no exception.[13] In 1776 he had committed himself to exile on a romantically styled estate after losing a dispute over an inheritance. His move into a 'paradise back to nature' was an expression of the widespread escapism of the European nobility. The grounds contained

nothing to remind him of the political problems that plagued him. Ruins styled on ancient Rome, concert rooms, baths, grottoes, caves, garden pavilions and country huts were his diversion. His three-winged iron conservatory around a masonry core was filled with tropical plants and became a winter retreat.

IN 1799 Josèphine de Beauharnais sought refuge from Paris at Malmaison, an estate she acquired near Versailles. There she commissioned architects Jean Thomas Thibaut and Barthelemy Vignon to design a large south-facing conservatory of 6 by 50 metres with a masonry back wall, heated with twelve charcoal stoves. The construction was started in 1803 and completed in 1805. Along with her vast rose collection, Josèphine's passion for tropical plants was such that she spent approximately a quarter of the cost of the entire estate on the conservatory. Originally a Creole from the Caribbean island of Martinique, Josèphine took advantage of the Peace of Amiens and enhanced her collection by buying from nurseries in England and throughout Europe. It also contained species from Australia, Egypt and the American states. Delahaye was her head gardener in 1805 and this position was taken over by Aimé Bonpland, the botanist on the Humboldt Expedition. Alexandre de Laborde, in his *Description des nouveaux jardins de la France* of 1808, describes the conservatory as a fine collection of the rarest foreign plants, the true botanical garden of France, on a par with Kew and Schönbrunn; according to him some 180 species unknown in other gardens flourished at Malmaison. It was isolated deep in the garden far from the château, which was the fashion, and he criticized this as inconvenient. Behind the sloped glass plant-chamber was a gallery for paintings from which the plants could be viewed. Josèphine used these adjoining salons for social occasions including breakfasts. In 1809 her marriage with Napoleon was dissolved and in 1814 she died from a chill while boating with Tsar Alexander I. Her son, Eugene, then lived at Malmaison, and on his death in 1824 the plant collection was sold and many species were obtained by British collectors.

GLASSHOUSE designers on the Continent were certainly not ignorant of the developments made by their British counterparts. Architect

48

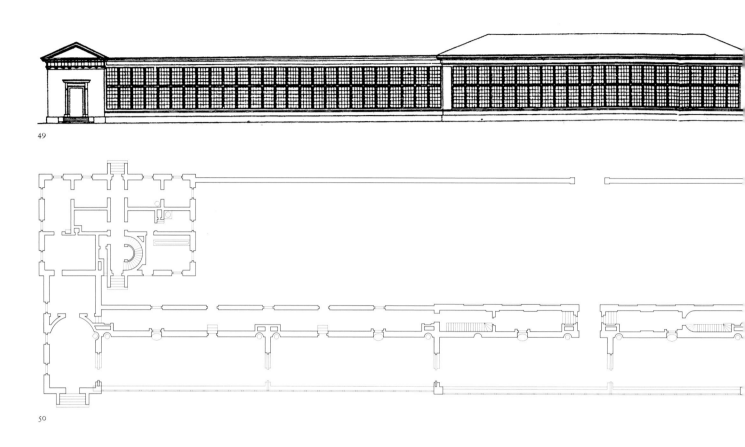

49

50

49, 50 Front elevation and
ground plan of the
demolished
conservatory, Old
Botanical Garden,
Munich, Friedrich
von Sckell, 1818.

Friedrich Ludwig von Sckell was well aware of the English use of curvilinear and sloped glass buildings, preferring more pragmatic forms and technology appropriate to the Bavarian climate in Munich. Von Sckell could be described as a functional classicist attracted to the symmetry of rational buildings with little superfluous detail. For this reason, his buildings appeal to us today. Kohlmaier has even placed Von Sckell's development of glasshouses in Germany on a par with Loudon's in England and suggests that his buildings have had a lasting affect on the European glasshouse designers of the nineteenth century.[14]

AS the superintendent of King Maximilian's royal gardens, Von Sckell argued that the snow and cold in Germany rendered English glasshouse details inappropriate. Empirical observation led him to favour tall vertical south-facing glass with solid insulated roofs and enclosing masonry walls on the north, west and east. He preferred wood structure, window sashes and mullions. The one exception is the lengthy, 262-foot, extant Iron Conservatory at the Nymphenburg Palace in Munich, built in

1807. Its pitched glass and iron roof was meant to accommodate tropical plants. His later work did not mimic this metal conservatory and he returned to wood. One of the classical pavilions at the end of the facade was said to be used by the king, and the other as a shed for the gardener – function and symmetry not always making good bedfellows. The restrained decoration makes it elegant and appealing to the contemporary eye. A clever detail is the cast-iron decorative frieze that masks the gutter and also serves as a snow guard.

IN 1809 Von Sckell was asked to lay out a new botanical garden in Munich. He used geometry reasoning that codifying and displaying plants should be done in an ordered, symmetrical and unified way. The conservatory, which was demolished in the 1860s, was the grandest of Von Sckell's glasshouses; it was 400 feet long with a large central chamber and architectural pavilions at each end. The linear plant-chambers were formed with a vertical wood and glass southern wall, insulated roofs and a solid curved back wall. Stoves, fed from the rooms behind,

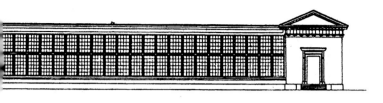

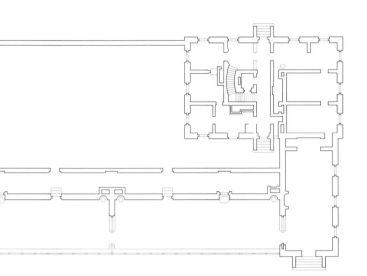

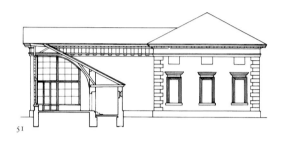

51

52

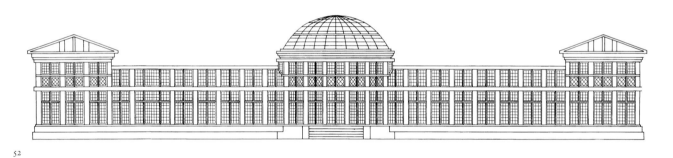

53

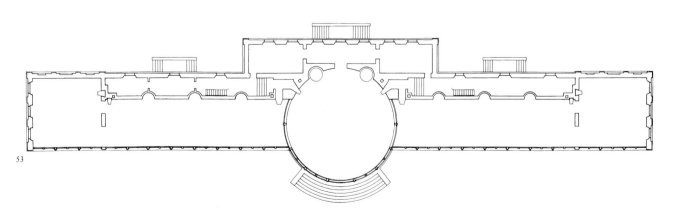

THE GRAND PRIVATE CONSERVATORY

were spaced along the back wall. Von Sckell, exceeded by no other glasshouse designer, was able to marry scientific botany and formal aesthetics. In 1820 he designed the elegant, extant Palm House, constructed in line with the Iron Conservatory at the Nymphenburg Palace. It has lines similar to the Conservatory in the Munich Botanical Gardens. Perhaps in no other building did he exercise greater skill in integrating the functional response to climate for internal environmental control with architectural classicism. As in the glasshouses of the Imperial Botanic Gardens in St Petersburg, built at around the same time and with similar climate considerations, the plant-chamber is narrower than its counterparts in more temperate climates like Britain. Also, as at St Petersburg, in the absence of roof glass, plants had a tendency to curve to the light; Von Sckell experimented by curving the back wall of the plant-chamber and painting it white. He reported that all the plants grew upright, even those at the back. Today the building has been converted into a delightful café for visitors to the Palace.

THE Wilhelmshöhe Great Conservatory, in Kassel, by Johann Conrad Bromeis, was built in 1822 for Elector William II and then extensively renovated in 1887. Bromeis was head architect to the Elector until the end of his reign in 1831. His original building was in the classical style similar to the conservatory in the Botanical Gardens by Von Sckell, with the exception of the sloping glass and the innovative circular central pavilion dome, built out of iron and glass. It was similar to a plan that had been proposed by Cambridge University Professor of Botany Richard Bradley, a century before. The style was severely non-decorative with the building relying on imposing proportions rather than ornamentation, though there is a decorative railing on the architrave, which is probably a snow guard. In a quest for light, the south stone columns that supported the stone architrave were designed so thin that they had to be substituted with cast-iron in the actual construction. Again, the north wall of the plant-chamber has heating niches backed by service rooms and chimneys. The central-domed pavilion was

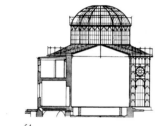

54

55

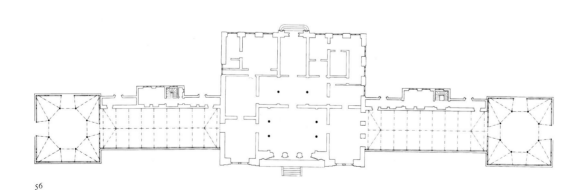

56

57

demolished in 1887 and then replaced by one of rectangular stone and spanned by the glass and iron vault that we see today.

SITUATED in the Rosenstein Royal Park at Cannstatt near Stuttgart, the Wilhelma summer estate with living quarters and ornamental plant houses in the Moorish style represents the extreme affluence, or decadence, enjoyed by some German nobility in the nineteenth century. The glasshouse ranges were key features in this late feudal estate built by Württemberg's King Wilhelm I. The central villa, colonnades, gazebos, banqueting hall and quarters for domestic help were in grounds filled with flower beds, fountains and basins, laid out in a formal manner with plantations of trees on the periphery. The architect Karl Ludwig von Zanth described the total design for this commission in his published work *La Wilhelma, villa mauresque* of 1855. From 1837 to 1853 there was a continuous building programme in the Moorish style on a scale and romance comparable to the Prince Regent's Brighton Pavilion by John Nash, decades earlier. Von Zanth explained that

the Moorish style was Wilhelm I's choice. It was easier to apply in the masonry villa, than in the glasshouses as there were no historic precedents for iron and glass structures in the Moorish style. The conservatory was set in the middle of a terraced south-facing slope on an axis with the villa, its central pavilion having a view of the Neckar River. Von Zanth wisely set the conservatory below the top of the hill to protect the glass from the cold north winds. Other south-facing vegetable and fruit-producing glasshouses were set in a line nearer to the villa.

THE construction of the conservatory began in 1842 and was completed in 1846 in time for a festival related to the marriage of the Crown Prince of Württemberg to Princess Olga of Russia. The colonnaded walks and stairs, gazebos, streams, terraced beds, lawns, tree plantations and the banqueting hall were completed in subsequent years.

VON ZANTH outlined his dilemma with the Moorish style; on the one hand he wanted to adhere to its romance and on the other he had many functional requirements to solve.

57 Glass house exterior, Wilhelma.

These were associated with the climate and his classical upbringing:

to my knowledge no earnest attempt has been made, in Germany at least, to adapt the Moorish building forms, which are suited to the climate and conditions of their homeland, to essentially different latitudes. There were no signposts put out to indicate the correct path to take for the solution of this problem; one had to seek out the correct directions oneself, and to my mind these were only to be found in the basic principles of Greek art, which have proved their full value irrefutably in the most outstanding, the most diverse concepts.[15]

THE result was much more restrained than that of Nash at Brighton, which had been extravagant, even shocking. Von Zanth went on, ' it is therefore important to affect the imagination strongly by exploiting the exciting characteristics of this architecture without using anything which went against reason and taste'.

THE layout of the Conservatory is typically German, with a dominant central building and side wings ending in pavilions. The original central building was called the Summer House and arranged with living rooms around the central dome. Its Moorish glass dome and arched masonry base probably fulfilled the King's oriental dream better than the glass and iron wings. These had superimposed horseshoe-arched glazing bars and cast-iron details, which could not be seen from a distance because of their transparent backdrop. The domes over the pavilions are hardly Moorish and may have been redesigned as a cost-saving measure.

WILHELM did not live at Wilhelma regularly and only the chosen few ever saw it, in fact the King gave strict orders that no person should be allowed to enter without his personal permission. The beautiful dome over the central building was destroyed in the Second World War. Unfortunately, it has since been replaced by a simple glass roof.

THE curvilinear conservatory at Liechtenstein Castle, in Lednice, in the Czech Republic, is an excellent example of iron and glass construction based on the English principles professed by

59

60

58–59 Shots of the Moorish-style interior of a glasshouse at Wilhelma, Stuttgart, Ludwig von Zanth, 1842–6.
60 Exterior of a glasshouse at Wilhelma.

61 Curvilinear conservatory,
Liechtenstein Castle,
Lednice, G Devian,
1843–5.

62–3 Ground plan and section
of the curvilinear
conservatory,
Liechtenstein Castle.

64 Detail of the glass
conservatory,
Liechtenstein Castle.

Loudon. Erected in 1843, the structure of this large private conservatory is based upon arched iron ribs supported by a double row of slender bamboo-shaped columns at 12-foot intervals along the 302-foot length. The width of the house is 44 feet and it is built over a basement area. The glazing bars support small overlapping leaves of glass as found in Loudon's buildings such as at Bicton Gardens. The bars at the hemispherical end do not, however, reduce in number as they rise to the apex, as they do in the houses of Loudon and the Baileys. The structure relies on its rounded arch shape to resist horizontal wind loads. Kohlmaier says that the winter-garden was built by an Englishman Mr Devian and that this house carries on the 'highest traditions of British hothouse architecture'.[16]

THE private conservatory at Stuttgart-Berg, designed by architect Christian Leins in 1845, was one of the first iron curvilinear houses outside Britain to follow Loudon's principles. Leins had worked with Von Zanth, architect of the huge cast-iron Wilhelma glasshouses, and with Henri Labrouste in Paris. Adjacent to the

Rosenstein Royal Park, the Stuttgart-Berg Conservatory afforded a view of the Wilhelma gardens. The curved glass arms of the conservatory grew out from the masonry central building, an orangery with a summer residence above for the Prince. The plan was a symmetrical arc with rather basic cylindrical pavilions at each end. To the right were the temperate plants and a rock mass with a waterfall. The other temperate wing contained camellias and azaleas and the glass cylinder had tropical plants.

ONE of the most renowned gardens and palm collections was situated in the Berggarten of Georg II August, Elector of Hanover, at Park Herrenhausen, near Hanover. In 1846, the architect George Ludwig Friedrich Laves was commissioned to design a new palm house for the expanding collection. He created a tall plant-chamber with a circle superimposed on a rectangular plan and, true to the German tradition, elevated the south, east and west glass walls to assure that sunlight would penetrate deep into the plant-chamber. The roof, however, was only partly opaque, being fitted with glass

61

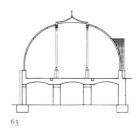

63

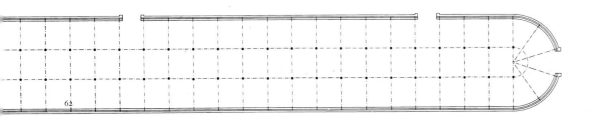

62

64

THE GRAND PRIVATE CONSERVATORY

65 The Palm House in the Berggarten, Park Herrenhausen, Hanover, built by George Friedrich Laves, 1846.

66 Glass passage conservatory, Schwarzenberg Castle, Hluboká nad Vltavou, Franz Beer, 1840–7. This links the castle with the stables.

65

66

on the north and south slopes and in the roof cone over the circular bulge in the plan. The north face of the plant-chamber was built of masonry and contained two levels of rooms for entertainment, service and access stairs. The building was replaced in 1879 by a larger palm house, again because of the expanding collection. This rational though cumbersome iron and glass chamber built with lattice members appears to derive its proportions from clumsy engineering rather than architectural design; the architect, Auhagen, being obsessed with strength and durability.

IN 1847 a glass-passage conservatory was built at Schwarzenberg Castle in Hluboká nad Vltavou, in the Czech Republic, by architect Franz Beer. Constructed in a mock-Gothic style, it used the precision of cast-iron decoration to establish an ornate south front between the previously built castle and riding school. The north wall is masonry, and the gable roof spans the 33-foot width for most of its 141-foot length. Kohlmaier calls it an 'expression of feudal prestige', in contrast to the architectural acts of the wealthy middle class, who became important through manufacturing and trade: 'The nobility had to demonstrate the wealth of its estates, its traditional base.'[17]

AT Karlsruhe, the glasshouses were integrated into the centripetal design of the geometrically planned city, which was begun in 1715 with the castle at its centre. Heinrich Hubsch's orangery is 197 feet long and 49 feet wide. It was built from 1853 to 1857, east of the castle, facing towards the town and connected to his semicircular winter-garden. At the centre of the orangery, the glass palm house has red-sandstone walls and a pyramidal glass roof supported by stone caryatids. A wooden Victoria Regia house, now removed, was directly south of the palm house and leant on it. The larger wintergarden's plan, a segment of a circle, is nearly 400 feet long. Its lean-to glass roof is removable in the summer. The winter-garden and the orangery were originally constructed of wood and, in 1868, J F Dyckerhoff replaced this with iron and added a central pavilion to the wintergarden, which can be seen today.

106

THE most extensive private conservatories were built at Laeken Palace, in north Brussels, by the arch-imperialist and lover of plants, Leopold II, King of the Belgians. In 1865 Leopold II succeeded his father and enthusiastically created the park at Laeken, which grew from 70 hectares to 200 hectares during his reign (1865–1909). The one-mile-long conservatories and the flower-lined glass corridors are extraordinary. Nearly 5 acres of varied climates exist under 10 acres of glass surface. On Leopold's accession there was a beautiful orangery but few glass buildings. Behind the Orangery he constructed a large glazed corridor, the Camellia House, that led to the great rotunda Winter Garden constructed later in 1876 and designed by the architect and Professor of the Académie des Beaux-Arts, Alphonse Balat (1818–95). Balat's glass rotunda is today the most grandiose in Europe. Its diameter is nearly 60 metres and its height to the top of the cupola crown is nearly 30 metres. Tuscan-style marble columns, 18 metres high, support an exo-skeleton of ornamental curved iron ribs that pierce the glass skin and form the upper

dome. The external structure is reminiscent of Balat's Victoria Regia House for the Jardin Zoologique de Bruxelles built some twenty years before. An extensive heating plant was built next to the rotunda, its chimney disguised as an oriental minaret, and pipes were laid under grates on the periphery of the Winter Garden. In the central room formed by the columns the floor was handsomely tiled for use as a ballroom, with fountains on each side and the great plants all around. Visitors reap the legacy of those early and repeated plantings, for the palms are spectacular.

DURING the ensuing years Leopold built an extensive array of glass environments along the connecting corridors. The large Congo House, enclosing palms and tropicals, commemorated his newly acquired lands in west central Africa. He had a yellow star mounted at the top in celebration of the event. Next to this another house makes a transition to the underground gallery that was dug out and then covered with glass, so that the walk could pass below a service road. The glass corridor then climbs the hill to another group of conservatories culminating in

67

67–8 Exterior views of
the glass passage
conservatory,
Schwarzenberg Castle.

68

another Balat palm house, constructed in 1892. THE King's extravagance did not end with this palm house, for further on and also connected to the corridor system, Leopold built a glass and iron church that was used regularly for services. Constructed in 1894, the round church is approximately 140 feet in diameter and 100 feet high. Ten pairs of polished red-granite columns support the main dome. A 20-foot corridor around the periphery had on its outer side glass niches planted with palms and flowering shrubs that were replaced on each occasion. Between the circle of columns, an altar, an organ and a centre aisle with seating generated the religious atmosphere among the palms; an observer at the time described the church as a great conservatory. By 1894 all the glass buildings, including this crystal chapel, were lit with electricity.

LEOPOLD was fanatical about gardens, flowers and exotic plants. Perhaps the most notorious of nineteenth-century imperialists, his infamous Congo policies taint the history of that time. His exploitations were no doubt forgotten in the glazed dream-world he created at Laeken.

Ironically, he died in his glasshouses – in the small palm pavilion near the palm house on the hill, in 1909.

THOUGH it is difficult to trace the exact origins of the Art Nouveau work practiced by Balat's pupil Victor Horta, as seen, for example, in the Maison Tassel of 1892, Horta was certainly fascinated by plants and their structure, and in his library were botanical books, including one describing the Laeken conservatories. According to Marcus Binney, Horta, as Secretary to the Society of Architects, described a visit to the Laeken houses.[18] He enthused about the tropical plants and the curvilinear metal frames of the Winter Garden. He praised Balat for not using iron in shapes 'only governed by the slide rule', but in forms with 'artistic character' and with 'ornament which is perfectly appropriate to the purpose of the building, and which despite its richness does not detract from the simplicity of the whole'. Horta, like the painter Henri Rousseau who often visited and sketched in the Jardin des Plantes, had been impressed by the beauty of the tropical world under glass.

70

69

71 Night-time illumination
of the Congo House at
Laeken, 1886.
72 Interior of the
Conservatory, Laeken.
73 Plan of the glasshouses,
Laeken, with the Winter
Garden at the bottom
right, and the Chapel
at the top left.

71

72

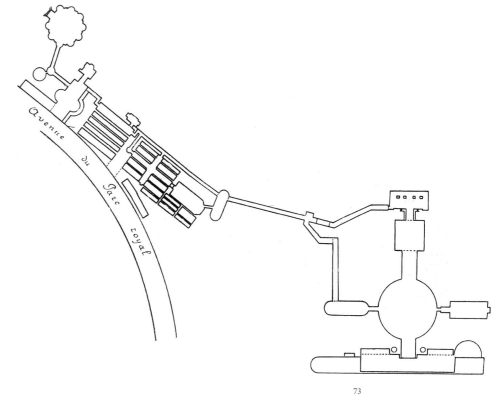

73

THE GRAND PRIVATE CONSERVATORY

74

74 The Congo House, Palm
Corridor and Winter
Garden at Laeken,
Brussels, Alphonse Balat,
1886 and 1875–6.
75 An unusual
underground-greenhouse
corridor leads to the
landing stage, Laeken.
76 Palm House, attributed
to Alphonse Balat, in the
huge range at Laeken,
1885.

75

76

BUILT in 1910, the Conservatory of the Palais Burnay, Lisbon, has a modern style that is reminiscent of the thriving contemporary Vienna Jugenstil. It is also representative of the delicate structure possible when there is no risk of a snow load. The glass barrel vault is terminated with a delicate and beautiful coloured rose window. The stone architrave on the Ionic columns contrasts this style, which indicates that the glass had been built over it at a later time.

WITH a few early exceptions, the conservatory came later to the United States than to Europe. However, after the Civil War it rapidly became a ubiquitous fashionable additon to the houses of the wealthy. For the self-made men of the New World, the conservatory became a means of expressing social aspirations rather than withdrawing from society. Industrialists, thriving in a time of peace and influenced by Victorian taste, demanded this symbol of perpetual spring for their homes in the quiet suburbs of Boston, Pittsburgh, New York and Philadelphia, or on their estates in Connecticut, upstate New York and the Hudson Valley. Client references in

the catalogues of two major conservatory manufacturers, Lord & Burnham of Irvington, New York, and Hitchings & Co of Jersey City, read like a social register: names included Warren Delano jun, Helen Gould, John D Rockefeller, John A Roosevelt, W K Vanderbilt and J P Morgan, to list a few. Later generations of glasshouse enthusiasts included John Jacob Astor jun, William Buckley, Jascha Heifetz, Mrs Thomas A Edison, Dr W J Mayo, E H Maytag, H S Firestone and W E Boeing.

THIS private glass heritage can be seen both at the spectacular Longwood Gardens, originally the private conservatory of Pierre S du Pont, near Kennet Square, Pennsylvania, which is now open to the public, and at the semipublic, and equally interesting, glass gardens of the late Doris Duke near Somerville, New Jersey. She carried on the tradition of her father, who maintained his private interconnected glasshouses with eleven distinctive themes including tropical jungle, American desert, Japanese, Chinese, Persian, French parterre, Edwardian and English summer garden.

77 Front entrance of the Conservatory, Palais Burnay, Lisbon, 1910.

THE American conservatory was in no way a shuttlecock in the game of style as it was in England at the end of the nineteenth century. The structural simplicity represented at Chatsworth, Kew and Hyde Park, which was soon abandoned in England, generally remained an ideal. Mail-order conservatory businesses from American catalogues, with limited styles, flourished all along the East Coast and later in the suburbs of Chicago, San Francisco and Seattle.

WHEN the wealthy New York merchant George Merritt bought a notable Gothic Revival house from a former mayor of New York City, he hired the original architect, Alexander Jackson Davis, who had designed the house in 1838, to build a conservatory, tower and other additions. Known as Merritt's Folly, the conservatory was, at its construction, the largest in the United States. This great greenhouse, in a modified Saracenic and Gothic style, was one of the few to be built using a decorative theme. Its dimensions were enormous for a private conservatory at 380 feet long, with two wings on either side of the central portion. The

central hall was 95 feet long and 80 feet wide. On the north side were a carpenter's shop, bedrooms and games rooms for billiards, a gymnasium and a bowling alley; in the cellar, there were boiler rooms, coal rooms, a mushroom cellar, water tanks and various potting rooms. But most spectacular was Merritt's 100-foot tower behind the central hall. It was topped with a glass cupola, affording an elevated view of the surrounding estates. Merritt was said to have invested $100,000 in his horticultural ventures, which included 250-foot-long forcing-pits to the north of the conservatory and his collections of exotics and grapes. When he died in 1873, the plants were disposed of and the estate was offered for sale. It lay derelict until it was purchased in 1880 by Jay Gould, the railroad magnate, who refitted and restocked the glass structures. Soon after, in December 1880, the great greenhouse caught fire from beams built into the chimney and was ruined. Undaunted, Gould hired Lord & Burnham to rebuild on its existing foundations. These curvilinear structures are the first steel-framed greenhouses built

78

78 Conservatory for P M Warburg, Hitchings & Co.

79 Rooftop glass garden erected on 7 East 96th street, New York. Several greenhouses were built on the top of skyscrapers in the 1920s.

80 Sunshine room and pool in Toronto, Canada.

79

80

81 This conservatory and swimming pool in Los Angeles, built in 1913 by Lord and Burnham, recreated the Garden of Eden in the 1920s.

82 Sunshine Room in a western United States resort in the late 1930s, from Lord and Burnham's catalogue, *Glass Gardens*.

83 Greenhouse over a garage in Richmond Hill, Long Island, from Lord & Burnham's catalogue.

in the United States. Unfortunately, Lord & Burnham's horticultural factory burned to the ground while the new Gould conservatory was being prefabricated. However, Gould offered a loan to rebuild the factory and gave additional time to complete the contract.

THOUGH grand conservatories and associated glasshouses were built worldwide in the nineteenth century, they came about only with the great affluence of a few. The conservatory's delight, as we have seen, was brought on with the efforts of gardeners, butlers, maids and labourers attached to each estate and city dwelling. This dependence on armies of cheap labour eventually contributed, of course, to the decline of the grand private conservatory. As glass began to crack and paint flaked from the sashes, which then rotted, as boilers burnt out their tubes and fireboxes, decisions were made to do away with many great conservatories. Industry lured gardeners with higher wages, and fuel rationing in the First World War killed many of England's vast botanic collections. The Second World War brought the *coup de grâce*, for

81

82

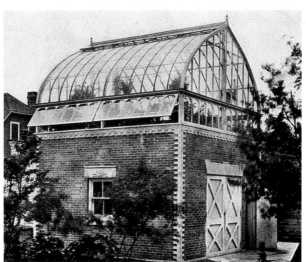
83

84

survival was at stake and art, whether painting or horticulture, fell by the wayside. The twentieth century brought with it new and exciting forms of entertainment. Transportation also enabled people to look beyond the home for recreation. The conservatory seemed dull and mundane compared to illustrated magazines, the cinema, the motor car and the aeroplane, which made trips possible even to the origins of the exotic plants.

THE increased availability of foreign produce, especially with the introduction of refrigerated ships and rolling stock, brought a marked price reduction in foods once reserved for the rich. Market-gardens of vast proportion began to grow under glass in the Lea Valley north of London and in other areas away from smoke and pollution. Glasshouse nurserymen responded to the demands of the city's Victorian middle class who had money to buy produce but no land. By the turn of the century, the major cities were ringed by large market nurseries, which reduced the need for private glass, resulting in its dismantling and destruction.

84 Main entrance to the conservatory, Duke Gardens, New Jersey.
85 The central portion of Merritt's folly, Lyndhurst, Tarrytown, New York, in *c* 1870, before it was burnt down by fire in 1880.

85

86 The Lyndhurst
glasshouses as rebuilt by
Jay Gould and Lord &
Burnham after 1880. It
is apparent from this
photograph how difficult
it is to maintain such
extensive glass ranges.

86

MOREOVER, tastes had changed; in 1883
William Robinson wrote an important book,
The English Flower Garden, and argued for a
return to nature instead of the artificiality of
the conservatory. His ideal was the English cottage garden. Robinson had caught a new
mood, against the conservatory, for the book
sold out eight editions and had six reprints
by 1903. There is no doubt that Robinson had
a great deal of influence on the changing gardening scene and was instrumental in ending the
Loudon-Paxton era with remarks such as these:

*A few years ago, before the true flower garden
began to get a place in men's minds, many of the
young gardeners refused to work in places where there
was no glass. A horrid race this pot and kettle idea
of a garden would have led to; men to get chills if
their gloves were not aired. I met the difficulty
myself by abolishing glass altogether … To bloom
the rose and carnation in midwinter, to ripen fruits
that will not mature in our climate, to enable us to
see many fair flowers of the tropics – for these
purposes glass houses are a precious gain; but for*

*a beautiful flower garden they are almost needless
and numerous glass houses in our gardens may
be turned to better use.*

BRENT Elliot marks the fate of Paxton's Great
Stove at Chatsworth as the turning point for the
conservatory.[19] The Duke of Devonshire's
application to the wartime government for
exemption from coal rationing to keep the conservatory heated was turned down and most of
the plants died during the winter of 1917. After
the war it was decided to demolish the shell
filled with dead plants instead of restocking it.
In 1920 it took five dynamitings to mark the
end of the extraordinary glasshouse epoch.

BY the time of the private conservatory's
demise, it had also lost its elite connotations.
New popular types of glasshouses had become
commonplace. As shall be shown in the next
chapter, the key factor to the emergence of both
cheaper, smaller private conservatories and big
public exhibition spaces was the adoption of
industrial methods of glasshouse production
and assembly.

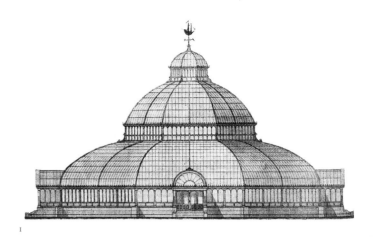

1

INDUSTRIALIZATION
AND MASS-MARKETING

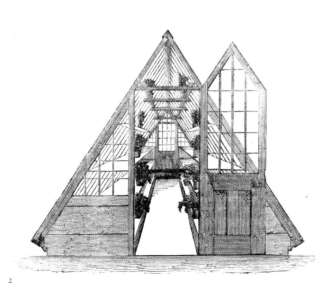

VI

2

THE industrialization of manufacturing processes in the nineteenth century that were used to make glass and iron allowed the mass-marketing of glasshouses. Whereas the wooden structures of the previous century had been individually fashioned, cast-iron space-frames could be broken down into component parts. Even in the earliest stage of industrialization, producers were quick to realize the commercial possibilities of the innovatory application of iron. After his invention of the wrought-iron sash bar in 1816, used in conjunction with cast-iron columns, Loudon started producing custom-designed glasshouses with W & D Bailey. If, however, Loudon and the Baileys were catering only for a select clientele on a relatively small scale, the development of the iron, railway and shipping industries quickly enabled glasshouses to bridge wider spans and to reach broader markets. By the end of the century the iron industry had become vast and the components available for construction endless. Iron foundries were producing parts for all sorts of structures, including bridges, railway stations, factories, sewage systems and street furniture. The consolidation of the railway network in Britain, and then abroad, facilitated the transportation of materials and the finished goods, and

4

5

6

also the communications necessary for selling to a world market through mail-order catalogues.

THOMAS Clark was an early prefabricator and builder of metal glasshouses, who also, like Loudon, sold to an exclusive and wealthy client list. He founded his business in the autumn of 1818 in Lionel Street, Birmingham; the first page of his initial order book from that time shows two lean-to forcing-houses, one a pineapple house for the Duke of Newcastle, at Clumber Park, Nottinghamshire. Subsequent order books are filled with sales to nobility. They included the 1844 glass sashes for Queen Victoria's Frogmore kitchen-gardens, near Windsor. The Clark firm's first foreign order was in 1839 for: 'Two ranges of hot water apparatus for heating a pine house for His Majesty the King of Württemberg, Stuttgart'. This was possibly for Wilhelm 1 who began his summer estate Wilhelma that same year.

ORIGINALLY the firm traded under the name Clark & Jones. It provided the components for the Camellia House at Wollaton Hall in Nottinghamshire, 1823, and for The Grange in

Hampshire, 1825. The Wollaton glasshouse, which has an engaged classical order on the elevation, is one of the earliest pre-fabricated metal structures existing today and clearly depicts the spirit of the early nineteenth century. It has an irregular plan, a result of a fall in the site, which required an irregular masonry retaining-wall on the north. The hollow structural columns, which double as a rainwater collection system, are laid along paths supporting the double-skinned sheet-iron barrel vaults. All were pre-fabricated in the Clark shop and assembled on the site. Approximately half of the large 49-by-96-foot roof is covered with the glazed elongated pyramids set over the planting beds between the metal-vaulted paths. This reduced glass area is ideal for cold-house plants like camellias and azaleas, although the original purpose of the conservatory was probably for growing tropical plants, fashionable at the time it was built. The Conservatory at The Grange in Hampshire, built two years after that at Wollaton Hall, has so many details similar to Wollaton's that it again demonstrates the

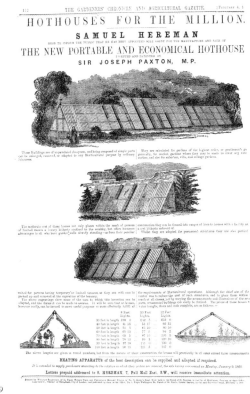

important role of the manufacturer. Although the glasshouse is often attributed to the architect C R Cockerell, as mentioned in the 1875 Henry Hope catalogue, it is probable that Cockerell only dealt with the style of the masonry, making it compatible with the mansion.

IN 1858, Sir Joseph Paxton designed a glasshouse system for a more modest market. He adapted the folding-frame portable tent that he had developed for the Crimean War campaign into a patent for 'Improvement in the Manufacture of Horticulture Buildings or Glazed Structures for Horticulture and Other Purposes'. They were a collection of hinged wood frames, which could be shipped flat, unfolded and glazed. Inexpensive and practical, they perfectly suited the middle classes living in the expanding suburbs around major cities. The mass-produced glass frames afforded these new suburbanites the opportunity to own glasshouses, a luxury previously confined to the wealthy. The possibility of refolding the glass modules appealed particularly to those with temporary or limited tenures. According to law, plant houses fixed in the soil

4 The roof of the Camellia House, Wollaton Hall, Nottinghamshire, by Clark & Jones, 1823. There are double-skinned iron vaults over the pathways and glass over the flower beds.

5 Exterior of the Camellia House, Wollaton Hall.

6 Joseph Paxton's A-frame design as a tree-filled conservatory, S Hibberd, *The Floral World and Garden Guide*, III, 1860.

7–8 Further examples of uses for the Paxton A-frame design: left, a span-roof vinery for summer and autumn, S Hibberd, *The Floral World and Garden Guide*, 1871; right, an orchard house-cum-aviary complete with fountain.

9 Sir Joseph Paxton's patent 'hothouses for the million', an advertisement by Hereman and Morton in *The Gardener's Chronicle*, May, 1876.

10 Ewing's Patent Glass
   Walls in the garden of the
   Horticultural Society,
   Chiswick, *Illustrated
   London News*, 28
   August 1852.
11 'Elevation of conservatory
   now being constructed
   for a nobleman', Weeks's
   advertisement in *The
   Gardener's Chronicle*,
   February 1860.

were the property of the freeholder. Tenants could fold and move Paxton's glass frame at the termination of their lease.

THE sole agent for manufacturing and marketing Paxton's glass tents was Hereman & Morton of 7 Pall Mall East, London. Hereman wrote do-it-yourself instruction manuals, such as the *Handbook of Vine and Fruit tree Cultivation under Glass, with a Description of Sir Joseph Paxton's Hot Houses*. He obviously expected the new glass gardeners in profusion according to optimistic advertisement, 'Hot Houses for the Million'.

PAXTON'S was one of a host of prefabricated glass structures produced for the middle-class and commercial markets. The glass tax repeal in the late 1840s combined with new techniques for producing glass cheaply enabled glass to be one of the least expensive roofing materials. Novel applications of inexpensive glass were being devised; one of these was Ewing's Patent Glass Walls, which appeared in the 1850s. Masonry walls, every gardener knew, trapped solar heat and protected fruit trees espaliered along them. Ewing argued that the grey skies

and fickle British climate, however, often dampened the gardener's reliance on brick walls. The solution was Ewing's linear cast-iron and glass cases for fruit and vines with sliding or casement fronts; they had glass side panels, as high as 9 feet, that could be removed in the summer. The gardener Charles McIntosh praised these narrow glasshouses as a substitute for inelegant and expensive brick and stone walls but, rightly, he questioned their heat retention as compared with masonry mass.[1] The morning or evening light refracting through a garden of Ewing's glass prisms, however, must have been an added delight.

COMPANIES manufacturing horticultural buildings flourished in the 1860s, 1870s and 1880s and continued until the First World War.[2] Some, like Weeks & Co and Ormson & Co, were located in the Kings Road, Chelsea, which had a long horticultural tradition, not only with the Chelsea Apothecaries' Garden but also at several nurseries including the huge Veitch's nursery. The manufacturers provided prefabricated buildings, satisfying current taste,

10

11

and also boilers and ventilation devices usually made under their own patent. Some of the designs were unique; W H Lascelles attained popularity for curved wood and glass roofs (previously only possible with metal bars), which were produced by steam bending the wood. Wood, for glazing, had regained its popularity. WEEKS & CO built a display winter-garden next to their Kings Road shop, representing the complete conservatory package – iron and wood glazed structures, heating and ventilating equipment, even the plants. Horticultural magazines of the 1870s and 1880s are filled with Weeks's designs, including, for example, the glass at Hampton Court and the Folkestone Winter Garden, erected for South-Eastern Railway at their Royal Pavilion Hotel in 1885. BY the 1880s, the marketing strategies of shop-fabricated conservatories were well established. Designs presented in brochures, pamphlets and catalogues were distributed throughout Britain and the Empire. In 1880 Messenger & Co, horticultural builders from Loughborough, hired the architect Edward William Godwin and his

12

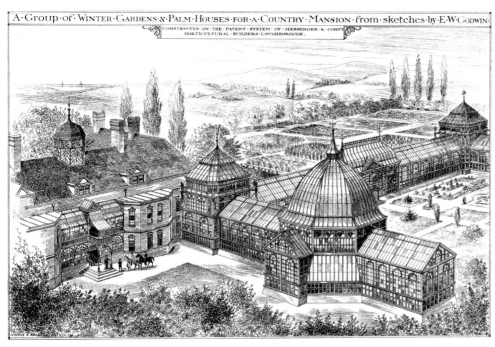

13

12 The Folkestone Winter Garden, attached to the Royal Pavilion Hotel, Weeks and Co, c 1885. This building was a health garden for those who had come to the seaside for recuperation. The expansion of the railways enabled health resorts to develop along the coast within easy reach of London.
13 E W Godwin's country mansion, with winter-gardens and palm houses, constructed by Messenger & Co, *Artistic Conservatories*, 1880.

14 E W Godwin's
Anglo-Japanese-style
conservatory, built by
Messenger & Co, 1880.

15 Conservatory in the
gardens of the Royal
Horticultural Society,
South Kensington,
designed by Sydney
Smirke and Captain
Francis Fowke, and built
by Handyside & Co,
1860.

PLAN

WINTER · GARDEN · IN · THE · ANGLO · JAPANESE · STYLE   CONSTRUCTED · ON · THE · PATENT · SYSTEM · OF · MESSENGER · COMPANY · HORTICULTURAL · BUILDERS · LOUGHBOROUGH · 1880   FROM SKETCHES BY E.W. GODWIN, F.S.A.

14

15

assistant Maurice B Adams to make a series of designs for their booklet *Artistic Conservatories*. It contains the 'packaged' private winter-gardens that could be assembled from their patented construction system, often in the Anglo-Japanese or Anglo-Italian styles popular at that time.

THE glasshouse had to be as maintenance free as possible, particularly for the emerging middle class, with less domestic help than the landowning classes, who spent most of their time in offices and factories. In the latter half of the nineteenth century, such a house was patented and manufactured by a Mr Beard at Bury St Edmunds, Norfolk. Beard's prefabricated house was a forerunner of the standard dry-glazed buildings that can be purchased today. Its unique feature was Beard's wrought-iron glazing bar, for small conservatories had previously relied on putty and wood glazing bars. The glass was sandwiched between thick asphalt strips and held in place with a baked-enamel metal bar. The erection of the house was simple and rapid. Similar to Paxton's glass frames, the house

122

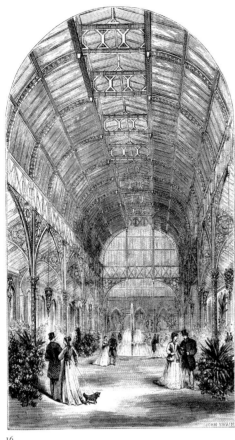

16

17

was popular with tenants who could disassemble and transport it to another garden.

IT was not only small glass buildings that were being prefabricated and site assembled. The 1860s saw many iron foundries producing large conservatories and winter-gardens. One of these, Handyside & Co, built the cast-iron conservatory in the gardens of the Royal Horticultural Society, which had returned to South Kensington from Chiswick for the 1862 Exhibition. Designed by Sydney Smirke RA and Captain Francis Fowke RE and erected in 1860, the building was 100 feet wide and 270 feet long and used 157 tons of cast-iron and 70 tons of wrought-iron. The central 75-foot-high space supported a glazed lean-to and a corrugated-iron roof veranda, which enclosed over 27,000 square feet.

ANOTHER of Handyside's many buildings was an 1868 addition to Henry Bessemer's mansion at Denmark Hill, Camberwell, which was designed by the architects Robert Banks and Charles Barry (son of the architect of the Houses of Parliament, Westminster). Seventy tons of wrought- and cast-iron were used to assemble the elaborately ornamented structure.

THE engineer R M Ordish was involved with several iron constructions, including the Albert Suspension Bridge over the Thames. He worked with Owen Jones on an iron structure to be marketed and transported throughout the Empire. With the architect Alfred G Jones and the engineer Le Feuvre, he designed the Exhibition Palace and Winter Garden in Dublin in 1865; and he engineered another winter-garden for the Infirmary at Leeds, designed by Sir George Gilbert Scott and built by Handyside & Co in 1866.

BY the 1880s, hundreds of foundries employing thousands of men were casting the integrated components as a 'kit of parts' to build the bridges, railway stations and factories that are still used in the twentieth century. One of these companies, Walter MacFarlane's Saracen Foundry in Glasgow, and later of London, was founded before the 1850s, casting rainwater-goods, kiosks, street urinals, park benches and sewage piping. Their catalogues show an early integration of varied components and. By their

16 Winter-garden for the Leeds Infirmary, designed by George Gilbert Scott and R M Ordish, built by Handyside & Co, 1866.

17 Iron conservatory in the garden of the Royal Horticultural Society, South Kensington, with the Albert Hall under construction in the foreground.

18–20 Illustrations from
MacFarlane's castings
catalogue, sixth edition,
showing: top, the
application of scalloped-
shaped castings for a
curved roof in a
zoological garden; and
centre and below, the
exterior and interior
of a hypothetical
conservatory, winter-
garden or flora. These
large structures could be
built from the list of
components in the
catalogue.

18

sixth edition, in 1880, they were manufacturing large iron and glass buildings that required the combination of many complicated parts. Orders were made by post for the sophisticated European and British styles from throughout the world, particularly the Empire. The MacFarlane catalogues whetted appetites in Johannesburg, Singapore, Cairo, Calcutta, Sydney and Toronto. The castings were often used as facades for existing buildings in the way that tin facades were shipped from St Louis and Chicago to the hardware stores in America.

THE complete packaged mail-order building, assembled for tropical climates, revealed a potential market that has never been so successfully exploited. Exported cast-iron and glass, combined with galvanized corrugated iron, were excellent materials for tropical and subtropical climates. Glass and metal roofs kept out the tropical rain and cast-iron resisted corrosion and termites. Structural components were readily assembled with wedges and bolts. A choice of varied crestings, terminals and frieze rails were easily attached for 'style'. Clear,

19

20

21

22

23

24

21, 24 Pages from MacFarlane's
castings catalogue, sixth
edition, showing the
application of ironwork
to the interior and
exterior of a building;
compare with figs 22
and 23.

22, 23 Interior and exterior
of the Barton Arcade,
Manchester, assembled
from Walter MacFarlane's
books by architects
Corbett, Raby and
Sawyer, 1870s.

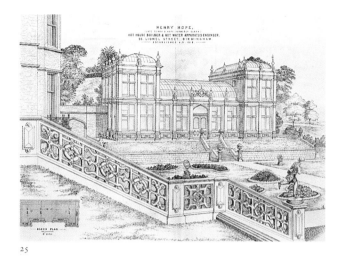

25

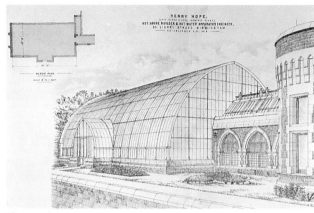

26

27

translucent, coloured and decorated flat glass infilled the iron lattices enclosing smoking rooms, arcades, aquariums, pavilions, conservatories and winter-gardens that are beautifully illustrated in the catalogues.

BEFORE the publication of their *Book of Designs of Horticulture Buildings* in 1875, Henry Hope (originally Clark & Jones) manufactured and shipped an elaborate conservatory to Buenos Aires. This marked the beginning of their export business, which was expanded to include prefabricated buildings and windows for Japan, New Zealand, Australia, Africa, Holland, Canada and the United States. The subsequent firm Crittall-Hope manufactured metal windows popular throughout the world in the twentieth century.

THE construction of prefabricated glasshouses in public gardens proliferated during the 1870s. In Florence, the Orto Botanico palm house, an elegant transparent structure by architect Giacomo Roster, was constructed in 1874 for an international garden exhibition. At this time the architect was the selector, not the director,

of a building's form. This was in the hands of the manufacturing company that prefabricated the components and site assembled them. The basilica form of the Florence glasshouse, with a central nave and side aisles, is a type that could be purchased from a catalogue and is similar to the Royal Horticultural Society's Kensington glasshouse prefabricated and built by Handyside & Company.

IN Madrid's Parque del Retiro, the Palacio de Cristal, a large glass structure on the lines of church architecture, was designed by architect Valázquez Bosco in 1887. It is reminiscent of English prefabricated catalogue buildings prevalent at that time. Botanical glass structures are unusual in warm climates, with the exception of arcades and small botanical houses. This building was meant to exhibit plants from the Philippines, a Spanish colony. The subsequent Spanish-American War made stocking this house difficult and it is now used for art exhibitions.

WHEN in 1875 James Lick ordered two glasshouses from England for his estate in San José, California, the pre-manufactured

buildings of corrugated, cast- and wrought-iron were shipped all the way around Cape Horn to San Francisco. However, Lick died in 1876. The crated buildings were bequeathed to the Society of California Pioneers, which in turn sold them to a business group that donated them to the San Francisco City Administration. Lord & Burnham of Irvington, New York, were hired to erect one of Lick's palm houses in what is now Golden Gate Park; Frederick Lord finished the work in 1879. The palm house's columns are cast-iron, but much of the building is wood. The whereabouts of the other glasshouse is unclear; it was said to have been assembled on an estate in Sacramento.

BY the late nineteenth century, the East and West Coast of the United States were connected by railroads opening up huge markets for manufacturers. Lord & Burnham, who later amalgamated with Hitchings & Co of Jersey City, became North America's most prolific manufacturer of glasshouses during the nineteenth and twentieth centuries. Their numerous catalogues are filled with glasshouses of

28, 29 Exterior view and detail of the Palacio de Cristal, El Retiro Park, Madrid, Valázquez Bosco, 1887.

29

30 Palm house, Golden Gate
Park, San Francisco, Lord
& Burnham, 1879.

every size and description. The prefabricated structure and glazing was manufactured in New York and shipped by rail throughout Canada and the United States; for example a 'Tropical Garden and Palm house' for an estate in Menlo Park, California, was ordered by a client who saw an advertisement in a newspaper in around 1910.

ONE of the larger commissions for glazing from Lord & Burnham's sales office and factory in St Catharines, Ontario, was the Crystal Garden, built in connection with the Canadian Pacific Hotel in the early 1920s, now The Empress in Victoria, British Columbia. The Crystal Garden centred around a large saltwater swimming pool, it had two ballrooms, an art gallery, a concert hall and extensive meeting and tea rooms designed by architects P L James in collaboration with F M Rattenbury. Another public glasshouse typical of Lord & Burnham's work is in Toronto's Allan Gardens.

THROUGHOUT the nineteenth century, cast-iron became a refined building material.[3] The art of casting intricate shapes enabled the designers to pursue a 'battle of styles', while hidden under the decorative foliage lay the pure structural criteria for the columns, brackets and beams. The cast-iron component, be it a truss, rain gutter or column, could be cast with a sophisticated connecting joint which minimized assembly time on the building site. Charles Fox's 'snap-on' joint between the cast girder and column connectors, used on the 1850–1 Crystal Palace, was secured only by an iron wedge which enabled its rapid assembly.

THERE are lessons to be learned from the great Victorian glasshouses, including the Crystal Palace, the Winter Garden at Regent's Park, the Palm House at Kew, and the numerous and often vast buildings from companies like MacFarlane. However large, they were made from components limited in size by the manufacturing process and the available transportation facilities. Victorian engineers relied on the column to overcome the span limitations of cast-iron. Spans were relatively modest, but when combined, they formed buildings of vast size. Recurring components conveyed a human

30

31 Tropical palm house for an estate in Menlo Park, California, Lord & Burnham, c 1910. This palm house was ordered by a client who saw an advertisement in the newspaper.

32 Palm house, Sefton Park, Liverpool, MacKenzie and Moncur, 1896. Henry Yates Thompson, who gave the house to the city of Liverpool, filled it with sculptures of famous botanists and explorers, like Christopher Columbus and Captain Cook.

31

scale to the large enclosed space, harmonizing the whole. The Crystal Palace was built essentially from one spanning component – a truss 3 feet deep by 23¼ feet long, weighing 900 lbs and easily manoeuvred by a few men with a jib crane and a block and tackle. Today's building components are often too large to store and transport.

VICTORIAN firms (like Fox & Henderson who built the Crystal Palace) designed, prefabricated and built turn-key structures with an efficiency not known in the latter half of the twentieth century. The eighteen-acre Crystal Palace took only six months to complete. Today, the construction process is segregated into disparate groups and this is not as efficient as in Victorian times when one company with a casting works did it all. Contemporary contractors prepare tenders from architects' plans based on philosophies that they do not understand. Then, they hire subcontractors to do the work. These subcontractors are so specialized that little component integration is possible. Thus, our contemporary construction sites are filled with disparate companies doing fragmented work. Compared to nineteenth-century glasshouse construction, we have digressed and reverted to elementary practices without integrated components and skills.

CURRENT-DAY construction is limited to a narrow selection of standardized parts. There are fewer 'off-the-peg' components available. This small pallet of choice forces today's architects to create idiosyncratic designs and detail. The nineteenth-century designer could choose from a greater array of manufactured components, which were far more sophisticated and varied. Components today are devoid of the finesse found with cast-iron, where the structure, the connection and decoration were accomplished in one intrinsic building element. Only a few manufacturers now remain and they produce the same sheet goods and components with little concern as to how or where they will be used. During the course of the twentieth century, mergers and takeovers have ensured that the rich texture of the industry created by small manufacturers has been lost.

32

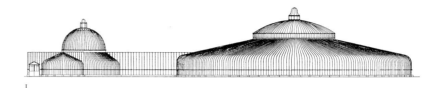

1

GLASS IN THE PUBLIC GARDEN

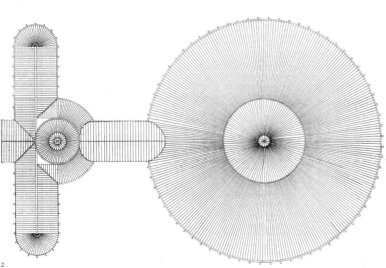

VII

2

IT was in the nineteenth century that the idea of constructing glass spaces for the general public first gained currency. Previously, there had been technical and economic obstacles to building on a grand scale – the problem of bridging large spans was unresolved and glass was heavily taxed. Wealth also tended to be concentrated in the hands of the nobility and landowners built glasshouses on their estates for their own private enjoyment. More-over, it was only with the maturity of the social forces which were a product of the industrial revolution that a greater population of middle- and working-class city dwellers emerged; these new urban inhabitants, with holidays to amuse themselves and a greater combined spending power, sought new diversions and places to visit.

THERE is no single evolutionary thread running through the glasshouse in the public garden. Botanical hothouses were built from the begin-ning to the end of the century, sometimes even in similar styles. However, particular trends can be identified; for instance, many of the earlier British glasshouses tended to be curvilinear while their later German counterparts were built in a rectilinear classical style. Certainly it is true to say that the capacity for

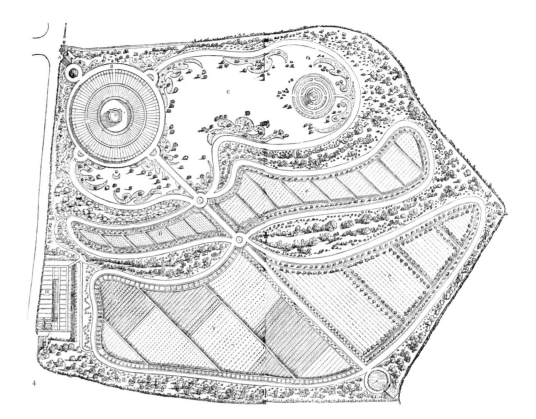

4

5

larger structures grew as the century progressed, allowing a larger cross section of the public to be accommodated. Many of the early botanical gardens, which were responsible for the first glasshouses, were founded by royalty or horticultural societies who only allowed access to a select elite, but by the end of the century they had opened their doors to the general public. The popularity of botanical glasshouses was such that it was not long before their use as purely recreational centres was realized. Winter-gardens and German floras were built throughout the mid- and late nineteenth century, which attracted crowds to the cafés, restaurants and assembly rooms within their exotic glazed surroundings.

A FORMATIVE scheme for a botanical garden with glasshouses was designed in 1831 by Loudon for the Birmingham Horticultural Society. It was planned for a 16-acre site at Edgbaston, two miles from the city centre. Much to Loudon's disappointment the design was never carried out. It would certainly have been one of the finest gardens, far ahead of its time. Loudon's plans included functional glass domes of great beauty, which pre-dated even those at Chatsworth and at Kew Gardens. Their size, the heating, ventilating and rainmaking apparatus and unique construction sequence, can be attributed to the justified confidence of this inventor, gardener, encyclopedist and editor of gardening periodicals.

PUBLIC access to the garden would have been a matter of economic necessity. The Horticultural Society wanted a commercial nursery to be included in their plans for the scientific ornamental garden. There would have been an admission charge, for this was before the advent of free gardens later in the century.

LOUDON developed two glasshouse designs in detail.[1] Both had circular plans calculated to look good when seen from all sides and from the highest corner of the garden site. The first design was a circular glass corridor that surrounded a central tower. The steam-boilers were located in the tower's basement, and coal was transported there by an underground passageway. A second boiler stood by in case of an emergency. Above was a potting and tool shed

132

4 Plan of a garden for the Birmingham Botanical Horticultural Society, J C Loudon, 1831, illustrated in *The Gardener's Magazine*, 1832. Loudon's huge greenhouse is in the upper left.

5 Conservatory, Birmingham Botanical Gardens, F B Osborn, 1869. Loudon's own greenhouse proposals were unfulfilled.

6 The first circular glasshouse proposed by Loudon for the Birmingham Horticultural Society's garden, *The Gardener's Magazine*, 1832.

7 The second design proposed by Loudon if expense were no object, *The Gardener's Magazine*, 1832.

8 The St Louis Climatron, designed by Murphy and Mackay, 1959–60. Loudon's proposal for Birmingham was considerably larger than the Climatron.

and a water tank for the glasshouse and garden fountains. Water was to descend to a pond at the lowest area of the garden and be recirculated by steam-pumps. The glasshouse had inner and outer rings of glass-covered pits for smaller plants. Trees were to be planted inside directly in the ground and other plants set around in pots. Cast-iron cisterns under the pathways were to collect rainwater from the roof. Heated water would flow through pipes pierced with holes to imitate a shower as at the Loddiges's tropical house at Hackney. A walkway at the ridge of the glasshouse was designed to store mats that could be rolled down over the glass during cold weather.

AS an alternative Loudon proposed a multi-storey structure, which could be built 'if expense were not an object'. It covered nearly an acre with its conical roof, which was 200 feet in diameter and 100 feet high. The ground level was laid out in concentric beds and walks, with four radiating partitions that separated four artificial climates. At the centre, in a glass chamber 30 feet in diameter, the most

rapidly growing and tallest tropical trees, 'their trunks and branches clothed with epiphytes and climbers', would have been planted and the ground covered with ferns; surrounding this tropical cylinder a spiral ramp, its railings draped with creepers, would have connected the various plant galleries. As in the more modest design, the conical roof had walkways to enable the gardeners to cover the glass on winter nights with matting or oil cloth. Immediately under the glass were pipes heated by steam, while over the glass there was even a system of conducting rods for 'guarding against the effects of electricity' (lightning). The glass was arranged in separate panels supported by rafters and could be removed during the summer months, for, as Loudon correctly believed, this strengthened the vegetation. The glazing design followed the method invented by John Jones of Birmingham, who Loudon considered the best hothouse builder in Britain.

LOUDON's ambitious proposal was substantially larger than the St Louis Climatron built in 1959, which is 175 feet in diameter and 70 feet high.

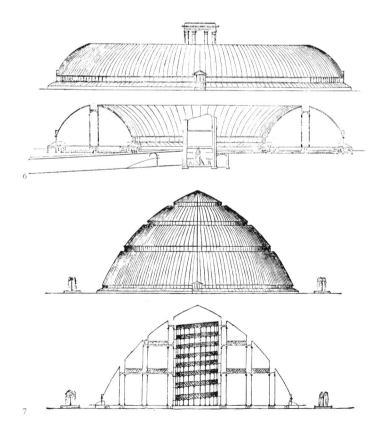

Still, he told the Birmingham Horticultural Society that 'there would be no difficulty in erecting such a building' and, he claimed, it would have been easier to heat than his less expensive design.

IN his discussion of the Birmingham project Loudon also predicted the advent of public gardens:

when towns and their suburbs are legislated for
and governed as a whole, and not, as they are
now, in petty detail, by corporations and vestries;
and when the recreation and enjoyment of the
whole society are cared for by their representatives;
public gardens, with hothouses of this sort, or
even of far greater magnificence, will be erected,
for the general enjoyment, at the general expense.

However, Loudon was never to see the realization of his prediction in the Crystal Palace or the Palm House at Kew, for he died in 1843, the year that Queen Victoria drove through the Duke of Devonshire's Great Conservatory at Chatsworth in her carriage.

THE Sheffield Botanical and Horticultural Society was formed in 1833, a year after Loudon described his ill-fated glass and garden designs for Birmingham in *The Gardener's Magazine*. The garden was designed in 1833–4 by Robert Marnock who had been working at the Botanical Gardens in Regent's Park, London. The architect for the glass pavilion, B B Taylor from Sheffield, gained the commission through a competition that was judged by a committee which included Joseph Paxton. The elegant glass domes rising above the masonry back wall and south-facing columns are similar to the glass shell construction instigated by Loudon and emulated by W & D Bailey. The glass domes are examples of the few remaining buildings that illustrate the technical prowess also found in the structural glass skin enclosing the Bicton Palm House and certainly in Loudon's prototypes at Bayswater, the Loddiges's nursery and the Conservatory at Bretton Hall.

THE central pavilion, connected to two smaller pavilions by corridors covered in ridge-and-furrow glazing, was 52 feet wide, 33 feet deep

9

9, 10 The Glass Pavilion, Sheffield Botanical Gardens, B B Taylor, 1833–4. The original glass corridors, which were similar to Joseph Paxton's designs and linked the pavilion as one building, have now been removed.

10

11 Interior of the Glass
Menagerie, Surrey
Zoological Gardens,
Henry Phillips, 1830–1,
illustrated in *The Mirror
of Literature, Amusement
and Instruction*, 1832.
12 *The Royal Surrey
Zoological Gardens*,
lithograph by F Alvey,
c 1840s.
13 Plan of the Glass
Menagerie, Surrey,
built 1830–1.

11

12

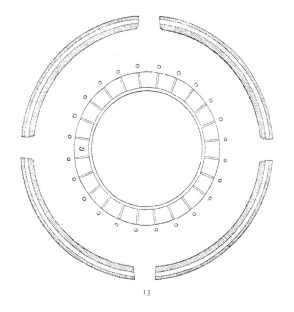

13

and 33 feet high. It is interesting to note that the construction of Paxton's Great Conservatory at Chatsworth began in 1836, when the Sheffield pavilions and gardens were opened for the pleasure of Horticultural Society members and, on occasions, the public. This is not to say that the Sheffield design was necessarily an inspiration for Paxton, but that the glass designers of the time kept in touch with what was happening throughout England and Europe by travel, correspondence and horticultural magazines.

IF public access was at first restricted to some botanical gardens, glasshouses were also being built as commercial ventures. With its varied attractions the Royal Surrey Zoological Gardens was one of the most popular during the 1830s, 1840s and 1850s. According to an 1840 guidebook of London, a three-penny omnibus ride from Charing Cross towards Camberwell would deliver a visitor at the gardens. On an average day eight thousand visitors promenaded around the grounds and on special occasions this figure was doubled. The caged and roaming animals were the main attractions, but

there were also concerts, balloon ascents and a five-acre model of Rome. Edward Cross, the founder, had previously kept his huge menagerie at Exeter Exchange, a three-storey building that jutted into the Strand. When the street was widened in 1830, Cross was forced to move his animals temporarily to King's Mews, on the site of Trafalgar Square, while the new zoological gardens were under construction on the eighteen-acre site of Walworth Manor House. Henry Phillips, a schoolmaster turned horticulturist and author of *Sylva Florifera* and other plant histories, laid out the garden and arranged to have built for Cross what was then regarded as the largest glass conservatory in England. At the time few people knew of Mrs Beaumont's similar conservatory of 1827 at Bretton Hall, Yorkshire, by Loudon and the Baileys.

THE zoological 'conservatory' as it was called, was actually a glass menagerie for Cross's 'wild beasts'. The greatest attraction was the cage shared by an Indian tigress and an English spaniel, a curiosity viewed by Queen Victoria and Prince Albert. The compartments or cages

14 The Metropolitan Meat Market at Smithfield, designed by Sir Horace Jones, 1868.

14

for animals were arranged in a circle towards the centre of the building. Around them was a colonnade, which supported the glazed roof and contained hot-water pipes. It was only beyond this that there was an open paved area for spectators. The Surrey menagerie lasted beyond Cross's retirement in 1844, but the animals were sold in 1855 and the structure was torn down in 1856 to provide the site for the Royal Surrey Music Hall, an ugly Victorian design by Sir Horace Jones, also the architect for the cast-iron and glass Smithfield Market in the City of London.[2] In 1825, prior to his involvement in the Surrey Zoological Gardens, Henry Phillips had designed an oriental garden near his home in Brighton. The garden centred on a large glass conservatory, the Athenaeum, which could house palms in its steam-heated tropical section. It was also to have a 'literary institute' comprising a library, a museum, a reading room and a school of science, where Phillips proposed to lecture, and in this way it anticipated the German floras. A start was made on the building, but it was abandoned in June 1827 due to lack of funds.

IN 1832 the oriental garden project was revived at Hove near Brighton. A domed conservatory, now called the Antheum, was to excel anything of its kind, enclosing full-size trees with birds, a lake with fish, a hill of rocks and an amphitheatre for eight hundred people. By July 1833, Joseph Paxton, on a visit to the Duke of Devonshire's house in Brighton, was able to inspect the nearly completed structure. The dimensions were formidable. The 60-foot-high glass dome had twenty cast-iron ribs forming ten elliptical arches spanning nearly 170 feet. Each rib was 3 feet deep at its base and 2 feet deep at the top and was assembled from six castings held together by bolts and flanges. A circular casting, 7 feet in diameter, held the ribs together at the top and each base was encased in a 12-foot-high pier, part of a brick circular wall. Light cast-iron purlins spanned between the ribs forming concentric circles at various elevations. A wooden scaffolding was built in the interior to hold all the structural members in position until the building had been bolted together.

AN unfortunate oversight in the design, the lack of diagonal braces between the ribs, was detected by the supervising architect Amon Henry Wilds. But, as no provision had been made in the ribs to receive this bracing and to make it would have resulted in considerable expense, the contractor refused to provide it. Thus, when the scaffolding was removed the weight of the glass and iron immediately caused the unbraced ribs to swerve in serpentine lines, cracking the purlins. Loudon made a visit to inspect the great glass bubble on 12 September 1833 and found that the whole centre had collapsed; 'breaking with a report like the running fire of light artillery, giving out sparks, as to produce the effect of a powerful flash of lightning', to quote an observing architect, Charles Augustin Busby, in the *Brighton Herald*. The shock of the collapse was said to have sent poor Phillips blind and he died seven years later. However, half the ironwork and all the brickwork remained intact; Busby, who was often a collaborator of Wilds, undertook to rebuild the Antheum, but nothing came of the scheme. The wreckage remained until the mid-1850s when Baron Goldschmid had the ground cleared to lay out Palmeira Square.

THE history of the London Horticultural Society's gardens at Chiswick during the first half of the nineteenth century is central to the development of the glasshouse in the public garden. It is indicative of the economic and practical obstacles that glasshouse builders still had to overcome. More important than this, though, the garden provided Paxton, one of the glasshouse's most influential designers, with his initial horticultural training, and brought him into contact with his greatest patron, William Cavendish, Duke of Devonshire.

IN 1822, London's Horticultural Society, originally founded in 1804, gave up its small garden at Kensington and leased a 33-acre plot from the Duke of Devonshire, adjacent to his Chiswick estate. The Duke, keenly interested in botany, had previously built there a 300-foot-long hothouse with a conservatory in the middle. The society built a more substantial establishment with new roads, paths, walls, glasshouses and offices containing a council room. By 1824 a national school for the propagation of horticultural knowledge was established, Paxton's name being one of the earliest entries in its log book. Paxton was soon upgraded from labourer to under gardener in the arboretum where his work apparently attracted the eye of the Duke, a frequent visitor. In 1826 he lured Paxton away to Chatsworth, where the gardener's remarkable career flourished.

THE 1830s saw the gardens at Chiswick become a popular place for horticultural exhibitions and competitions, as well as a fashionable place to promenade. The horticultural competitions, for which the gold Knightion and Banksian medals were awarded, became so popular that twelve thousand tickets could be sold for a single show.

THE Horticultural Society had been interested originally in indigenous plants, but exotics were being sucessfully brought back to the gardens, mainly through the efforts of the society's collectors, like Theodore Hartwick, and with the Duke of Devonshire's economic support and fanatical interest. A controversy began about the collection of orchids and other tropical exotics because they required expensive new glass, but the taste for foreign tropicals won the day. The society's members wanted tropical propagation, the seeds and cuttings for their own collections.

IN 1838 Thomas Knight, who had become renowned as the society's president, died. He was succeeded by the Duke of Devonshire, whose famous interest in glass building had already resulted in the Conservatory at Chatsworth and was to emerge again in plans for a large conservatory at Chiswick. It was to have a central dome 100 feet in diameter and four wings 185 feet long and 30 feet wide. Unfortunately, only one wing was constructed by D & E Bailey in 1840, owing, for one thing, to the exorbitant tax on glass at that time.

BY 1857 many of the large exotics were too tall for the conservatory and it was converted into a vinery and wintering house for camellias, oranges and other half-hardy potted trees. In a good season it produced 4,500 lbs of eighty-three varieties of grapes, such as Black Hamburg and Muscat of Alexandria. Such a bountiful harvest required machinery, and a wrought-iron ladder, curved to the shape of the glass and mounted on wheels, was built. A continuous ridge ventilator, with an aperture and butterfly shutters, provided ventilation similar to the

15

16

15 The Conservatory, Royal Horticulture Gardens Society, Chiswick, constructed by D & E Bailey, 1840.
16 The glasshouses at Chiswick today.

17

Bicton Palm House in Devon. In 1861 the society leased grounds in South Kensington for a new garden and Chiswick was neglected. During the 1880s there was a return to Chiswick when the lease at Kensington was given up. However, it was abandoned again after the Wisley Garden was purchased in 1903. THE early British prototypes discussed here were all built in glass and iron. Though the uses of the glasshouses were not always purely botanical, the designers all had horticultural backgrounds. They worked from the gardener's point of view and they did not regard their chief concern to be one of architectural style. It was only when large-scale prestigious commissions arose, like that of the Palm House at Kew, in the middle of the nineteenth century, that architects became involved. The application of the new materials, iron and glass, made it necessary for architects to work with engineers, upon whose design and fabricating skills they were inordinately dependent. This close collaboration has led to the questioning of authorship of iron buildings previously credited wholly to architects. Two

major nineteenth-century glass gardens, in Kew and Regent's Park, are popularly attributed to the architect Decimus Burton and little is said of the contractor Richard Turner. Yet Turner engineered, fabricated and to a considerable extent designed these two structures, working from his Hammersmith Iron Works in Dublin, built in 1834, where the components were made. They were undoubtedly the finest glass and iron conservatories ever built in Britain. Although Joseph Paxton is rightly acclaimed for his marvellous crystal palaces, it must be remembered that they were clad with glass and timber while Turner built structures totally of cast-iron with elegant spans of curved wrought-iron ribs and iron trusses. The resulting glass buildings, unsurpassed even today, were formulated by an engineer who understood well the construction potential of iron in all forms.

TURNER'S first known work is the Botanic Gardens Palm House in Belfast. This was begun in 1839, and by the next year two wings were completed. The design, however, was not by Turner, but by the Antrim County surveyor

17 Interior of the Chiswick Conservatory, from *Knight's London*, vol v, 1843.

18 Conservatory and fruit house for Colonel White at Killkee, Co Dublin, designed by Richard Turner, illustrated in Charles McIntosh, *The Book of the Garden*, 1853.

19 The Conservatory at the Royal Horticultural Society's garden in Chiswick, built by D & E Bailey in 1840.

18

19

20 The conservatory at Ballyfing House, County Laois, was added to the house by Richard Turner in 1850.

21 The domical conservatory designed by Richard Turner, and illustrated in Charles McIntosh, *The Book of the Garden*, 1853. The split pilasters in this design also appear in Turner's Regent's Park Winter Garden and Ballyfing.

20

Charles Lanyon. However, when Young & Co of Edinburgh constructed the central building years later in 1853, it differed considerably from Lanyon's original design and showed the influence of Turner's Palm House at Kew, completed five years before.

THE Belfast Palm House was followed by the Palm House and curvilinear range at Glasnevin near Dublin, built by Turner for the Royal Dublin Society in 1843 and enlarged in 1869. This was the prototype for many of the details found in his extant Kew Palm House and his demolished, and little-known, Regent's Park Winter Garden.

THE Royal Botanic Society of London was incorporated by Royal Charter in 1839. In the following year the society acquired the 18-acre 'inner circle' of Regent's Park, previously owned by Jenkin's nursery, and it commissioned Decimus Burton to design a winter-garden.[3] Burton suggested a huge, 315 by 165 feet (1.2 acres), wood and glass construction, made with five spans of ridge-and-furrow roofing. The centre span was to have a curvilinear

dome.[4] A model was made, but nothing was done until Burton submitted a revised plan in April 1845, with an iron ridge-and-furrow roof. The dome had been replaced by a curvilinear apse in the middle of the facade. Bids were submitted for the central portion of the large enclosed garden, one from Cubitt & Co for £5,500 partly of wood, and the other from Richard Turner, which cost less and was made entirely of iron and glass. He outlined this in his bid to Burton on 16 April 1845 disproving the latter's claim that wood was cheaper.[5]

THE society made some modifications to the design, replacing the end wall with curvilinear lean-tos for strength and appearance. This was acceptable to the cooperative Turner who coveted the commission.

OPENED to the public on 20 May 1846, the Winter Garden protected 19,000 square feet and was truly a glass garden, for the floor was earth, covered with gravel and topped with 'pounded' seashell. Access to the light, elegant structure was through rows of outward-hinged French windows, giving views in all directions,

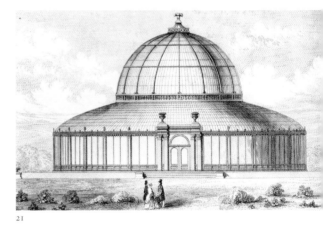

21

22

22, 23 Exterior view and
interior detail of the Palm
House, Belfast Botanical
Gardens, designed by
Charles Lanyon and built
by Richard Turner,
1839–53.
24 Plan of the Winter
Garden in the Inner
Circle of Regent's Park.

23

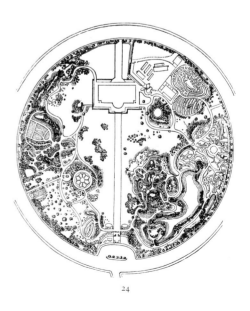

24

and also ventilation. Turner's divided pilasters, infilled with red and blue ground and polished glass, must have delighted Victorian visitors. The curvilinear ridge roofs were all supported on 14-foot cast-iron columns that transferred rainwater to the cisterns below. The internal planting was a departure from the customary formal style; the plants were grouped in clumps, growing through the white seashell, and valuable specimens were allowed to stand on their own. Small iron tables were filled with hyacinths and narcissi, and flowers of all description formed what the 1851 edition of Knight's *Cyclopaedia of London* called:

a veritable fairy land transplanted into the heart of London an actual garden of delight, realising all our ideal. From the keen frosty air outside, and the flow-eriness aspect of universal nature, one steps into an atmosphere balmy and delicious … The most exquis-ite odours are wafted to and fro with every movement of the glass doors. Birds singing in the branches … make you again and again pause to ask, is this winter? Is this England?

25

26

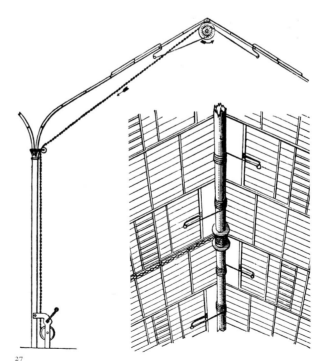

27

25 Glasshouses, Botanic Gardens, Glasnevin, Dublin, Richard Turner, 1842–9.
26 Interior of the Winter Garden, Royal Botanic Gardens, Regent's Park, Richard Turner, 1846.
27 Turner's ventilation system for the Regent's Park Winter Garden. A rod extended the length of each ridge, and metal sashes opened by their own weight as the rod turned.

TO create this climate the temperature was regulated by two Burbidge & Healy ribbed boilers, feeding water into nearly a mile of four-inch pipe. Six hot-water pipes followed the periphery in a 3-foot-deep channel and four pipes ran down the middle. The warmed air rose in shafts placed at intervals throughout the area and was controlled by iron grilles. The boiler house and the chimney were located some distance away and the main pipes were led through an outside covered channel. A portion of the glass garden was partitioned off and kept warmer for the tropical exotics. In addition to the heating pipes, a water-filled tank also went round the wall just below the glass. It was covered and fitted at intervals with dampered grilles to control the moisture in the air.

QUEEN Victoria was the first patroness of the society and took great interest in encouraging ladies to become members and attend lectures and meetings. Large flower shows and evening fêtes were held in the summer. In 1871 Turner's company added an east wing, an apse and a connecting corridor and in 1876, a west wing and

an apse, completing the 210-foot symmetrical facade with its three-crowned half domes. The original lease came to an end in the late 1920s, and increasing financial difficulties forced the society to auction its rare plants in September 1931. Despite the efforts of Queen Mary, who was particularly interested in saving the Winter Garden, the society disbanded in 1932. The grounds were taken over by the Royal Parks Department, and the Winter Garden was eventually demolished.

A CONTROVERSY surrounds the contributions of Burton and Turner to the Winter Garden. The constructed building had the curvilinear ridge roofs proposed by Turner, instead of Burton's ridge and furrow, and an apse instead of a dome to save money. The open pilasters filled with coloured glass, the iron casement-window detail and the sliding iron-ridge vents were Turner's trademarks. Burton seems to have become the go-between for the society and Turner. The Botanic Society's secretary at the time, J de C Sowerby, wrote, 'this building, constructed of iron, was designed and built by

28 *An Evening Fete at the Winter Garden in Regent's Park*, M M Runciman, 1876.

28

Turner, of Dublin'. But, as at Kew, Decimus Burton influenced the overall form, which was based upon his early designs.⁶

THE Kew palm collection had been ill-housed for many years in the old stove at the Royal Botanic Gardens. In the same year that Queen Victoria visited Chatsworth, 1843, the Director of Kew Gardens, Sir William Hooker, also inspected the recently completed Great Conservatory, the largest in Britain and Europe. Hooker wanted to initiate the construction of a larger structure at Kew. The gardens had recently been made public and they became increasingly popular with nearly 64,000 people visiting them in 1847, and 327,000 in 1851, the year of the Great Exhibition.

THE design process for the Palm House involved a laborious and drawn out metamorphosis, an arduous interplay between Turner (the designer-contractor), Burton (the designer-architect), the gardens' commissioners and Hooker. The 2 September 1848 and the 7 August 1852 issues of the *Illustrated London News* attribute the building to the design of Decimus Burton, and the ironwork to Richard Turner – as does the 15 January 1848 *The Builder*.

Great praise is due to Mr. Turner, for the manner in which the work is done. A correspondent on his part remarks – 'As nearly all the work of this building has been executed by Irishmen, who are grateful for the employment it has afforded them, I hope you will consider it a proof that the mechanics of that country are disposed to earn their bread in honesty and peace, and are capable of executing works of that kind to the satisfaction of the professional gentlemen of this country.'

HENRY-RUSSELL Hitchcock began to sow a seed of doubt when he questioned 'whether the ornamental restraint, combined with a real degree of expression should be credited to Turner or to Burton'.⁷ George F Chadwick also questioned Burton's contribution to the Great Conservatory at Chatsworth, seeing him as a supervisor and as providing working drawings for Paxton's main idea.⁸ (Burton's office also produced drawings for the Kew Palm House.) An article in *The Architectural Review* by Peter Ferriday seems to re-establish Richard Turner in his position as designer,

prefabricator and builder at Kew.⁹ However, the former librarian and archivist of Kew, R Desmond, credits Burton with the overall form of the Palm House in a well-researched article: 'Who designed the Palm House in Kew Gardens?'¹⁰ Desmond reveals the following events based on pertinent quotations from the Kew Archives:

In 1844 Decimus Burton prepared sketch designs for the new Palm House, but Kew's director, William Hooker, and the curator, John Smith, rejected them because of the number of columns. Burton set about preparing an alternative design. About this time Turner arrived from Dublin and showed Hooker and his Commissioners a scale model with a central house and two wings. His design package, complete with estimates, was approved and it was agreed that he should make full drawings. Turner also was shown Burton's design which he confirmed as extravagant and 'encumbered with immense trussed arched columns'.

BURTON had similar criticisms for Turner's plans, though he approved of the general scheme of central space and wings. He criticized Turner's inner row of columns, objecting to the proportions and to Turner's 'Ecclesiastical or Gothic style'. He forwarded a second design of his own and altered the central section of Turner's scheme so that it was similar to the Chatsworth Conservatory, and added a lantern roof, while suggesting a 'conventional horticultural style'. Later, Turner, with the contract for the ironwork in his hand and working in collaboration with Burton, was able to write to Hooker, 'I am glad to inform you that Mr. Burton is determined to make a most magnificent and beautiful range for you.' In short, Turner had suggested the overall layout of the building, while Burton was responsible for the proportions of the central section as we see it today. Moreover, these great conservatories, such as at Kew, were sophisticated engineering feats requiring detailing, structural prefabrication and construction techniques natural to an engineer like Turner. After the initial form and style of an iron building had been decided, the architects' task appears to have been over. A similar situation occurred with Paxton's Crystal Palace, which could not have been built without

30

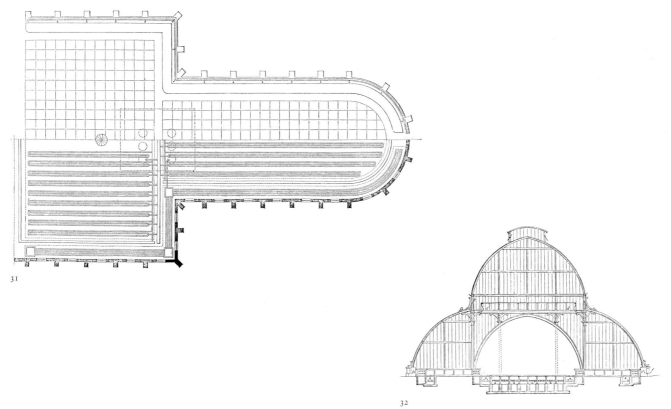

31

32

29 Interior of the Palm House, Royal Botanic Gardens, Kew, Decimus Burton and Richard Turner, 1845–8. This photograph was taken during the house's recent restoration when it was emptied of all the plants.
30 Exterior of the Kew Palm House.
31 A half plan of the Kew Palm House, *The Builder*, 1848.
32 Design of a section for the Kew Palm House, signed by Decimus Burton, 1844.

Overleaf
33 The Kew Palm House in the snow. To the right can be seen the Victoria Regia House.

the admirable skill of Charles Fox, whose firm, Fox & Henderson, was the contractor.

THE dimensions of the Palm House are most impressive. The entire length is 362½ feet, with the central space 137½ feet long, 100 feet wide and 63 feet high, exclusive of the 6-foot lantern. Concrete foundations, by Grissel & Peto, supported large granite blocks, which had cast-iron sockets for the main nine-inch-deep wrought-iron ribs of the framework. The structure, which Turner substituted for the original cast-iron, is a significant point in the development of wrought-iron. The wrought-iron 'bulb and tee' ribs had been patented by Kennedy & Vernon for ship building in 1844, and their application here makes it the first building to use a rolled I-shape section. They were fabricated in England as lengths of about 12 feet, and welded together in a blast furnace in Dublin by Turner, where they were drawn to the required curve. In the central space, the tops of the side-aisle ribs are supported by cast-iron columns and brackets, which in turn support the upper ribs and the balcony. The span of these ribs and wings is a

clear 50 feet. These ribs are braced together with wrought-iron tie-rods, inside cast-iron tubes, which act as purlins. The wrought-iron rods were drawn taut after the building was assembled. This put the unique hollow purlins in compression, knitting the post-tensioned structure together, a novel solution which formed part of a patent granted to Turner in December 1846; it was used by him on several railway station roofs of the late 1840s.

THE Palm House was to be one of the first structures of considerable size to be clad in tax-free glass, after the repeal of the glass tax by Sir Robert Peel, which came into effect in April 1845. Over an acre of 21-ounce sheet-glass patented and made by Chance & Co of Birmingham, in panes of 3⅙ by 9½ inches, was used. It was stronger than the common and cheaper crown-glass, but the irregular surface, it was believed, could cause concentrated scorching. A pea-green tinge was infused into the glass with copper oxide to counteract this. The plants, however, did not flourish for lack of light and the building was later reglazed clear.

34

34 The 550-foot tunnel that links the Palm House in the Royal Botanic Gardens, Kew, to an Italianate service tower.

35 The construction of the Kew Palm House, c 1847.

36 Print of the interior of the Kew Palm House, as illustrated in the *Illustrated London News*, 1852.

36

35

37 View of the Kew Palm
House with the Victoria
Regia House.
38 The iron and glass roof
over Lime Street station,
Richard Turner, 1850.

37

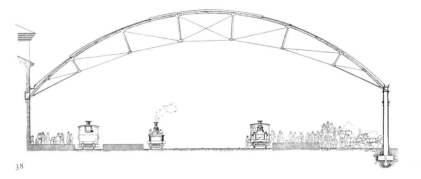

38

THE upper roof of the central space is supported on tubular cast-iron columns that drain the rainwater collected in the gutter of the upper roof into tanks formed around the whole interior of the building. The water from the lower lean-to roof is received into a gutter forming the upper part of the plinth and is carried into the same tanks.

THE Palm House created an artificial climate for exotic and utilitarian plants from throughout the world. The specifications required that the heating maintain 80°F when the external air was 20°F. Twelve Burbidge & Healy boilers in zoned pairs, placed in vaults below, fed nearly 5½ miles of pipe on the periphery and in loops under the perforated cast-iron floor. Each boiler had its own set of pipes, so that, according to the temperature required, one or both boilers could be fired. Tanks were placed in the basement below the stone walkways to assure maximum humidity.

IN marked contrast to modern architecture like the Lloyd's Building, the Victorians went to great lengths to hide mechanical services. Decimus Burton specially designed an Italianate tower to contain the flues for the boilers and a water tank about 500 feet to the east of the Palm House. The boiler rooms were linked to the coal yard and the chimney campanile by a tunnel, which, besides containing the smoke flues, housed a railway, with iron wagons to carry coal and to remove ashes. The water tank was filled by a steam-driven pump. It supplied water to a series of perforated pipes that made artificial rain in the house. Controversy of authorship aside, the Palm House is one of the most beautiful in the world, and was extensively restored in the late 1890s.

TURNER went on to design and build the original roof of the Broadstone station, Dublin (1847), and the second train shed at Lime Street station, Liverpool (1849–51), which has been demolished; he received international recognition in the 1850 competition for the Great Exhibition building in Hyde Park. His entry and that of Hector Horeau received the only two 'special mention' awards among the 245 submissions.[11] In spite of his defeat in the building competition, Turner had a big show at

39

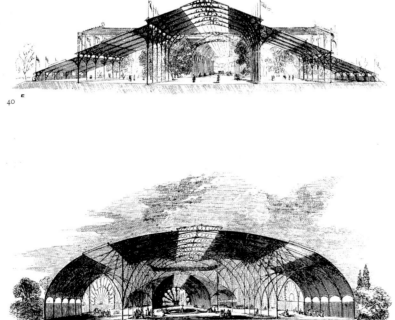

40

41

39 Temperate House, Royal Botanic Gardens, Kew, Decimus Burton, 1859–63. The rectangular wings were added between 1895 and 1897.

40 Hector Horeau's glass and iron competition entry for the 1850 Great Exhibition Building. This was a simple shed in a basilica form, with four side-aisles and a transept. The nave ended in a domed, semi-circular apse.

41 Richard Turner's submission for the 1850 Great Exhibition competition, which received a special mention.

42–44 The roof, interior and exterior of the Palm House, Royal Botanic Gardens, Edinburgh, R Matthienson, 1858.

the Exhibition. Along with models of several iron-roofed buildings, including two to house a man-of-war, he displayed scale models of the Lime Street station, the Kew Palm House, the Regent's Park Winter Garden, both of his designs for the Great Exhibition building, a range of glass conservatories (including a round one), and a brass model covering half an acre of a winter-garden designed for the King of Prussia in Berlin.[12]

CHARLES McIntosh, who published a number of Turner's designs in his *The Book of the Garden* of 1853, rightly described him as 'one of the first hothouse architects of the day'. An exuberant and enthusiastic proponent of wrought-iron and glass, he produced designs that show potential beyond his own prolific building career. A structural visionary, but also an enterprising businessman, he made full use of his engineering background, his manufacturing company and his team of Irish workmen to build a 'package deal' answering the customer's demands.

WHEN, in 1859, £10,000 was granted by Parliament for a new temperate glasshouse at

Kew, Turner's erstwhile partner Burton was at last able to design a scheme dictated by his choice of architectural language rather than 'horticultural convention'. He prepared plans for five interconnected buildings. Cubitt & Co constructed the main central space and the two octagonal buildings on each side, the remaining two rectilinear buildings were built later. The central space is 212 by 137 feet and 60 feet high, and the two octagons are 50 feet in diameter. The whole range sits on an acropolis of about 4 feet high and 528 feet long. It covers 48,400 square feet and is approximately double the size of the Kew Palm House, making it one of the largest groups of glasshouses in the world. Burton used a masonry-base wall and a projecting portico to endow it with architectural 'style'. The low sloping roof allowed a series of ridge vents along the length of the rectilinear buildings, which are opened in favourable weather. A contemporary writer in *The Garden* of 15 June 1872 was not as complimentary as he might have been, when he complained that: 'the huge mass of iron pipes piled up along the

central walk completely spoils that air of repose which a noble conservatory ought to possess. Indeed, the great number of exposed pipes looks more like what one might expect to see in a factory-yard than a garden.'

THE palm houses in the Royal Botanic Gardens, Edinburgh, are a far more successful example of architectural styling. Both Old and New Palm Houses are incorporated into a classical scheme in which glass domes spring from wide architraves that are part of temple-like stone arcades. The first palm house in the Royal Botanic Gardens was opened in 1834. Octagonal in plan, it is approximately 65 feet in diameter and 46 feet high. Soon after its completion it became apparent that this house was too small for the burgeoning collection – some of the palms were even growing through the glass roof. Professor John Hutton Balfour commissioned the design of a new building by architect R Matthienson, with the unusual height of 71½ feet, which was approved by Parliament in 1855 and was built in 1858. Though raised on masonry walls, the section of the glass roof is almost perfectly

42

43

44

45

46

47

modelled on the Palm House at Kew. The old pyramidal wood and glass roof of the previous palm house was replaced in 1859 with a iron and glass dome, and a glass partition was built to separate the two buildings; the new house is now used for tropical plants and the old octagon to contain species from temperate climates.

THE enthusiasm for public botanical gardens with glasshouses was just as intense in the rest of Europe as it was in Britain. In Paris, the Musée d'Histoire Naturelle de Paris, or Jardin des Plantes, endured continuous rebuilding programmes from the eighteenth century until well into the twentieth century. The glass range always surrounded the long central ramp that compensated for the large fall in the site to the south. A watercolour by Hiloir in 1794 shows a wind-protected south-facing specimen garden with two glass orangeries towering on each side of the ramp in the back of the garden; service rooms and storerooms were located below. The painting does not show the sloped-roofed glasshouse to the east. By 1821 menageries were added to the garden and by 1837 the architect

Rohault de Fleury published his newly constructed designs; in 1854, because the plant collection needed more space and in anticipation of the Universal Exhibition of 1855, further designs were made under his direction but not carried out; in 1882 an east wing was added by the architect André; and in 1908 the pavilions were rebuilt as we know them today.

IN 1833, construction started under Rohault de Fleury's direction on the new iron and glass houses that were to replace the existing structures. In 1834, before they were finished, he visited England to study iron construction and heating in glasshouses, including those of the Loddiges brothers in Hackney, the Coliseum in Regent's Park, the Royal Botanic Gardens in Kew, the Horticultural Society at Chiswick, Covent Garden Market, those built by the contractors W & D Bailey and Loudon's glasshouses in London. At Regent's Park a particular double-vaulted glasshouse seemed to have influenced Rohault de Fleury, though his design was also directed by the fall in the site and the existing foundations. However, he claimed that

MUSÉUM D'HISTOIRE NATURELLE

GRANDE SERRE DE

48

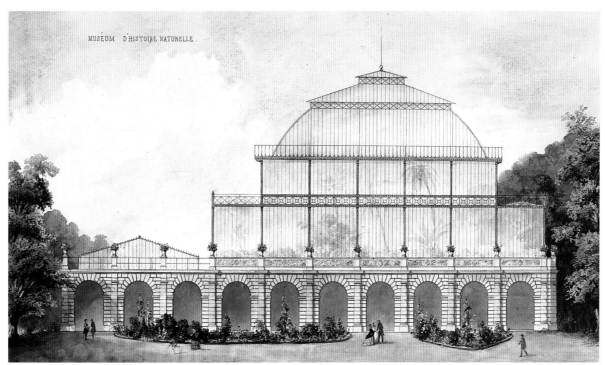

MUSÉUM D'HISTOIRE NATURELLE

49

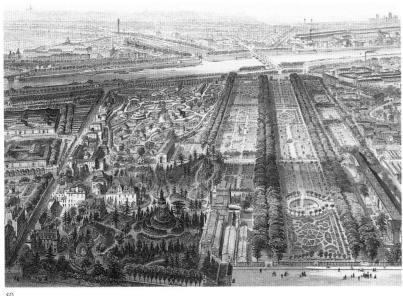

50

51

50 Aerial view of the glass
range in the Jardin des
Plantes after the 1833
building programme.
The Seine and the
zoological gardens are
in the background.

51 Charles Rohault de
Fleury's design for
glasshouses in Liège,
Belgium, *Revue Générale
de l'Architecture et des
Travaux Publics*, 1849.

claimed that the form of the Paris houses had
already been decided before he left.

SIGFRIED Giedion in *Space, Time and Architecture*
describes the De Fleury glasshouse as 'the prototype of all large iron-framed conservatories', and
as 'the first large structure consisting mainly of
iron and glass'.[13] There is no doubt that these
public conservatories influenced other architects
in Europe, but in England, where many fantastic
schemes were being devised and built on grander
scales, scant notice was paid to the De Fleury
houses.[14] However, we know that Paxton visited them in the year of construction while on
Grand Tour with the Duke of Devonshire.[15]

IN 1849 operational difficulties with the steam
heating in the Jardin des Plantes caused De
Fleury to visit three Belgian towns, Brussels,
Gand and Liège, and report that he had learned
a great deal about heating in their gardens, particularly those in Brussels, which had been
operating successfully for many years. De Fleury
also showed drawings in *Revue Générale
Publiques de l'Architecture et des Travaux*, 1849,
illustrating how the glasshouses in Liège 'had

been copied from' and the one at Gand
'inspired by' his glass at the Jardin des Plantes.

AT the conclusion of his article in the *Revue* of
1849, he expressed his desire to go again to
England to see the many new and wonderful
constructions. Perhaps this was in anticipation
of the ambitious building plans outlined by a
contemporary, Gottfried Semper – a scheme for
completely covering the Jardin des Plantes with
an immense portable glass roof, which could
be removed in the summer. However, De
Fleury's original construction had only consisted of the two pavilions and the west wing;
in 1854 the two-tiered curved shape was
retained, the east wing was added and the
interior of the west wing was renovated.
Neglect, in addition to the bombardment of
Paris and the uprising in 1870, caused the collection and the glass at the Jardin des Plantes to
go into decline. In 1882 an east extension was
built to the design of the architect André, which
represented the conflict between horticultural
requirements and aesthetics. Horticultural
journalists criticized the design for being

52 Plans and elevation
of the Tropical House,
Botanical Gardens,
Brussels, drawn by
Charles Rohault de
Fleury and illustrated
in the *Revue Générale
de l'Architecture et des
Travaux Publics*, 1849.

53 The central conservatory
of the Tropical House,
Botanical Garden,
Brussels, Jean-Paul
Meeus, 1826–9.

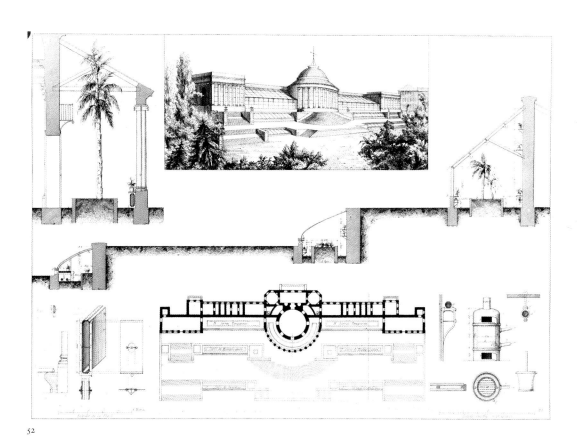

52

detrimental to the plants and having too many glazing bars and too little glass.

DURING Rohault de Fleury's visit to the Brussels Botanical Garden in 1849, he would have seen an extensive range of glass buildings with a large central conservatory, one of the oldest existing today. Built in 1826–9, some years before the curvilinear houses at the Jardin des Plantes, it is a formal composition of a large central glass rotunda with subordinate wings each ending in temple porticos with Ionic columns, all set on a plinth high above the garden. Designed by Jean-Paul Meeus, an administrator of the Royal Horticultural Society, and Pierre-François Gineste, it is about 400 feet long with curvilinear plant-frames stepping down the front. A striking feature is that the boulevard rue Royale runs parallel and overlooks the length of the garden, so that it can be viewed even without entering it.

IN 1872 the Copenhagen Palm House and glass ranges were built in the same form as the Brussels Botanical Garden, but with a continuous masonry wall of service rooms protecting the

53

54

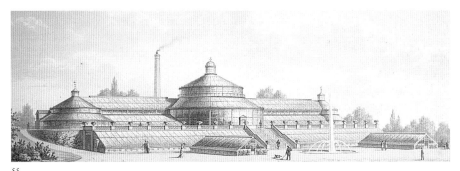

55

54, 55 Palm House,
Copenhagen, Botanical
Garden, Tyge Rothe and
Johann Carl Jacobsen,
1872–4.
56, 57 Elevation and section
through the Palm House,
Copenhagen.

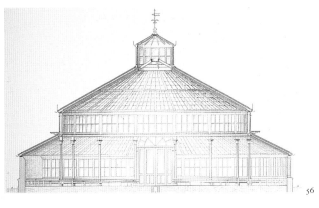

56

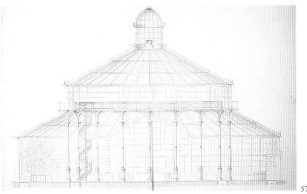

57

garden on the north. The design is attributed to the architect Tyge Rothe. However, it has been suggested that its benefactor, Johann Carl Jacobsen, who had previous experience with his own glasshouses adjoining the residential part of his Carlsberg Brewery, had much more to do with the design than simply to help pay for it.

DURING the winter the climate in Copenhagen can be rigorous and the glass garden was built with a form of double-glazing that uses wood to discourage condensation drops that are injurious to the plants. The space between the glass panes could be heated to discourage these problems. Double-glazing ruled out the possibility of curved glass; however, the circular areas in the plan and the truncated-cone roofs create a pleasing and rational building. As with most grand glass-houses of the time it is raised above the garden giving it an increased presence, but also providing a lower terrace for young stock and bedding plants which are so important to any garden.

IT is often difficult to determine whether a nineteenth-century garden and its architecture

58 *Palm House Interior,
Pfaueninsel Island, Berlin,*
Karl Blechen, 1832.
59 Great Palm House, Royal
Botanical Garden, Berlin,
Carl David Bouché,
1857–9.

58

were initially intended to be accessible to the public. Many of the gardens that originated in the private domain of the anxious European nobility in the period after the French Revolution were shortly transferred to the public. This is particularly true of Germany and Central Europe, where the rulers of the various small kingdoms displayed perhaps the greatest extravagance in glasshouse construction before their political and economic power finally waned. In 1822 Friedrich Wilhelm III transformed the Pfaueninsel, on the Havel in Berlin, into a zoological island, only thirty years after his father, Friedrich Wilhelm II, had first directed that the area be laid out as an English-style informal park. When a private collection of large palms trees and other exotics became available, Friedrich Wilhelm III directed that a palm house be built in 1832 to house them together with an Indian pagoda. Karl Friedrich Schinkel, the popular royal architect, was involved in the direction of the project, but most of the work was carried out by Albert Ketrich Schadow, his student. The interiors of the buildings were

obviously influenced by the Bengali pagoda and the current taste for Romantic-style botanical and recreational buildings, which was also prevalent at the time in John Nash's Royal Pavilion and Humphrey Repton's drawings and designs for Sezincote.[16]

IN 1809 the administration of the Berlin Royal Botanical Garden (now known as the Old Botanical Garden) was transferred from the Prussian royal family to the new University of Berlin. Over the years many glass buildings were added until it was moved to the Dahlem district in 1897 because of urban pressures. In 1821 a palm house was designed by Schinkel. Other houses followed for orchids, ferns, the Victoria Regia water-lily and the Great Palm House, which was designed by Carl David Bouché and built in 1857–9. Bouché had invaluable experience working with tropical plants as head gardener on the Pfaueninsel, particularly in the Schinkel and Schadow Palm House. Though he was not an architect, as Inspector of the Royal Botanical Garden he was well equipped to provide design criteria and

59

60 Sundial House, Park
   Schönbrunn, Vienna,
   1885. This was built
   behind the Great
   Palm House.

details based on his previous experiments. There were many architects and draughtsmen willing to put his ideas on paper for construction. The Palm House, raised on a terrace, had impressive dimensions. It was 57 feet high at the centre and covered over 10,000 square feet with a 48-foot central span. The roof glazing was ridge and furrow and the house had many other features, such as a system for collecting water that had been devised for the Crystal Palace of 1851 and the Munich Glass Palace of 1854. The roof glass was structurally conservative being half-inch wire glass. Bouché devised extensive steam heating for the spacious house and, because of the climate in Berlin, a back-up hot-water system was used when the temperatures were unusually cold. The Palm House was dismantled in 1907 and some parts were moved to the New Botanical Gardens in Dahlem.[17]

THE archetypal Central European botanical glasshouse was symmetrical with a larger central pavilion and side wings that usually terminated in pavilions and a masonry north wall with service rooms protecting the plant-chambers. Exterior walkways were built to facilitate glass and ventilation maintenance and to access the shades, which could be rolled down. These rational plant factories, often associated with university botanical gardens and stripped of ornament, had a curiously functional beauty. A few of the many examples were to be found at Breslau, Munich, Strasbourg, Tübingen and Innsbruck. The German and Austrian designers, though aware of the English curvilinear houses, did not use curved glass roofs to any extent, but preferred what they regarded as a rational recti-linear approach that was easier to build and to double-glaze for winter conditions.

THE Breslau Botanical Garden Conservatory, demolished except for one wing, was built in 1861 on the edge of the Botanical Garden. It had masonry back rooms and a pyramidal roof over the central pavilion. Ridge-and-furrow glazed roofs spanned the side wings from the masonry back wall to the cast-iron columns built into the skin of the solar side of the house. The style was more attuned to the rational neo-classical than to its own more romantic period.

MUNICH'S Great Palm House in the Old Botanical Garden by August von Voit, was built in c 1860–5 near the Von Voit Crystal Palace of 1854. The glasshouse sheltered behind the museum to the north. As with most European houses the central pavilion was designed as the warmest for tropical palms and ferns, and the side wings, being further from the centre, were cooler. Kohlmaier considers this building to be one of the most significant in Europe, while Koppelkamm claims that Von Voit desired to raise the tone above the glass palace with additional extraneous decoration; 'Putting span roofs side by side with domes and conical roofs gave the exterior a lack of clarity and did not do away with the stiffness of the building.'[18] Because of a fall in the site, the conservatory had a masonry basement containing the service rooms and the heating plant. The external skin was double-glazed with a five-inch gap and metal gutters that were suspended below all projecting structural elements to channel away condensation.

THE glasshouses in Strasbourg's New Botanical Garden were built in 1877–82 by Hermann Eggert. Following the European model, they were designed on a strictly functional and rational basis, as described by Eggert. He claimed that plane, flat surfaces made construction easier and required fewer elements that blocked light. Functional buildings were cheaper to construct and kept operating and maintenance costs low.

IN Tübingen, the Great Conservatory in the Old Botanical Garden was built in 1885–6 to the designs of Albert Koch. The glasshouse, with the traditional protective masonry buildings at the rear, replaced an older house from the early nineteenth century. Situated near Tübingen University, it had the typical central pavilion for large plants and symmetrical sloped glass side buildings with gabled masonry ends.[19]

THE Innsbruck Botanical Garden Palm House, which was constructed in 1905, is proof that there was little variety of design in the rational archetype for glasshouses in botanical gardens. The central pavilion and the sloped glass wings are fitted with gangways and steps for maintenance and to facilitate the rolling down of shades in the summer. The low-sloping glass and the small internal air volume of the side wings necessitated mat shades to compensate for the maximum heat gain in summer at this

60

61 New Winter Garden,
Burggarten, Vienna,
Friedrich Ohmann, 1900.
62, 63 Exterior and interior of
the Old Winter Garden,
Louis von Remy,
1823–6, lithographs
c 1840.

latitude. The early rational knowledge about light and heat had been lost in such houses.

THE Sundial House of 1885 in Vienna's Park Schönbrunn, is built beside the contemporary Great Palm House. However, it lacks the Palm House's curvilinear structural exuberance. Arched lattice trusses span 48 feet from the solid north wall and continue down behind the south facade, creating an uninterrupted simple elegant hall.[20]

IN 1900, Friedrich Ohmann was commissioned to build a winter-garden in the Burggarten, Vienna. This replaced the Old Winter Garden designed by Louis von Remy in 1823–6, which now only survives through lithographs that show both its exterior and interior. Ohmann was a student of Otto Wagner and he built in the style of the period with grand Corinthian columns lining the central building. The New Winter Garden was 425 feet long. Ohmann had the original challenge of having to build on the old foundations, which retained a fall in the site. It is not clear whether this was possible for all the foundations, though the newer glasshouse

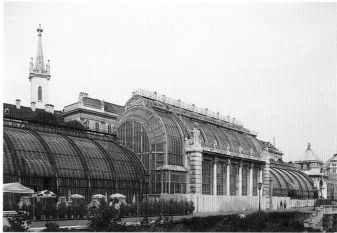

61

62

63

64–5 Glasshouses in the
St Petersburg Imperial
Botanic Gardens, built
in the 1880s.

THE GLASSHOUSE

has a central pavilion and side wings just like the old. Clearly in the Viennese Jugendstil, but leaning towards classicism, the central pavilion has a barrel vault of riveted iron and ventilators at the top. The curved side buildings lean against the back masonry wall and upper ventilators.[21]

A MORE rectilinear-style construction was often more appropriate in severer weather conditions. However, it was not the only design solution. The St Petersburg Imperial Botanical Gardens had been situated alongside the River Neva for many years, when, in 1845, the architect Fischer-Uralsky designed a curvilinear iron glasshouse to replace the old complex of glass hothouses. It was one large space 266 feet long and 79 feet wide. In the 1880s the two large glasshouses were built that exist today. One is a curvilinear glass building on the lines of the Palm House at Kew and the other is a simple volume with an octagonal plan. Building in a city as cold as St Petersburg, with the likelihood of heavy snow loads, necessitated caution. Nevertheless, the stronger structure caused by these live loads is, understandably, not expressed on the

exterior, as it is in the palm houses at Berlin, Dahlem and Schönbrunn. Expressed exo-structure encourages thermal bridging and thermal movement. Nevertheless double-glazing and wood cladding on the glazing bars were inevitable at St Petersburg.[22]

DURING the late nineteenth century, city corporations built the greatest number of glasshouses in their newly formed public gardens. Even the Ecole Nationale Supérieure des Beaux-Arts, with its rigid adherence to classical forms and materials began to perceive that the avante-garde materials, iron and glass, could be acceptable candidates for the Grand Prix de Rome. One such recipient was the architectural student Pascal's adventuresome rendering of a winter-garden inspired by the Jardin des Plantes in Paris. There was a proliferation of glazed, often temporary, exhibition buildings in Paris during that period. In 1877 the first prize at the Ecole des Beaux-Arts was awarded for a glasshouse, an 'Anthenaeum for a Capital City', by Adrien Chancel. The design had meeting rooms, a library and a grand conservatory:

65

64

66 Design for an
'Athenaeum for a
Capital City', Adrien
Chancel, 1877. This
won the first prize at the
Ecole des Beaux-Arts.

67 Phipps Conservatory,
Schenley Park, Pittsburgh
Botanic Garden, built by
Lord & Burnham. This
was a gift from the
philanthropist Henry
Phipps to the city.

66

clearly masonry, iron and glass had merged within an acceptable vocabulary.

IN the United States, public gardens were being endowed by the wealthy families that had enjoyed prosperity and low taxes for many years. The Druid Hill Park Conservatory in Baltimore was planned in the early 1870s by park commissioner John H B Latrobe and architect George Frederick. It was not, however, constructed until 1887–8. The Phipps Conservatory, Schenley Park, was philanthropist Henry Phipps's gift to Pittsburgh's Botanic Garden. It was constructed by Lord & Burnham and shown in their *Catalogue of Greenhouse Heating and Ventilating Apparatus*, 1903.

THE New York Botanical Garden Conservatory of 1900–2, in the Bronx, New York, is representative of the many glasshouses built in major cities. It was designed by the architect William R Cobb. The creation of the 653-acre Bronx Park in the 1890s offered a home for two grand ideas in search of a site: a zoo and a botanical garden. The New York Zoological Society took over most of the south half of the park and

the New York Botanical Garden was given control of over 250 acres to the north. The conservatory plan is arranged in a C-shape with the principal entrance to the large dome centred at the rear. It was built by Hitchings & Co who merged with Lord & Burnham. The conservatory, modelled after curvilinear English examples is typical of the many houses built by these companies well into the twentieth century.

THE New York Botanical Garden came into being largely as the result of the vision and tireless energy of Nathaniel Lord Britton, Professor of Botany at Columbia University, who enthused to the Torrey Botanical Club about his recent visit to Kew Gardens, in 1888. Among the forty-eight public-spirited citizens listed in the Act of Incorporation, fully subscribed in 1895, were John D Rockefeller, Seth Low, J P Morgan, Andrew Carnegie, Cornelius Vanderbilt and Samuel Sloan.

LONGWOOD Gardens, at Kennet Square, near Philadelphia, is typical of the great North American display gardens. It ranks as one of the outstanding display gardens in America, and has

67

68–9 New York Botanical
Garden Conservatory,
designed by William
R Cobb, 1900–2, and
built by Hitchens &
Company, a company
that merged with Lord
& Burnham.

70, 71 Exterior detail and
interior view of the
dome of New York
Botanical Garden
Conservatory.

68

69

70

71

been under development since 1906 when the property was acquired by Pierre S du Pont as a country estate. Besides the arboretum, flower and water gardens, coloured-light fountains and pools developed by Du Pont, the gardens have some four acres of connected conservatories of varied climates filled with species from throughout the world. More specifically there is an emphasis on seasonal flowers: acacias, amaryllis, azaleas, camellias, chrysanthemums, cymbidium orchids, poinsettias and early spring flowers. A small conservatory was built in 1914. By 1921 the main conservatories were built under the guidance of Du Pont and J W Cope, an architect working for the Du Pont Company. The gardens have been popular since 1921 when the conservatories were opened to the public. Rivalling the Laeken Gardens in Brussels in their splendour, they are also more accessible.

THOUGH many of the early botanical gardens incorporated zoos or other amusements to subsidize themselves, the middle of the nineteenth century saw the emergence of a new glass building type that was dedicated solely to public

entertainment. Often embracing dance halls, cafés and restaurants, the winter-garden enabled city-dwellers to promenade among lush vegetation under glass throughout the year. Although the first so-called winter-garden was the one in Regent's Park, the second, Jardin d'Hiver in Paris, was the first true winter-garden established for public entertainment. A big business, it was financed by a joint stock company and could attract seven to eight thousand people on public holidays. Paris had two winter-gardens, in fact, in quick succession on a site between the Rond Point and the avenue Marboeuf on the Champs Elysées. The first ill-fated glass garden was erected in 1846, built with eight fountains in a scheme to decorate the alleys of the Champs Elysées. The building had a reading room at one end and the Salles des Bouquets and office at the other. In between was the gable-roofed winter-garden, 120 feet long, 30 feet wide and only 18 feet high.[23] To the Parisians the garden was not grand enough for a winter promenade and social meeting place; the low roof produced a 'heavy' effect.

72 New York Botanical Garden Conservatory.

73 East Conservatory,
   Longwood Gardens,
   Pennsylvania, designed
   by the firm Richard
   Phillips Fox, 1969–73.
   It replaced an earlier
   building on this site.
74 The T-shaped Main
   Conservatory, Long-
   wood, constructed for
   Pierre Samuel du Pont
   and designed by J Walter
   Cope, 1921.
75 Glasshouses at Longwood
   Gardens.

74

75

76, 77 Exterior and interior
        view of the Jardin
        d'Hiver, Paris, 1848.

THE GLASSHOUSE

Consequently the house was pulled down within six months and another was started. This new house's success is well conveyed by the Englishman, W Bridges Adams, in 1850, writing about the kind of winter-garden the Crystal Palace ought to be:

Something of the kind has recently been established at Paris as a private speculation and has become one of the most popular places of resort in that city. Public dinners, balls and concerts, are continually held in the Jardin d'Hiver of the Champs Elysées, and with frost out of doors, and the snow covering the ground, visitors there find themselves in another and more genial climate, surrounded by tropical trees, flowering shrubs and plants, interspersed with statues and fountains.[24]

THE new Jardin d'Hiver in Paris was magnificent, with its ballroom, Jardin Anglais, promenades, fountains, reading room, café and patisserie; the perfect rendezvous on a winter's day. Though Hector Horeau has been credited with its design, this now seems unlikely.[25]

A contemporary writer, Gottfried Semper, mentions the architect Hippolyte Meynadier des Flamalens as the originator of the design, and Charpentier being hired by the Garden Company to carry on from him and oversee the execution of the design during the construction (with the help of the engineer Moehly).

THE new winter-garden was opened to the public in January 1848. With the gardener's house to the right, the entrance led through a ballroom, sky-lit and hung with pictures and works of art for sale. The covered garden was a grand 300 feet long and 180 feet wide at the crossing. A raised promenade on its periphery afforded views of the other promenaders and those relaxing, reading and writing at the tables below. Four ornamental fountains framed the main space and on one side bouquets, coffee and pastries were sold. The whole was filled with camellias, ericas, azaleas and orange trees. Down the nave, the Jardin Anglais had a lawn interspersed with large shrubs and trees and the 50-foot *araucaria excelsa* from the Jardin des Plantes.[26] The Jardin Anglais ended in a dramatic fountain ascending almost

76

77

78, 79 Transverse and
longitudinal sections
through the Jardin
d'Hiver, Paris, 1848,
renovations attributed
to the engineer Rigolet
during the 1860s.
80 Plan of the Jardin
d'Hiver, Paris, 1848.

78

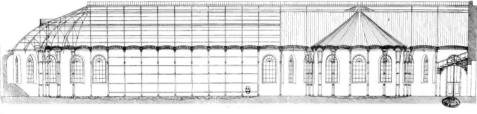

79

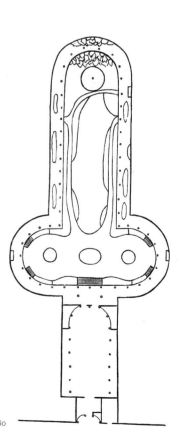

80

to the roof and cascading on to the rocks below. The delicate iron and glass roof hovered 60 feet above and was supported by double- and quadruple-iron columns, which also supported a narrow gallery filled with rhododendrons and dwarf palms. The curved walls of the cross and both ends of the building were covered with mirrors set in filigree. Along the promenades were basins of goldfish and aviaries of ornamental and song birds; the immense building was steam heated to a minimum of 56°F on the coldest days.

PAXTON was inspired by the Jardin d'Hiver. This probably accounts for his wish that the Crystal Palace be turned into a winter-garden following the closure of the Great Exhibition (he visited the Paris garden in its opening year).[27] With its combination of art and botany, it also became a model for the floras that were to follow in Europe. Later, in the 1860s, the engineer, Rigolet, was probably responsible for the renovation work that made the floor one level plane and accommodated a niche for a sculpture in the form of an imperial eagle.

IF Hector Horeau was not responsible for the design of the Jardin d'Hiver in Paris, he was, perhaps, the most enthusiastic proponent of glass structures. He proposed designs for many fantastic glass-covered boulevards, the Paris City Hall and Les Halles market. He seemed to be plagued with unbuilt or unbuildable schemes, as most of his designs were not constructed. A notable exception was his Jardin d'Hiver in Lyons, on the left bank of the Rhone, which started in May 1847 and formally opened seven months later in time for Christmas. The central hall was filled with flowers, shrubs, trees, fountains and kiosks for selling bon-bons, birds and curiosities. Around it was the raised promenade and on the north side, overlooking the Rhone were a restaurant, café and the covered principal entrance. To the south were two warmer conservatories facing the summer garden. The west wall housed glass-enclosed rock work, covered with tropical shrubs and flowers, with a stream of tepid water issuing and cascading down its top and flowing into and irrigating the winter-garden.

81 Covered streets of Paris,
Hector Horeau, 1866.
Horeau proposed
covering the streets of
Paris with richly
decorated arcades.

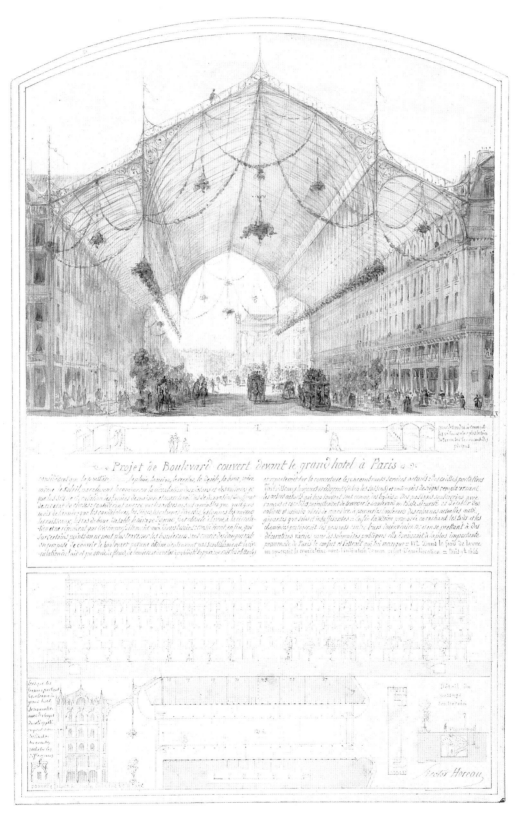

82–3 Covered streets of Paris,
Hector Horeau's scheme
for a Grande Hôtel, Paris.
84 The Conservatory in
the Buxton Pavilion
Gardens, Edward
Milner, 1871.

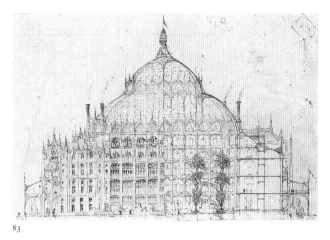

83

82

THE 1848 Jardin d'Hiver in Paris had been the earliest model of a winter-garden in which other rooms devoted to recreation and arts were added. Owen Jones's 1859 design for the People's Palace proposed at Muswell Hill, and the design of Alfred G Jones and Le Feuvre for the Exhibition Palace and Winter Garden in Dublin of 1865, followed this programme. The Muswell Hill winter-garden was unusual as it was expressed as a glass building, whereas most others were hidden behind a facade of masonry.

DURING the 1860s and 1870s many speculative companies were formed to build these multi-use pleasure gardens that combined masonry rooms for art and concerts with glass and iron winter-gardens. The developed archetype of exotically styled architectural masonry usually fronted the building and contained the function rooms for exhibitions, refreshments and concerts. The glass, steel and iron winter-garden was hidden behind. Once inside the winter-garden became the centre of activity like a romantic fairyland – the essence of recreation being the escape from everyday life.

A RECREATIONAL complex that did not conform to the masonry archetype was the Buxton Pavilion Gardens. Built in 1871, these glass and iron buildings that interconnected with glass corridors, contained a large octagonal concert hall, a theatre, a restaurant and a café. The pavilions included many of the elements that can be found in the Crystal Palace's structure, such as the characteristic inscribed semicircular window arches. Their designer was Edward Milner, who, according to George F Chadwick, was an assistant to Joseph Paxton when he was working on the Great Conservatory at Chatsworth.[28]

THE commercial potential of winter-gardens meant that glasshouses captured the imagination of many entrepreneurs. One such man was the versatile inventor John Kibble. The son of a wealthy Glasgow merchant, who described himself as an engineer and whose talents included astronomy, photography and botany, Kibble introduced a new method of propelling vessels on the Clyde by fitting the steamer *Queen of Beauty* with chain-paddle floats. He made a large glass-plate camera, which was

84

85

said to be horse-drawn and able to produce photographs with a degree of perfection never before attained. His sun pictures gained him a gold medal at the Great Exhibition in London in 1851. However, his significant architectural ventures began on his retirement from Glasgow business, when he moved to Coulport House on the shores of Loch Long in about 1865. At Coulport he built a private iron and glass conservatory designed by Boucher & Cousland, which was made in the casting yards of the well-known Scottish glasshouse contractor James Boyd of Paisley. The conservatory was later moved, and became the extraordinary Crystal Art Palace at Queen's Park in Glasgow Royal Botanical Gardens.[29]

THE original conservatory was much smaller than the one found in Glasgow today. The overall shape was similar, but the two side arms were originally only short compartments and the large dome was supported on fewer columns. A few years after its construction at Coulport, John Kibble proposed to extend the structure and give it to the Glasgow

Corporation. With good business sense he suggested terms profitable to himself for twenty years. He agreed to move the building, re-erect it and increase its size at his own expense; after twenty years he would hand the building over to the corporation in perpetuity. During the twenty-year period he would have the right to manage concerts and other entertainments and to charge an entrance fee. In May 1872 the conservatory was dismantled and put on a raft to be towed by a Clyde 'Puffer' up the River Kelvin. As Kibble had promised, he increased the diameter of the main dome to 146 feet, the link corridor to 36 feet and the two side arms to an imposing front elevation of 150 feet. As at Coulport, there was a rock-work island, shrubs, statues, fountains and rare plants, but on a much grander scale. With exaggerated enthusiasm, Kibble described his Crystal Art Palace as a magnificent concert hall capable of containing six thousand people. In fact it was an attraction, at least for the middle-class Glaswegians who lived in the West End around Queen's Park. It could have been a 'People's Paradise'

85, 86 Interior and exterior of Kibble's Crystal Art Palace, Glasgow Botanic Gardens, constructed by Boyd & Sons of Paisley for John Kibble, 1872.

86

and not just a 'West-End Pleasurance', had it been built, as originally intended, in the South Side Park, a poorer district, where it would have been 'seen of men', according to a crusading newspaper.[30]

KIBBLE proposed for his Crystal Art Palace a light and sound show with a 'powerful view-dissolving lantern' that would cover a 40-foot disc. He had some hundred slides of exquisitely prepared natural objects and a 'oxyhydrogen microscope', which would show microscopic animalculae enlarged to 3 feet. In the centre of the main dome was a large pond, under which he wanted an orchestra chamber, as 'music would form a melodious mystery to strangers', he said. The chamber was constructed so that the sounds could be admitted or shut out of the dome at will to create diminuendo and crescendo effects from the invisible performers. When this device was not in use, a fairy fountain in the middle threw forty jets 35 feet in the air, while coloured lights played on the rising and falling spray. The pond could be drained in one hour and boarded over to accommodate eight hundred people for concerts. Underneath the cast-iron fretwork floor were timber sleepers and three miles of three-inch copper heating tube. Six hundred gas jets lit the large glass dome, which must have made a magnificent spectacle at night, both inside and out. The Kibble Crystal Art Palace was officially opened with a capacity house promenade concert in late June 1873, just one year and a month after it had been dismantled and towed from Loch Long. In the following years many shows and meetings were held in the palace. In November 1873, the year of its opening, Benjamin Disraeli made his inaugural address there as Lord Rector of the University to an audience of four thousand as did his political opponent William Gladstone in December 1879.

A NEW building type that developed out of the winter-garden was the flora. Particularly popular in Germany, its layout differed from that of its predecessors, such as the Jardin d'Hiver in Paris. To prevent the humidity of the main plant halls affecting the flora's other facilities, assembly rooms were built in separate, often multistorey complexes, in front of or alongside the central hothouse.

AN example of the flora's direct descent from the winter-garden is the Frankfurt Flora. The original winter-garden was built by Prince Adolf von Nassau at Biebrich in 1846. Filled with exotics, the glasshouses were a series of parallel roofs building up to a domed palm house at the rear. The glass area was enclosed on three sides by a masonry ambulatory, which formed the entrances, and ended with masonry exhibition and recreational rooms behind the dome. In the 1860s the exhibition rooms were improved in keeping with the times when the complex was opened to the public. The Prince of Nassau's reign had come to an end by the late 1860s and the plant collection and the glass was sold to the City of Frankfurt.[31] When the plants, palms and the glasshouses at Biebrich became available in 1868, the newly formed Palm Garden Company purchased the collection. They leased approximately thirteen acres of land from the City of Frankfurt and hired the architect Friedrich Kayser to design and build the flora, which was finished in 1871. It combined assembly and banqueting rooms with a large palm court, spanned by 99-foot elliptical arches of riveted iron. The form of the building was similar to railway stations of the day with a masonry-facade building in front and the clear-span glazed space behind. A contemporary description of the palm garden was of a 'phantasmagoria of the Orient', and of romantic tropical foliage. At the height of its glory, two concerts were performed daily by the palm garden's own orchestra and it became the venue for many festivals and balls. The building is extant though it has gone through many renovations in its 120-year history.[32]

THE Cologne Flora, designed by the architects H Martens and Georg Eberlein, was the first complex in Germany to combine a tropical environment with dining, music and recreation in a single space.[33] It did not have the typical large separated rooms for art exhibitions and concerts. An early palm court, it followed the lines of previous winter-gardens. Its combination of service rooms and small assembly rooms at the masonry periphery had several functional drawbacks, including inadequate side light for the plants. A private company had built the glass garden as an adjunct to its successful zoological

87

88 Exterior of the assembly
room building, Palm
Garden, Frankfurt,
H T Schmidt, 1878.

89 Palm house interior
of the Palm Garden,
Frankfurt.

90 Section through the palm
house, Palm Garden,
Frankfurt. The 99-foot
span was single glazed,
which caused problems
with condensation and
injury to the tropical
plants from the cold.

91, 93 Exterior and interior
of the Cologne Flora,
Cologne Botanical
Garden, H Martens and
Georg Eberlein, 1864.

92 Lithograph of the site
plan of the Cologne
Flora.

88

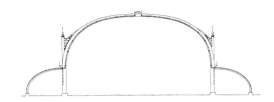
90

89

91

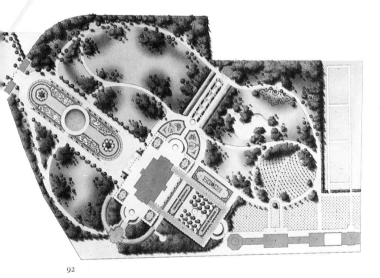
92

93

94, 95 Drawing and site plan of exterior of the Berlin-Charlottenburg Flora, Hubert Stier and Johannes Otzen, 1871–3.

gardens. An extensive garden with formal promenades and fountains in axis with the building, as well as a park-like *jardin Anglais*, was also developed around the acropolis of the flora. Two glass barrel vaults intersected, forming a magnificent space of 187 by 95 feet and 66 feet high, each vault ending with a rose window reminiscent of the Crystal Palace. It was demolished in 1914.

THE Berlin Flora in Charlottenburg, built in 1871–3, followed the floras in Cologne and Frankfurt and was the largest and most extensive of its kind. The original architect was Johannes Otzen and his design was an assemblage of two buildings, one of masonry in a Gothic-Renaissance style centred on a large banqueting and assembly hall with service and entertainment rooms around it, the other an enormous palm house, 70 metres long with a span of 37.5 metres. The architect Hubert Stier, who also designed the German Parliament building, took over the interior detailing and revised the layout and the structural systems. With the help of engineers H and O Grenier, he emphasized the trussed-arch construction of the glass and iron palm house. The palm house was designed as a neutral background for the inherent decoration of the plants and was modelled on the Berlin railroad station. Extensive double-glazing with a sixteen-inch space between the glass layers provided extra protection for the humid warm climate required for the tropical plants. The heating equipment had been modelled on the Palm House at Kew and was by Ormson, an English manufacturer. This flora was demolished in 1902.[34]

THE Berlin Central Hotel was a new kind of hotel providing not only accommodation but also entertainment. A very large banqueting-cum-entertainment hall accommodated music and theatre in a garden atmosphere, every day of the year no matter what the weather. The hall of the winter-garden was 247 by 75 feet and was said to seat a thousand diners. The hotel was designed by architects Hermann von der Hude and Julius Hennicke and was built in 1880–1. It represents the conjunction of the protected palm court with a Parisian café atmosphere that

94

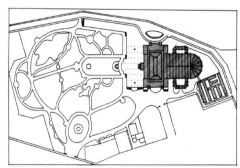

95

96

97

98

was so popular throughout Europe at the end of the nineteenth century, particularly in hotels.

ANOTHER flora developed from the botanical glasshouse was Le Jardin d'Acclimatation in the Bois de Boulogne, Paris. The interior of the great glasshouse was planted in the informal style with a meandering stream. Later, a large 'Palmarium' and a masonry structure for concerts with a café-restaurant, salons and galleries were added.

AN existing example of a flora archetype, the People's Palace in Glasgow Green, was built in *c* 1880 for the Glasgow Corporation. Like the Kibble Crystal Art Palace before it, it was constructed by Boyd & Sons of Paisley, who enjoyed business throughout the British Empire and most notably in South Africa. The palace was intended for the pleasure and enlightenment of the working class of Glasgow who did not have their own gardens or greenhouses. The main building was a museum-cum-exhibition building. With its large winter-garden of 178 by 117½ feet and nearly 60 feet high, it became very popular for organized events and

as an escape from the drudgery of factory and tenement life. The cast-iron pillars support latticed arched girders with a lean-to side aisle, making the People's Palace one of the last great surviving curvilinear glass spaces.

THE central feature of the Ny Carlsberg Glyptotek in Copenhagen was also a glass-domed winter-garden. Built in 1897 and extended in 1906, the flora was constructed under the direction of Vilhelm Dahlerup with the support of the Carlsberg-brewer Johann Carl Jacobsen, who had donated his art collection. Jacobsen was an enthusiastic supporter of botanical display, his family having also contributed to the construction of the glasshouses in the Botanical Gardens built in 1872. The Glyptotek like the floras combined art, knowledge and botany. The glazed winter-garden was surrounded and overlooked by the library, art galleries and assembly rooms that were separated from the humidity required in the garden.

IN 1877, during the same period as these floras, an extensive glass construction was proposed for Hyde Park to cover the Albert Memorial and

99

protect it from London's putrid and damaging atmosphere and pigeons. The project was suggested to Queen Victoria by John Wills, a nurseryman, florist and bouquet-maker to the Queen who had nurseries throughout London with his headquarters, the Royal Exotic Nursery, in South Kensington. He was extensively engaged in arranging and planting conservatories and constructing waterfalls and rockeries all over England and the Continent. King Leopold of Belgium had summoned him to Laeken to lay out and decorate his new palm house, orangery, and glass corridors in 1876. Wills's Hyde Park proposal had a huge iron, copper and glass dome, over the intersection of a cross 200 feet wide, which was surmounted by a lantern spire 350 feet high that covered the statue. Wings were placed on both sides and devoted to vegetation from various regions of the Empire, particularly plants that served mankind with food, medicine, clothing or building materials: 'The Prince Consort's idea of diffusing knowledge, and of binding different nationalities into one league by the bonds of

peace and reciprocal interest, would thus be fittingly illustrated. Horticulture, as the sister of Art, the handmaid of Science, and of ever-increasing commercial importance, would appropriately play its part.'[35]

WILLS is not expressing Prince Albert's personal philosophy or the *zeitgeist* of the age here, he is evoking the spirit of the Great Exhibition of 1851 – the Consort's major achievement. The Crystal Palace was a direct descendant of the botanical glasshouse and represented the horticultural advances of the nineteenth century in its form and function. The exchange between it and the botanical house, moreover, was two way. The Crystal Palace as an exhibition hall and recreational centre is the missing link in the history of the glasshouse in the public garden. It ignited a glass mania in the latter half of the nineteenth century, which saw many more hothouses being built for public use. The widespread adoption of glass for monumental structures, like winter-gardens, floras and other crystal palaces was emulated throughout the western world.

1

THE CRYSTAL PALACE
AND AFTER

VIII

THE Great Exhibition building of 1851 has now become symbolic of an age of industrial and imperial expansion. In the more specific history of glass architecture, however, the Crystal Palace is a watershed construction – a pivotal building between a former period of experimentation and a later period of confident design and engineering. The competition for its design in the mid-nineteenth century presented designers and building contractors with the opportunity to draw on their previously accumulated experience and produce a project on a vast and ambitious scale, which had to compete against other more traditional forms of architecture. When Joseph Paxton and Fox & Henderson won the contract for the exhibition building the time-scale, size and cost involved forced them to develop often untested methods of construction and mass-production.

AT the outset, it was Richard Turner rather than Joseph Paxton who appeared the keenest contestant for the Great Exhibition contract. In conjunction with his son, Turner designed and constructed a model of an exhibition building and submitted it to the Building Committee of the Royal Commission for the Great Exhibition as early as its third meeting on 24 January 1850. It was obviously Turner's

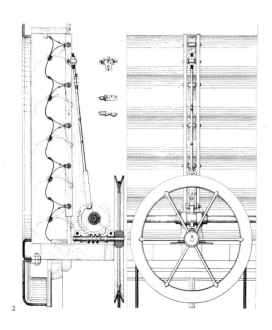

2

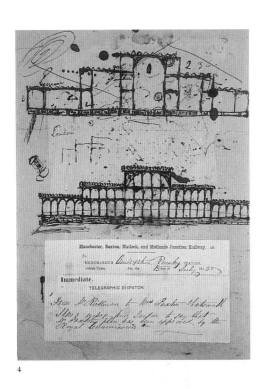

4

hope that the commission would be favourably impressed, and appoint him as the designer-builder. But the newly formed building committee very properly thought that the acceptance and adoption of any one person's design without competition was not in accordance with the spirit and nature of the whole undertaking, which was, after all, an 'Exhibition of the Works of Industry of All Nations'.[1] Turner's original model was a huge rectangular glass conservatory of 1,440 by 1,060 feet, with five domes rising out of the roof, the central dome being 200 feet high and the others 150 feet. Within the structure, a miniature railway was proposed to carry the public among the exhibits. The estimated cost was £300,000 – unfortunately far more than the commission had collected from subscriptions.

ON 21 February 1850 the building committee announced an international competition for the design and construction of the large exhibition building on a piece of land in Hyde Park.[2] Only one month was allowed for preparations. Among 245 submissions, Richard Turner and the French architect Hector Horeau received 'special mentions'. These two commended entries were in cast-iron, wrought-iron and glass. Following the committee's guideline, Turner's entry provided for one uninterrupted space about 1,940 feet long and 408 feet wide. Semicircular wrought-iron supporting ribs made three avenues: the middle one 200 feet wide and 127 feet high, and the side ones 104 feet wide and 77 feet high – impressive dimensions for the time. A transept cut across the centre of the building and a huge glass dome was proposed at the crossing of the main avenue. The ends of the building, as well as those of the transepts, were filled in with tracery in the upper half, and a colonnade below protected the entrances; galleries could be placed in the side avenues. The building was to have been principally constructed out of wrought-iron, of a visual delicacy that would have delighted a Victorian visitor. The use of large quantities of wrought-iron, though, was the scheme's downfall, for the difficulties of producing and assembling such an enormous amount in such a short period was considered impossible by the building committee.

WHEN, in April 1850, the building committee rejected the competition designs of both Hector Horeau and Richard Turner on the grounds of cost and a justified fear that they could not be built in time, the committee's task was to produce the largest building the Victorian world had ever seen without a workable design in just thirteen months. The exhibition building was to open its doors to thousands of visitors on 1 May 1851. The committee delegated Matthew Digby Wyatt, Owen Jones and Charles Heard Wild to create a new design based on the ideas from the competition. The result was a huge brick structure with a vast iron dome by the engineer Isambard Kingdom Brunel, but it did not meet the competition criteria since it would take a long time to build, be difficult to dismantle, cost a great deal and probably collect moisture in its massive brick walls that had to be laid during the damp English winter. Nevertheless, the building committee's design was presented in the *Illustrated London News* on 22 June and was sent to various contractors for bids to erect and later remove it. This was a disappointing result for so grand a project, a Great Exhibition of the Industry of all Nations, initiated by Prince Albert at his Peace Congress. W Bridges Adams described its purpose: 'to proclaim to all foreigners that England should no longer be misunderstood'.[3]

PAXTON's influence in the House of Commons and the committee's lack of confidence led to a clause in the specifications that allowed other bidders to submit alternative designs and costs.[4] Paxton himself had an alternative proposal, although time was short. He had already developed ridge-and-furrow roofs and other construction techniques for the Great Conservatory and the Victoria Regia House at Chatsworth and had strong communication with manufacturers and builders in the Midlands.

SENTIMENT had been favouring a dry method of construction (without mortar or plaster) as proposed by Paxton, and rumours were rife that the committee's massive design was seriously flawed. As early as April 1850, while the building committee's designers were preparing their drawings, W Bridges Adams, in his *Westminster and Foreign Quarterly Review*, suggested criteria for the committee and future uses for the build-

4 Joseph Paxton's first
blotting paper sketch
for the Crystal Palace,
11 June 1850, together
with the telegram to
his wife a month later
disclosing the approval
of his tender by the
Royal Commision.
5 Sealing a joint in the
rainwater drainage
system, *Illustrated London
News*, 16 November
1850.
6 Erecting the laminated
wood arches designed to
allow the elms to remain
within the building,
Illustrated London News,
16 November 1850.

ing. Adams's rational statements on the industrial exhibition present him as a man of prophetic wisdom, ahead of his time in his proposition for a glass construction:

The design of the building should be as original as its object. It should not be suggestive of the ideas of a pyramid, a temple, or a palace; for it will not be a tomb, a place of public worship, nor a mansion of royalty. The object should determine the design. That is to say, the design should be altogether subordinate to the uses of the building, and should be of the kind that would express them, or at least harmonize with them.[5]

ADAMS then enumerates the requirements of the building; that, for instance, it be fireproof, allow 'an abundance of light', be transportable, and at least be useful past the duration of the Great Exhibition. Obviously influenced by the engaging designs of Turner and Horeau, Adams wanted iron and glass, 'open towards the south with a system of flues and ventilation for preserving an equitable temperature'. His suggestions fitted well into Paxton's plans. Assured that new designs would be considered, Paxton visited the Hyde Park site on the first week of June, and on 7 June he left London to visit Robert Stephenson's Menai railway bridge, which he saw on 10 June. On his return to Derby on 11 June he made his famous blotting-paper sketch of a section through a three-tiered structure with ridge-and-furrow roofing and a central nave with a laminated arch, reminiscent of his Capesthorne Hall Conservatory. Between 12 and 20 June, Paxton, with his staff at Chatsworth and the help of the Midland Railway engineer Henry Barlow, worked quickly to complete the drawings. On 22 June he had finished designs to show to Lord Granville of the finance committee and on 24 June he had a long interview with Prince Albert, only two days after the building committee had published its design in the *Illustrated London News*. The commission discussed both their designers' plans and Paxton's several times and a stormy debate followed in the House of Commons on 2 July. Paxton, full of confidence and impatient

5

6

7 This is one of the
watercolours that
Owen Jones painted to
demonstrate his proposals
for the interior
decorations of the Crystal
Palace, Hyde Park, 1851.

7

8 Glazing the roof on the lower areas of the Crystal Palace without the aid of the glazing wagons, *Illustrated London News*, 16 November 1850. The illustration shows the notches in the gutter and ridge that the sash bars were fitted into.

9 Testing the quality of the girders by weighing them, *Illustrated London News*, 30 November 1850. It was necessary to weigh each girder as it arrived on site because of the possibility of air pockets in the casting causing structural failures.

to get on with the work, appealed to the public by having his design published together with a long article in the 6 July issue of the *Illustrated London News*.[6] The article discussed the structure in great detail, explaining the ventilation 'by filling in every third upright compartment with lufferboard', using canvas on the roof and south wall as a shield from the sun and avoiding any 'interior division-walls' with 'the whole structure supported on cast-iron columns'. Paxton and Charles Fox had by then worked out precise and appealing details for the building.

A CONSTRUCTION of about eighteen acres with such a tight time schedule could come about only with intense team efforts and familiarity with construction materials and methods. George F Chadwick has confirmed Paxton's contributions to the overall idea and many of the roofing and glazing details.[7] On 22 June Paxton showed his drawings to Charles Fox of the contractors Fox & Henderson and to Robert Lucas Chance, the Birmingham glass manufacturer, who had previously developed the blown-cylinder method for producing glass

sheets of 10 by 48 inches for the Great Conservatory at Chatsworth. They agreed to a joint bid, which gave only eighteen days until the submission date of 10 July.

FOX & Henderson was a large engineering and construction firm located in London, Smethwick & Renfrew, which supplied railway stock throughout the world. After its work on the Exhibition, the company was involved in the construction of the roofs of the railway stations at Oxford, at Paddington and Waterloo in London, and at New Street in Birmingham.[8] However, when the tender was placed for the exhibition building, the company had no experience with Paxton's sophisticated ridge-and-furrow glass roof.

THE building committee had provided a bay of 24 feet for the exhibitors; Paxton's preliminary design proposal unfortunately assumed a building module of 20 feet. This was adjusted, and a joint bid was offered for £150,000 if the building components remained in the ownership of the commission, but, as an alternative, only £79,800 if all the materials remained the prop-

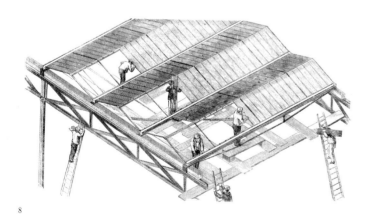

8

9

erty of Fox & Henderson. This bid was much lower than that of the building committee's designers, and Paxton had previously convinced the commission that his type of construction could meet the deadline.

ONE difficulty remained: a group of elms ran across the middle of the proposed site. A public outcry to save the trees forced the committee to request Paxton and Fox & Henderson to build over the trees without extra cost. This they were prepared to do for Henderson had already proposed a transept to enhance the beauty of the building, and the committee suggested that it cover the trees. But the proposed transept was lower than the elms, so Paxton suggested an arched roof, on the lines of his conservatory at Chatsworth. On 15 July the building committee advised the commission to accept the Paxton bid, which they did on 26 July.

AN extraordinary amount of work was accomplished in the month between Paxton's inkblotter sketch on 11 June and the final submission on 10 July. More incredible were the events to follow immediately after the acceptance of the proposal; events that characterize the courage of mid-Victorian industrialists. Charles Fox, with his railway background, immediately began working day and night to realize Paxton's design. He and his subcontractors had to detail and manufacture all the components and to assemble the structure in less than a year. Without a signed contract for the building, Henderson had subcontracted Cochrane & Co and Jobson, both from Dudley, to supply the cast-iron columns and girders; and Mr Birch of the Phoenix Sawmills, Regent's Park, to make the wood components. Fox & Henderson themselves supplied the wrought-iron work. Chance had to increase the output of his factory to make approximately 900,000 square feet of 16-ounce glass. The contract was officially signed on 31 October, though the first column had risen on the site some five weeks before.

CHARLES Fox submitted detailed designs and calculations to the engineer, William Cubitt, Chairman of the Building Committee for the Great Exhibition, who had been selected by the royal commission to supervise Fox & Henderson's construction. He was assisted by Charles Wild and later knighted along with Paxton and Fox, though there is some question as to what, if any, duties Cubitt had performed.

THERE was no question at all about the task that Fox & Henderson had ahead of them in constructing the 1,848-foot-by-456-foot structure, with 772,784 square feet of ground-floor area, 217,100 square feet of gallery space, 372 roof trusses, 24 miles of Paxton's wood gutter and 205 miles of wood sash bar devouring 600,000 cubic feet of timber. Charles Fox, after designing and integrating all the components, supervised the construction. The contract in which Fox functioned as a designer and builder was similar to 'turn-key' building contracts today.

FOR the commission, Cubitt was to keep his eye on the accounts and on the quality of construction, though he was fully aware that Fox & Henderson needed a free rein if the completion date was to be met. The actual detailing and construction with these new materials certainly had to be left in the hands of the engineer-builders. Architects had little to contribute to the construction, as Richard Turner had proved at Kew and Regent's Park in his collaboration with Decimus Burton. Fox and Turner organized, fabricated, and delivered materials unfamiliar to architects of the day and erected the structures.

IN his weekly periodical, *Household Words*, Charles Dickens expressed his amazement at the ambitious plans for the structure: 'to cover 18 acres of ground, with a building upwards of a third of a mile long.'

THE manufacturing techniques and the various systems in the building represent the sophistication that mid-century engineers and builders had attained since the first cast-iron frame construction by Boulton & Watt in Manchester in 1801. In today's building jargon, the exhibition building was the product of mechanization, mass-production, prefabrication, standardization, modular construction, systems-integration, critical path, rapid site assembly, dismantling and, of course, ingenuity, a quality they had in abundance.

THE Great Exhibition building was built with standardized prefabricated components, based on a 24-foot module. This module conformed to both the exhibition requirements and the smallest standardized element, the glass. Paxton's ridge-and-furrow roof-glazing system required a 49-inch length of sheet glass so that it could span 8 feet, furrow to furrow, with three ridges per 24-foot bay. The building had three tiers. A 72-foot timber-arched transept crossed the lengthy nave in the middle. The level above the ground contained a gallery in a space 264 feet wide by 1,848 feet, and the roof was ridge and furrow. All the dimensions, along with the later ground floor north extension (48 by 936 feet), are based on the module of 4, 8 and 24 feet. Ten staircases gave access to the gallery level, which was 1¾ miles long, and added another 5 acres of floor area to almost 18 acres at ground level.

THE cast-iron columns arrived on site with their ends turned on a lathe. This ensured an accurate length and a sealed joint, which when gasketted and bolted together, allowed rainwater to flow down from the roof. At each floor and at roof level, 3-foot cast-iron connection collars with integral connecting lips were bolted on top of the longer columns. This enabled the cast-iron girders with their specially cast projections to be slid between the lips and secured with two wrought-iron wedges. All the columns had the same outer diameter, enabling all the girders to be a standard length. The wall thickness of the columns, however, varied according to the weight that each had to support. One can imagine the detailed system Fox devised to ensure that a specific column arrived at its correct position on a building site a third of a mile long. The depth of all the spanning girders was 3 feet, except where the transept crossed the nave; there they were increased to 6 feet.

THE basic spanning girder was of cast-iron, nominally 24 feet long. It supported the gallery and its upper roof. The 72-foot roof span across the nave and the other 48-foot roof spans were carried with wrought-iron trusses, possessing better tensile strength than cast-iron. Wood trusses 24 feet long were used to support the roof above the single-storey main floor area, probably for economic reasons and the relatively light structural requirements. Across the transept, springing from a height of 63 feet, a series of wood-laminated arches spanned 72 feet, recreating the Chatsworth Great Conservatory in the sky, complete with the ridge-and-furrow glass skin.

10 Erecting the Crystal Palace, *Illustrated London News*, 16 November 1850.
11 Interior view of the Crystal Palace under construction, *Illustrated London News*, February 1851.

10

11

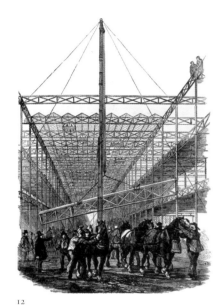

12

THE large amount of wood used in Paxton's ridge-and-furrow glazing system clearly belies any conception that the Crystal Palace (at Hyde Park or later at Sydenham) was an essay in glass and iron alone. Paxton's composite wood and iron rainwater gutter was the basic element that spanned the 24 feet between the girders. Its rain channel and condensation grooves, milled from timber of 5 by 6 inches, rested on main rain gutters supported by the girders. Dimensional stability required that sash bars and gutters used in this way should be made only of well-seasoned timber deal. Fox & Henderson, unable to secure enough, had to use green timber in some areas; shrinkage resulted in leaks and public criticism.

IN his original design Paxton used a patented, self-digging screw pile, which pleased the committee, concerned as it was to disturb the site as little as possible. This was, however, abandoned. The centre line of each row of columns was set out with a theodolite, and the centre-to-centre of the columns was measured with a wooden rod exactly 24 feet in length. A stake was driven to position the centre of the column,

and when it came time to dig the concrete footings, two stakes were driven into the ground at a distance of 6 feet from the column stake. A right-angled triangular wood template was then used to position the cast-iron base plate of 1 by 2 feet on the concrete footing. The footing was usually 2 by 3 feet, varying in dimension with the load ranging in depth and from 1 to 4 feet according to soil conditions. Fortunately there was a gravel stratum just below the surface, resulting in very few foundation problems. The site had a slight fall from west to east, so the whole building was constructed on an inclination of one inch in 24 feet and the columns deviated from being vertical by the same degree. This resulted in the east end of the building being 6 feet lower than the west.

AT 24-foot intervals on the outer skin, cast-iron columns supported the floors and roof above. Each 24-foot bay was divided by two wooden columns shaped to look exactly like their cast-iron counterparts. A decorative cast-iron frame held the columns together and produced three visually unified 8-foot wall modules per bay.

12 Raising the trusses of the Crystal Palace into place with block and tackle, *Illustrated London News*, 30 November 1850.

13 Details of the Crystal Palace transept construction made from Sir Charles Fox's working drawings, published in 1852. They include, left to right: a section through one of the built-up timber ribs, transverse and cross-section details of the vault and a plan of the roof.

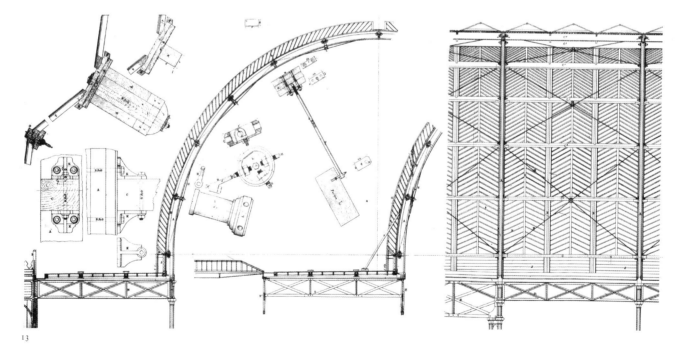

13

Behind this exo-frame were prefabricated panels of glass, wood boarding or doors to suit the functional requirements or the visual harmony. A 3-foot band of louvres ran around each tier at the top of the wall for ventilation. The main exhibition floor had a band of louvres at ground level, and the whole system was operated by wheels, rods and gears, enabling an operator to open or close 108 feet of sheet-metal louvres on each side of the mechanism. In the original design, plans were made to hang coarse canvas soaked with water in front of each louvre to produce cooling by evaporation.

THE ground-floor boarding, resting on sleepers, was spaced with a half-inch gap to facilitate easy cleaning with a machine devised by Paxton, involving water sprays and revolving brushes.[9] In practice this machine was not required, for women's long dresses performed this function admirably. The floorboards were brought to the site when work began and used as a temporary fence. Paxton was said to have devised a way to make the fence without nails so that the boards were not damaged.

PAXTON had first used his sash-bar machine in August 1838 to groove the wood for the Great Conservatory at Chatsworth, having previously visited workshops in London, Manchester and Birmingham for information on woodworking techniques. The sash-bar machine was combined with a Boulton & Watt steam-engine, which was also used for other tasks at Chatsworth. The whole cutting apparatus, including the table, cost him £20, and he estimated that by the end of construction he had saved £1,400 in manual labour for grooving the 48-inch bars. Having previously contrived many mechanized techniques in their railway work, Fox & Henderson and their subcontractors used all the labour-saving devices available on the Crystal Palace – both for cost and speed. Most of the machines were designed by Edward Alfred Cowper who was working for the contractors.

AT the Phoenix works, Birch had a number of machines for woodworking. First, a machine was used to adze and plane the rough timber. The square stock was then run through a gutter-

14 Wood stock drawn through a gutter cutting machine, *Illustrated London News*, 7 December 1850. The Machine milled the gutter and the side condensation channels, cut it to the desired 24-foot length and then drilled it ready to receive wooden dowels at the site.
15 The sash-bar painting machine, *Illustrated London News*, 30 November 1850.
16 The sash-bar cutting machine, *Illustrated London News*, 23 November 1850.

17

18

17 *Aeronautic view of the Palace of Industry for all nations from Kensington Gardens*, lithograph by Charles Burton, 1851.
18 *Building for the Great Exhibition in London, 1851*, Day & Son lithographers.
19 Plan of the Crystal Palace.

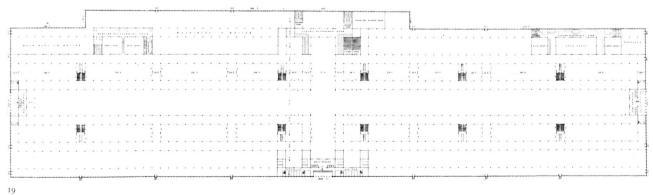

19

THE CRYSTAL PALACE AND AFTER

20 Proposed design for converting the Crystal Palace into a 1000-foot-high tower, lithograph by Charles Burton, published by Ackerman & Co.

21 Reglazing a transept of the Sydenham Crystal Palace, 1899.

22 Cartoon in *Punch* of the 'National Disgrace', John Leech, 1853.

20

21

22

cutting machine, which grooved the wood and cut it off at the required 24-foot length. Planks were run through a sash-bar machine and the bars drawn through a painting machine. The majority of the roof glazing was done from glazing wagons that moved on wheels in Paxton's wood gutters. Holes were punched through the wrought-iron bars with a steam-powered machine. These bars were used to assemble the iron trusses for the larger spans. The 24-foot cast-iron girders were weighed and tested with a hydraulic press to detect any defect in the casting before being lifted into position. Their design strength had been proved by the military who marched across them. The building was designed so that it was made of very few large pieces, the largest casting being the 24-foot girder weighing under a ton. This enabled a system of block and tackle, horse drawn or hand-winched, to manipulate and lift the elements.

THE Palace of the Great Exhibition was allowed to remain in Hyde Park throughout 1851 and into the next year, for Paxton influenced Parliament to vote for its retention until May 1852.

188

23 *The Exterior of the Crystal Palace, Sydenham*, Joseph Paxton, 1852–4, colour lithograph by George Baxter.

Meanwhile, controversy raged over what to do with the great glass building that had proved so popular. W Bridges Adams had anticipated the debate when he wrote in 1850 that it was rumoured that despite the enormous outlay of £100,000 the building was to be demolished at the close of the exhibition.[10]

In 1852, he then proposed a use that became increasingly popular for the great empty glass building: 'Why should the inhabitants of the metropolis not be enabled to command between the months of October and April of every year, the facilities a winter garden would afford for healthful enjoyment; and especially that large and invalid class of our population whom the first breath of a north-easterly wind now consigns to the imprisonment of their own dwellings?' Paxton also suggested that it become a people's winter-garden, enclosing winding promenades, equestrian exercise areas and carriage drives, among trees and greenery of perpetual summer. He proposed that the whole ground-floor facade be removed in summer to create a continuous uninterrupted vista of Hyde Park. But more importantly, Paxton discussed in a pamphlet the maintenance and operating costs of such a winter-garden, demonstrating its potential profitability.[11] Other proposals were to move parts of the building to Battersea Park or to Kew, but cost estimates made these seem impractical. A commission was formed by the government to review the matter. This was an opportunity for Paxton and another partisan of the Crystal Palace, Sir Henry Cole, to describe and illustrate their schemes for converting it into a winter-garden much finer than the one by Richard Turner in the inner circle of Regent's Park. With all the evidence collected, Paxton's statements were unfortunately mis-construed by Members of Parliament, who inferred that a new winter-garden could be built for less cost than converting the existing structure.[12] This, and Prince Albert's wish that the building not be retained, influenced the Commons to vote in April 1852 for its removal. PAXTON, not to be outdone, formed a public company in May, backed with £500,000 in capital, to relocate and run the Crystal Palace

23

24 Sydenham Crystal Palace,
1851–2. This photograph
was taken in the 1930s by
The Architectural Review's
favourite Modernist
photographers Dell
and Wainright.

for the benefit of the people of London and, of course, for profit. Samuel Laing, of the London, Brighton and South Coast Railway was appointed chairman and Paxton, Francis Fuller, Scott Russell and Matthew Digby Wyatt were among the directors. The Crystal Palace Company secured 349 acres of wooded parkland, including the east slope of Sydenham Hill and contracted Fox & Henderson to re-erect the palace there with a commanding view of the surrounding Surrey and Kent countryside. The company then sold 149 acres, and was left with a 200-acre pleasure ground conveniently sited on Laing's London to Brighton railway line and within easy reach of London.

THE Hyde Park Crystal Palace provided only some of the building components for Paxton's more grandiose design at Sydenham, which began construction in August 1852.[13] Paxton added several extravagances in the new building and gardens, which kept the company far from ever realizing any profit. The Sydenham site sloped so steeply that a basement floor had to be built to provide a level plateau for the iron and glass construction. Remembering Charles Barry's earlier suggestion of an arched roof over the main nave, Paxton adopted the idea for his 1,608-foot-long nave. An extensive raised 384-foot-long central transept was sprung from the summit of this arched roof, adding an additional two storeys, so that the three-storey building became six. Two more 336-foot-long transepts at each end of the nave balanced the composition. The new structure nearly doubled the glass area of the original Hyde Park building. The side aisles were divided into courts, representing the architecture of various epochs. The court idea gained the support of John Ruskin, adding credibility to the historic venture. Architects Matthew Digby Wyatt and Owen Jones scoured Europe for maps, drawings, models or casts to authenticate the Assyrian, Greek, Roman, Byzantine, Moorish, Egyptian, Chinese and Renaissance courts built alongside A W N Pugin's English Medieval court, which had been brought to Sydenham with the Hyde Park components. Paxton filled the nave with full-grown trees, exotic shrubbery, fountains

24

25 *The Crystal Palace and Park*, printed and published in 1854, showing the Sydenham Crystal Palace and Norwood Park.

25

and pools, at enormous expense. In the central transept a gigantic organ was built with a tiered concert platform large enough for four thousand performers.

THE new building, though a great technical achievement, was much more complex than the original at Hyde Park and, at 843,656 cubic feet it was nearly half again its predecessor's size. It was heated with twenty-two boilers paired and distributed along the basement under the nave and serviced by an internal roadway. These low-pressure hot-water systems, combined with special boilers for the tropical and aquatic plants, had nearly 50 miles of pipe.[14] This added greatly to the operational cost when compared to the unheated Hyde Park building.

IT was Paxton's idea that the gardens with their fountains around the Sydenham Crystal Palace should rival those at Versailles. In order to maintain water pressure for the fountains, the company commissioned Brunel to design two 300,000-gallon water towers, 282 feet high. These were located at each end of the great nave, so as to conform to the symmetrical composition and also to act as chimneys for the boilers under the nave and the steam-engine pumps at their bases.

QUEEN Victoria opened the building on 10 June 1854, and for a time the Sydenham Crystal Palace was enormously popular with London day-trippers. Besides the permanent displays and activities, the special concerts, balloon ascents, fireworks and sporting events lured thousands of visitors. These often included foreign royalty and heads of government, such as the Tzar of Russia, the Shah of Persia, Giuseppe Garibaldi and Kaiser Wilhelm II. But even with this popularity, the shareholders were losing money.

THE amount of wood used in the structure had been reduced; most of the arches were of lattice ironwork, not of laminated wood, as at Hyde Park. Many of the wood infill panels had been replaced with glass on the lower floors, though the slatted wood floor was retained in the new building. The glazing was still held in Paxton's wooden ridge-and-furrow construction, 21-ounce glass being substituted for the 16-ounce used before. In 1866 the north transept burned

26 Covered market, Bradford, Lockwood & Mawson, 1872–7, *The Architect*, 1872. This is typical of many public buildings in the 1860s and 1870s.

27 Proposed design for the roof of the Royal Exchange, Joseph Paxton, 1851.

28 The Crystal Sanitarium, Joseph Paxton, *Illustrated London News*, 5 July 1851.

26

to the ground, and with no spare funds it could not be rebuilt.

ON 30 November 1936, when another fire broke out, a strong wind from the northwest turned the central transept into a giant conflagration and the flames soon scaled the highest galleries out of reach of the fire hoses. It was visible to all of London and miles beyond (as far as Cambridge). This spectacle was the last anyone saw of the great Sydenham Crystal Palace. Still, it was remarkable that this structure, clad in glass thinner than horticultural glass used today, had stood for eighty-two years.

THE 1851 Crystal Palace caused an immediate glass mania in England. Smaller palaces were proposed for Manchester, Bath, Plymouth and London.[15] Engineers and cast-iron manufacturers saw the marketing potential of prefabricated construction. Glass arcades, markets and winter-gardens, were built all over England throughout the 1860s and 1870s; arcades were put up in Birmingham, Manchester and Newcastle, to name but a few of the shopping centres of the day. The architectural impact of the

27

28

29 Proposal for the Crystal
Way, William Moseley,
1855.

30 Proposal for the Great
Victorian Way, Joseph
Paxton, 1865.

Crystal Palace was also felt internationally; copying this new idea, exhibition buildings began to be built throughout the world.

PAXTON was a popular figure in the 1850s at the height of his glass building career.[16] Besides the Sydenham Crystal Palace, he proposed several glass constructions modelled on his previous work. Two of these were the Royal Exchange roofing and a 'Crystal Sanitarium'. Both were to be constructed from wooden arches patterned on the transept roof covering the Crystal Palace. In 1851 he presented the design for a glass roof to cover the court of the Royal Exchange. However, the design was rejected. Another unbuilt project was a sanitarium in Victoria Park for the City of London Hospital for Diseases of the Chest. Paxton offered this as a prototype for all city hospitals. The building, with a 72-foot arched span, would be 200 feet long and connected by two ridge-and-furrow corridors to the hospital, affording a large space for patients to exercise without being exposed to the open air. In support of this therapeutic design, he described the variable English climate, its humidity and the murkiness and impurity of the air, which could aggravate respiratory ailments, especially during London's winter months. Inside his curative conservatory, the climate would be temperate, pure and sunny without undue humidity. This anticipated the tuberculosis sanitariums of the early twentieth century.

ANOTHER of Paxton's ideas for the hospital anticipated complete air conditioning as we know it today: 'The ventilation should be constructed to afford a free circulation of air without direct currents; and no cold outer air should enter the building until it has been warmed, purified and rendered fit for easy respiration.'[17] Nor was Paxton content to confine these glazed health resorts to the infirm: 'I advocate their general adoption as promoters of public health, combined with pleasing instruction; and by this means some of the squares of London might, by being covered, form the most delightful and interesting places of resort at all seasons.'

IN 1855, Paxton put forward a proposal for 'The Great Victorian Way' to the Committee

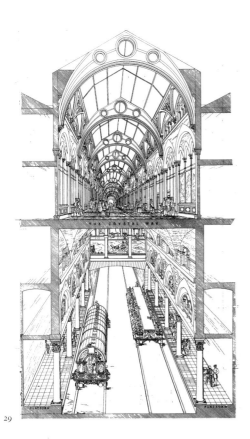

29

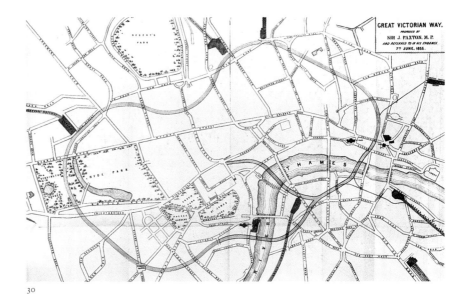

30

31 Project for an exhibition
   hall, St Cloud, Joseph
   Paxton, 1861.

THE GLASSHOUSE

on Metropolitan Communication.[18] Though an interesting glass-roofed structure, it was more important from a city-planning point of view and represents Paxton's railway interests and urban concern. The Victorian Way was to be a huge and lengthy glazed boulevard encircling the centre of London and connecting the railway stations. Crossing the Thames three times, its total length was to be ten miles. Its cross section, which was 72 feet wide by 108 feet high, covered a pedestrian pavement, a road and eight railway tracks running parallel to the glass arcade. The lower level was for dwellings, offices, entertainment and hotels. A similar idea, 'The Crystal Way', was also submitted by William Moseley in 1855 and followed part of the route of London's present underground.

PAXTON was to propose his finest and final great glass building in 1861 for an exhibition building at St Cloud, near Paris. George F Chadwick thinks it was an early proposal for the 1867 International Exhibition, which Paxton would have wanted to show to Louis Napoleon when they met in 1862.[19] Henry-

Russell Hitchcock suggests that the architect Owen Jones, who was to propose a separate design for St Cloud, influenced Paxton's design.[20] Jones had contributed greatly to the visual clarity of the Crystal Palace, advising on its colour scheme. He selected light blue for the structure, red for the underside of the girders, yellow cross-bracing and yellow and blue for the columns. He also designed the decoration on the gallery balustrades and stairs and suggested hanging oriental carpets over the galleries. Jones, because of his flair for decoration and his interest in Moorish art, became a major proponent of the Saracenic style, and was often referred to as 'Alhambra' Jones. With its three great glass domes bulging from the side of this building, which was to be 1,952 feet long and 304 feet wide, the dimensions of Paxton's St Cloud design were reminiscent of his palace in Hyde Park; the central dome was 328 feet in diameter and 360 feet high and the end domes were 216 feet in diameter and 250 feet high.

JONES was also a champion of glass architecture. As well as proposing his own exhibition build-

31

32

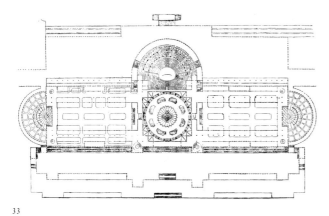

33

34

32 The central winter-
garden of a design for
a Palace of the People
at Muswell Hill, Owen
Jones, *Illustrated London
News*, 5 March 1859.
33 Design plan for the
Palace of the People.
34 Exterior view of the
Palace of the People,
Illustrated London News,
31 March 1860. The
railway terminus can be
seen below the north
front of the palace.

35 Interior of St Pancras
station, W H Barlow and
R M Ordish, 1866. This
long glass and iron roof
towered 100 feet above
the rails below.

35

ing for St Cloud, he designed and built a shopping arcade, the Crystal Palace Bazaar, in
Oxford Street using iron and glass. At this time,
as we saw in the last chapter, floras were also
gaining in popularity throughout Europe; they
were regarded as a marriage of the arts and
botany, often containing libraries, meeting and
performing halls together with winter-gardens.
Owen Jones's most exciting project, the 1859
design for the People's Palace, to be sited in the
north London suburb of Muswell Hill, was conceived in a similar spirit. The palace straddled
the top of the hill, surrounded by a gently undu-
lating wooded park with artificial gardens in the
Italian, French and Old English styles. Its high
position allowed the site to include a large railway terminal to be served by the London and
North-Western, the Eastern Counties and the
Great Western Railways, as well as the Great
Northern, which was sponsoring the project
with its subsidiary, the Great Northern Palace
Company. The link with the railways was obvious. It enabled 'visitors from the manufacturing
areas of all Britain to participate in the instruc-

tion and amusement, being transported by
excursion trains without the annoyance, delay and
expense of working their way through the
crowded streets of London'.[21] Though sited in the
country, the palace was to be connected to the
national transportation network, a link to this nineteenth-century vision of the workers' paradise.

A raised winter-garden with a diameter of 200
feet was to be in the centre of the palace,
between four viewing towers and connected to
the two upper galleries. There had been difficulty at Sydenham in maintaining the temperature for tropical plants. Here the winter-garden
was, like those of the German floras, isolated
from the rest of the building, so that heat and
moisture could not damage the other displays.

THE modern English- and Moorish-Style building was to be 1,296 by 492 feet and completely
covered with glass, either similar to Paxton's
ridge-and-furrow roofing or as flat sheets, particularly in the walls and the ornamental domes.
Though the People's Palace lacked the visual
clarity of the Crystal Palace, it would have been
one of the most exciting amusement complexes

196

of the nineteenth century and would have given 'Alhambra' Jones a great success.

WHEN the Royal Italian Opera House in London was destroyed by fire in 1856 the Duke of Bedford leased the empty site to Frederick Gye and a new theatre (Covent Garden Opera House, still in existence today) was begun in 1857, designed by the architect E M Barry, Charles Barry's son. By 1858 the Piazza Hotel, adjacent to the new theatre on the south side, was demolished and the site prepared for a new floral hall. Gye intended to lease stalls in the hall for the sale of flowers, plants and seeds. Building began in 1858, the architect was again Barry, the contractor was C & T Lucas, and the ironwork came from Henry Grissel. The hall extended about 230 feet from Bow Street to an iron and glass dome. The north side of this long nave abutted the Opera House. Another entrance faced the Covent Garden square. On the inside above each column, the cornice had a gas jet casting a romantic light on the activity below. The columns were perforated and provided ventilation for the building's deep cellars.

36

36 Paddington Station, I K Brunel and M Digby Wyatt, 1854, *Illustrated London News*, 8 July 1854. Brunel and Wyatt had both served on the Crystal Palace building committee that accepted Paxton's design. A Paxton ridge-and-furrow glass roof covered half the ribbed structure.

37 King's Cross Railway Terminus, Lewis Cubitt, 1852. The two semi-circular roofs, two thirds covered with plate glass are structured with laminated wood arches similar to those in Paxton's Crystal Palace, which was built the previous year.

37

FOR many years Gye and his successors sought permission from the Duke of Bedford, in their lease, to use the hall as a market, but without success. Licences were granted occasionally for concerts, exhibitions and for use as a drill hall. The West London Industrial Exhibition was held at the floral hall in 1865. The ninth Duke of Bedford finally bought the hall in 1887 and turned it into a foreign-fruit market, which relieved some of the congestion in the Covent Garden area. The floral hall exists today, at least up to the brackets above the columns, for the arched iron and glass roof and dome were destroyed by fire in 1956.

THE Crystal Palace had an immediate effect on those who saw it in Hyde Park, and the technical achievements displayed so dramatically on Sydenham Hill astounded contemporary observers and architectural critics. The palace's bare, unadorned modular bones, however, countered conventional decorative thinking too strongly, and even Paxton considered that framed-glass structures should be built only in limited or special circumstances.

PAXTON, like Loudon before him, made enormous contributions to horticulture as well as to glass architecture. Both men designed and improved glasshouses with a scientific and functional purpose that also produced magnificent structures. Both were architects without formal training. Loudon designed villas, cottages, farm buildings, inns and furniture; Paxton designed Italian and Tudor villas, Norman cottages, mock-Elizabethan country houses and utilitarian train stations. Except for their glass buildings, both produced rather mediocre buildings with little environmental understanding or experimentation; their domestic buildings were limited to matters of style. Utilitarian and rational use of iron, wood and glass was reserved for industry, transportation and exhibition buildings. What they considered permanent buildings were constructed of masonry or carved stone. Even utilitarian structures such as bridges and railway stations, when the budget could afford, were covered with Gothic, Greek, Egyptian or Saracenic decoration. Architect and engineer were in the same camp, accepting the

38

39 The entrance of Floral
Hall into the Piazza
Court, Convent Garden,
The Builder, 1860.
40 The Volunteers' Ball,
Floral Hall, illustrated the
white painted ironwork,
gilded decoration and
gas-lit chandeliers that
helped create a suitable
ball setting.

39

40

simplicity and functional form of utilitarian buildings, except when 'building' was to be considered as 'architecture'. The Crystal Palace of 1851, as we have seen, was built with techniques no less sophisticated than those of today. Those techniques resulted from step-by-step discoveries, which Paxton made empirically as early as 1828. They were ingeniously employed by a highly organized building industry, and nurtured by railway expansion requiring new methods and materials. Today we consider those results marvellous, but to the powerful legislator of style, John Ruskin, the Crystal Palace was no more than a feat of engineering. He wrote in *The Stones of Venice* (1851–3):[22]

*The quantity of bodily industry which that
Crystal Palace expresses is very great. So far so
good … The quantity of thought it expresses is,
I suppose, a single and very admirable thought of
Sir Joseph Paxton's, probably not a bit brighter than
thousands of thoughts which pass through his active
and intelligent brain every hour – that it might be
possible to build a greenhouse larger than ever was*

*built here. This thought, and some very ordinary
algebra, are as much as all that glass can represent
of human intellect.*

THERE is no doubt that as a precedent the Crystal Palace was a great influence on later exhibition buildings. Formative as it was, it was not always a model. The question of architectural style for glass buildings, despite the Crystal Palace's success, remained unresolved. For in 1860 Paxton proposed a winter-garden for Queen's Park, Glasgow, which with its neo-classical stone facade could hardly be called a glass building. The contrast between this building and his finest design, the exhibition building for St Cloud of 1861, represents the confusion and no doubt the controversy among architects and engineers over materials. The 1862 Exhibition building at Kensington, though with two bubble-like Saracen-style domes, was of massive brick, not unlike the 1850 building committee's abortive design. With hindsight it seems that the freshness of the Hyde Park Crystal Palace was only an interlude in the battle of styles.

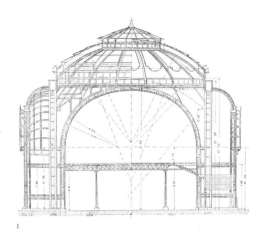

THE GREAT
EXHIBITIONS

THOUGH the influence of the London Great Exhibition of 1851 cannot be underestimated, it should not be looked at in isolation. World exhibitions were held with increasing frequency throughout the nineteenth and into the twentieth centuries and had been preceded by national exhibitions. One of the first was in Paris on the Champs de Mars in 1798. As Walter Benjamin has observed, 'this was the result of the desire to amuse the working class by holding festivals of emancipation'.[1]

THE Exhibition of the Works of Industry of all Nations, the brainchild of Prince Albert and Sir Henry Cole, was intended to marry industry with the arts, for Cole was in a sense one of the first theorists in industrial design. Prince Albert considered this 1851 exhibition a bid for universal peace because it might encourage the dropping of trade barriers, and allow for a complete industrialization of the earth. Again, W Bridges Adams gives a sympathetic account of the exhibition's ambitious scheme, which, he went on to claim, called for an equally ambitious and unique design:

> *And last came Prince Albert to proclaim*
> *that England should no longer be*
> *misunderstood; that from the ends*
> *of the earth foreigners should*
> *come to a universal jubilee*

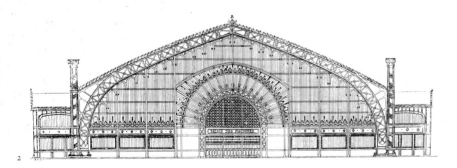

4

5

of the arts of peace; ... that unmistakably should be exhibited the results of many varying races: the artistry of the Celts and dark skins, and the mechanism of the fair-haired Saxons.[2]

SUCH was the spirit of the whole era of great exhibitions. Pilgrimages were made from all over the world to view this 1851 exhibition, which tended to emphasize the imperial and the imperialized, the civilized and the uncivilized, the haves and the have-nots. It glorified the exchange of commodities, hoping to create new markets in foreign lands. The exhibitions also promoted travel, for three different delegations of French workers went to London in 1851 and a second group in 1862. Victor Hugo published a manifesto for the Paris World Exhibition of 1867 – 'To the Peoples of Europe'.

THE international exhibition was contrived as a centre of distraction, created by what were often useless commodities and ephemeral experiences. The London Exhibition of 1851 was a showcase filled with bizarre objects, from an eighty-blade sportsman's knife to a floating church for seamen.[3] Visitors entered a phantasmagoria supposedly divorced from the realities of the world, a blend of machine technologies and paintings, war machinery and fashion, products and pleasure amalgamated into one thrilling visual experience.[4] Industrial objects were displayed like works of art, vying with gardens, fountains and statues for attention. The fairs were the origins of the pleasure industry, preparing the masses for advertising.

PRINCE Albert's plea for peace in 1851 set the stage for a crescendo of exhibitions in which politics presented itself with mythic powers capable of providing a future world of peace and social progress for the masses without revolution. Each successive exposition had to give visual proof of progress toward utopian goals by being more spectacular than the last. By the turn of the century governments were entrenched and were hardly distinguishable from entrepreneurs. Susan Buck-Morss sums this up: 'As part of the new imperialism, national pavilions promoted national grandeur, transforming patriotism itself into a commodity-on-display ...

202

World fairs claimed to promote peace, while displaying for government purchase the latest weapons of war.'[5]

THE 1851 Exhibition also set the scene for the great exposition halls that were to follow, each one bidding to outdo the statistics of its predecessors. The new materials, iron, glass and then steel, allowed ever greater volumes to be enclosed, although they were often cloaked in traditional 'architectural' skins.

BEFORE 1850 glass was a luxury. It was used with restraint, mainly because of the glass tax. By 1851, however, it was one of the cheapest cladding materials. It did not keep out the cold but it did keep out the rain and provided illumination for displays, for lighting was a challenge without electricity. Iron, as a structural material, had received a tremendous boost from the building of the railways. The large construction firms that had developed from this transport expansion were willing to consider any grand structure. Iron, however, was not yet considered suitable for the architecture of fashionable dwellings or public buildings. It was reserved

for industrial or engineering structures – arcades, railway stations, conservatories and temporary exhibition halls. The development of exhibition buildings in Paris demonstrates the ongoing struggle between the architect and the engineer, the decorator and the builder. With iron and glass, architecture outgrew art. The Palais des Machines and Eiffel Tower of 1889 attest to the supplanting of the Ecole des Beaux-Arts by the Ecole Polytechnique. Nevertheless, the plaster neo-classical halls of the 1893 Chicago World Columbian Exhibition had the last word – at least in North America. A new standard for exhibition architecture, established in Chicago, saw the pendulum swing back to dislodge the Crystal Palace as a stylistic model after little more than forty years.

COMPETITION among cities produced a number of international exhibitions; each strove to outdo the others in scale and cost. There was, indeed, a lot to compete with, including London 1851, Cork 1852, Dublin 1853, New York 1853, Munich 1854, Paris 1855, Kingston 1856, Manchester 1857, Toronto 1858,

4 The Palace of Industry, Toronto, Sir Sanford Fleming and Sir Collingwood Schreiber, 1858. It was built of wood with cast-iron columns and girders and roofed with tinned metal.

5 The Palace of Industry was moved to the Canadian National Exhibition site in 1878. It was reassembled by Strickland & Symons, and a second storey, large cupolas and a tower were added.

6 The Crystal Palace, Montreal, John William Hopkins, 1860.

6

7 Opening day souvenir of the New Orleans Exhibition, 1885–6.

8 The opening of the Industrial Exhibition Building, Dublin, designed by Sir John Benson, 1853.

Hamilton 1860, Montreal 1860, London 1862, Fredericton 1864, Dublin 1865, Paris 1867, Vienna 1873, Philadelphia 1876, Paris 1878, Toronto 1878, Sydney 1879, Melbourne 1880, Amsterdam 1883, Antwerp 1885, New Orleans 1885, Barcelona 1888, Brussels 1888, Copenhagen 1888, Paris 1889, Victoria 1891, Chicago 1893, Paris 1900 and Edinburgh 1903 to name a few.

THE Irish had held an architectural competition for the 1853 Great Industrial Exhibition in Dublin. John Benson from Cork, later knighted, won the competition with a structure covered mainly in wood with a huge glazed skylight over the centre of the principal nave. This great hall was proudly acclaimed to be 17 feet longer and 28 feet wider than the transept of the recent Great Exhibition building in London. The wooden arches spanning the hall were supported on iron columns cast in Edinburgh and transported to the Merrion Square site, where the building was erected in two hundred working days between mid-August 1852 and May 1853. Richard Turner, the Dublin

engineer and contractor, received third prize in the competition, and his only consolation was an order for his Hammersmith Works in Dublin for the wrought-iron trusses to support the upper galleries. Two smaller halls ran parallel to the great hall. These were filled with examples of the four categories of the exhibition – Raw Material, Machinery, Manufactures and Fine Arts – similar in content to the 1851 Exhibition in London, except that here oil paintings and watercolours were permitted entries. Several countries were represented, including Belgium, France and Prussia, with a major attraction being the side building with machinery in motion, again duplicating London. The Dublin Exhibition had too much wood to be in any real sense a glass building. Like the exhibitions of 1857 in Manchester and that of 1876 in Philadelphia, it owes a great deal to the Joseph Paxton and Charles Fox 1851 prototype.

THE first world fair in the United States also took place in 1853. New York City had initially invited designs for an industrial exhibition in 1851 in order not to be outdone by the Great

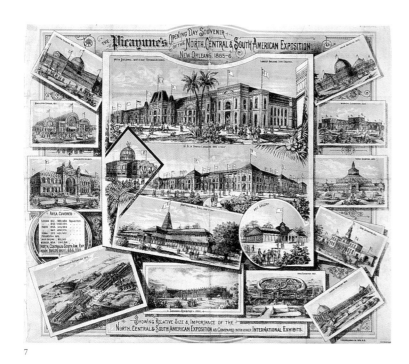

7

8

Exhibition in London. Joseph Paxton took part in the competition, but the prize was awarded to New York architects George Carstensen and Charles Gildemeister, beating an exciting entry by James Bogardus, the American master of iron-skeleton construction. The entries from Paxton, Bogardus and the winner did not carry roofs of glass, most probably because of the heavy snow falls along the eastern seaboard. Carstensen and Gildemeister's design was, however, completely walled in glass, following the precedent of the London Crystal Palace. The ground-floor plan, centred on a huge octagon 355 feet in diameter, was crossed by two main avenues with a dome 100 feet in diameter over the crossing. The main floor of 111,200 square feet, combined with two gallery levels above, provided 179,000 square feet for display, considerably less than the Crystal Palace. The construction was mainly of iron and glass, but a quantity of timber was also used, hence the spectacular fire that destroyed it in 1858.

THE following years saw other exhibitions in Europe and Britain. By 1854 the Glas Palast was

9

10

11 The Munich Glass
   Palace, August von Voit,
   1853–4, steel engraving
   by Johann von Poppel.
12 The Horticultural
   Exposition in the Palais
   de L'industrie, Paris
   Universal Exhibition,
   1867.

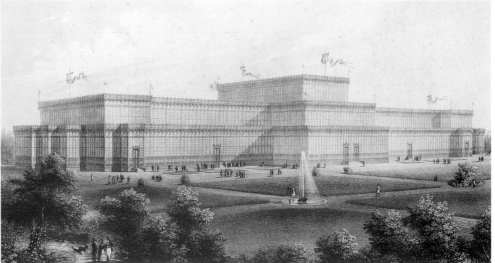

11

12

completed in Munich, designed by the Royal Superintendent of Works, architect August von Voit, and built by contractors Cramer-Klett, with Ludwig Werder in charge. The palace was located in the Old Botanic Gardens in the centre of the city near the station, a railway line was built adjacent to the site and the prefabricated components enabled the palace to be assembled in nine months. The building, approximately 790 feet long and 164 feet wide, was intersected by a 276-foot transept of similar width. The main space was spanned by 79-foot trusses, the height of the hall being 66 feet and 82 feet in the transept. The structural systems and building methods were similar to those found in Paxton's Crystal Palace except that more metal was used for example as in the iron sash-bar ridge-and-furrow glazing system. The palace served Munich for festivals, exhibitions and plays for many years until a fire destroyed it in 1931.

IN Paris, a grand glass and iron structure had been planned by Cendrier and Barrault for the 1855 French Universal Exhibition. It was decided, however, to surround the building with a covering of masonry. Behind this architectural facade Alexis Barrault built the largest known iron span over a 47-metre-wide hall, known as the Palais de l'Industrie, sited on the Champs Elysées and in use until 1906 when it was replaced by the Grand Palais. The roofs of the three long galleries were covered with so much glass that they dazzled spectators unused to such interior light intensity.

BACK in Britain, the building for the London Exhibition of the Works of Industry of all Nations, in 1862, would have pleased the 1851 building committee, as its masonry was similar to that of the committee's original design. Wide interest in Saracenic decoration had generated a number of designs with Moorish domes, such as Owen Jones's proposed People's Palace at Muswell Hill and Joseph Paxton's proposed exhibition building at St Cloud, and this 1862 exhibition building supported two such glass domes rising above the brick facades. Hidden behind the masonry, a system of cast columns, iron girders and a delicate triangular truss supported immense glass roofs. The designers were

13, 14 Interior and exterior
of the Exhibition of the
Works of Industry of
all Nations building
in London, Sydney
Smirke and Captain
Francis Fowke, 1862.

13

the architect Sydney Smirke and the engineer
Captain Francis Fowke, who also built many
provincial galleries. They also designed the
Royal Horticultural Society's large conservatory, on the Gore House estate, now occupied
by the Victoria & Albert Museum and the
Albert Hall. A plan of the Royal Horticultural
Society's garden in 1863 shows 'Albertopolis' as
the Prince Consort would have seen it. On the
left Prince Albert's Road (Queen's Gate) and on
the right Exhibition Road, both lined with
substantial houses whose rents were intended
to support the museums and institutions of
'Albetopolis'. In the centre of the great formal
garden, surrounded by arcades and bandstands,
the conservatory at the northern end provided
an entrance for the proposed Albert Hall.

IN 1865, an international exhibition of arts and
industry was organized in Dublin in the large
glass and iron Winter Palace designed by architect Alfred G Jones, and engineers Rowland
Mawson, R M Ordish and Le Feuvre. Ordish,
an expert in iron engineering, developed a
basilica section with a two-storey side aisle and

14

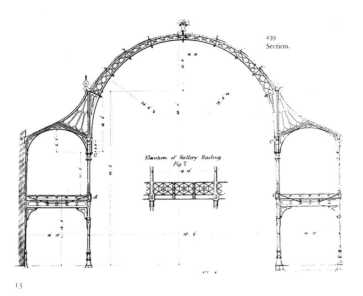

239
Section.

Elevation of Gallery Railing Fig 7

15

cast-iron brackets buttressing the thrust of the wrought-iron vault spanning 50 feet over the central winter-garden. The plan was L-shaped, with one wing 420 feet long and the other 210 feet. The complex contained two concert halls and rehearsal rooms for the orchestra, dining rooms, a large art gallery and a reading room. Ventilation was provided on top of the vault by a shaft that connected to a system of cables, which lifted two rows of glass panels, similar to vents in commercial glasshouses today.

THE second Universal Exhibition, held in Paris in 1867, was to be housed in a huge circular building symbolizing the globe, but there was not enough space for it on the Champs de Mars so the design was changed to an oval of 386 by 490 metres. The Second Empire was at its height, and Paris, also at the peak of fashion, attracted exhibitors from around the world who felt compelled to be represented in this artificial and temporary world of iron and glass. About thirty nations participated and over six and a half million visitors came. Seven concentric galleries formed a fantastic elliptical earth; the large

16

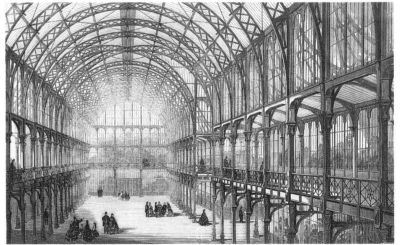

17

208

18 The Palais d'Horti-
culture, Paris Universal
Exhibition, Albert
Gautier, 1900.
19 Bird's-eye view of the
1867 Paris Universal
Exhibition.

outer gallery was devoted to machines and the
other galleries, in decreasing size and in strict
order, were devoted to clothing, furniture, raw
materials, liberal arts, fine arts and the history of
labour. In the centre was an open garden with a
pavilion for coins, weights and measures. The
building was divided into wedge-shaped seg-
ments occupied by the various nations, so that it
was possible to circumambulate the various galleries to compare similar commodities among
different participants or meander from the outer
gallery to the inner garden to see all the goods of
one country; all aptly described in the official
1867 publication: 'To make the circuit of this
place, circular, like the equator, is literally to go
around the world. All peoples are here, enemies
live in peace side by side. As in the beginning of
things, on the globe of waters, the divine spirit
now floats on this globe of iron.'

THE outer gallery, the Galerie des Machines,
had a span of 35 metres and was supported on
iron arches. Outward thrust was eliminated by
extending the pillars above the roof, creating an
exo-structure. This functional facade, bedecked

18

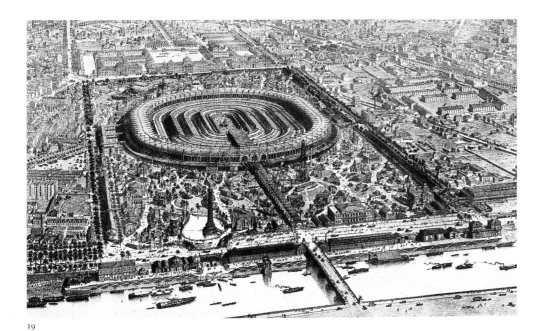

19

20

21

20 Destruction of the Palais
   de Cristal, Paris, by high
   winds, December 1867.
21 Interior of the Palais
   de Cristal, Universal
   Exhibition.
22 Commercial glazed
   pavilions built around
   the Palais de Cristal.
23 Galerie des Machines,
   Universal Exhibition,
   Paris, 1889.

22

with pennants and flags, was criticized by the Parisians, who were used to a more monumental style. The inner galleries were iron-trussed with glass-covered gable roofs. Designed by J B Krantz, the temporary building had a metal framework made by the company of the young engineer Gustave Eiffel, the major contributor to the detailed design.

A QUARTER of the grounds were reserved for horticulture and many commercial glazed pavilions were built around the 'Palais de Cristal', the central attraction of this 'Le Jardin Reserve'. Dramatically, in December of that year high winds destroyed the buildings, and the palms, which were on loan from the city of Paris, died in the severe cold.

THE most important exhibition, from the point of view of structural engineering and glasshouse design, was the exhibition in Paris in 1889 commemorating the centenary of the storming of the Bastille. Organized again on the Champs de Mars, it consisted of a series of interconnected buildings overlooked by Eiffel's famous tower. The Palais des Machines, designed by the architect Ferdinand Dutert and the engineers Victor Contamin, Eugène Pierron and Jules-Jean Charton, was the culmination of engineering confidence in steel structure and glass enclosure. Its great hulk dominated the exhibition complex, with a main hall measuring 115 by 240 metres surrounded by smaller vaulted side aisles. The main hall was spanned by rigid trusses, with pin connections at the top and at each base. The largest span attempted until this time had been the 73 metres of St Pancras station in London by Barlow and Ordish, where the arched trusses had been firmly secured at the foundations. These new pin connections disturbed many visitors familiar with structures securely planted into the earth; the gallery seemed to float above them. The north and south ends were enclosed with transparent glass walls supported by structural steel decoration that doubled as structure for horizontal wind loads. From inside, one could see through the glass wall to the sky, a sensation of space never achieved in the halls of the past. This gave a remarkable sensation of immensity, especially since the low pointed arches obscured the exact height. The roof was a design of translucent white and blue glass. There are recorded comments of visitors who found it disconcerting to see such a delicate skin of light purlins, glazing bars and glass supported by massive trusses, 3 metres in depth. The smaller arched side aisles and the two mobile trolleys that travelled the length of the space above the machines and exhibitions added some human scale to this vast volume. The exhibition was too large to be walked around, and travelling cranes carried as many as one-hundred thousand visitors on a busy day. Unfortunately, this marvellous structure was dismantled in 1910, though it remained for a much longer period a prototype of the exhibition halls and field houses built in the United States. Eiffel's 300-metre tower remains a tribute to what must have been a magnificent exhibition.

OUTSIDE Europe, Canada, like the rest of the Empire, looked to the 1851 Exhibition in London for direction. Sir Sanford Fleming and Sir Collingwood Schreiber collaborated to design the Palace of Industry in Toronto,

opened on 29 September 1858. The familiar rose window emulated that at the Hyde Park Crystal Palace. The structure was built of wood with cast-iron columns and girders and roofed with tinned metal. Exhibition buildings in North America had less glass because of the mitigating cold winters and hot summers. The glass for the roof lanterns over the exhibition spaces and side windows came from the Chance Brothers in Birmingham, the suppliers to the London and Dublin exhibitions. It was built in a very short time – only three and a half months – which was typical of prefabricated exhibition structures at that time. Sanford Fleming was an engineer doing considerable work for the Canadian Pacific Railroad at the time and gained fame as the inventor of Standard Time.

FOLLOWING the pattern of the Crystal Palace at Hyde Park, the Palace of Industry in Toronto was dismantled in 1878 and moved from its site on King Street just south of the Ontario Hospital to a new exhibition site for an annual fair, now the Canadian National Exhibition. The palace was reassembled under the direction of

25

architects Strickland and Symons and a second storey, large cupolas and a tower were added. The site was located where the present horticultural building is in Exhibition Park. The name Crystal Palace was established and it served as an exhibition building for twenty-eight years until it was destroyed by fire in 1906. NOT to be outdone, the Crystal Palace in Montreal of 1860 was designed for year-round use by John William Hopkins. Its main facades were of iron and glass and its side walls were of white brick with rose-coloured contrast. Severe winter climate considerations demanded that the roof was tinned as in Toronto.

IN 1876, the United States celebrated a hundred years of independence with the Centennial Exposition, an international exhibition in Philadelphia. Erected in Fairmount Park, which claimed to be the largest municipal park in the world, the main buildings were reminiscent of the Crystal Palace of twenty-five years earlier. The large aisles were covered with triangular iron trusses supporting a wooden roof, and the galleries were supported by means of iron lattice girders on cast-iron columns. The walls were extensively glazed, giving a delightfully open feeling. One of the lesser buildings, the profusely decorated Horticultural Hall, is representative of the break from the pragmatic functional styles of the 1850s and 1860s. It was a princely Victorian conservatory encrusted in Moorish, Gothic and Saracenic decoration, stylish at that time, but out of character with the Republican revolution brought about by the classicists Jefferson and Madison, whom it was to commemorate.

THOUGH often accompanied by stylized masonry, international exhibition buildings were liberated from the traditional constraints of 'architecture' as dictated by the Gothic or classical styles. Even a conservatory-like building, such as the Horticultural Hall at the Philadelphia Exhibition of 1876 represented a flight of fancy, integrating an improbable combination of Gothic and Saracenic decoration. However, it was the futuristic structures, like the Palais des Machines, that paved the way for the twentieth century when architectural style could become a matter of innovation.

EXPRESSIONISTS
AND BEYOND

X

GLASS is a magic material. It keeps out the wind and weather, collects the sun's warmth, looks like a jewel and awakens our fantasy. The crystal palaces built throughout Europe and North America in the nineteenth century were the manifestations of a fascination with glass. Susan Buck-Morss says, 'The Crystal Palace 1851 blended together old nature and new nature – palms as well as pumps and pistons – in a fantasy world that entered the imagination of an entire generation of Europeans.'[1] In 1900 Julius Lessing wrote:

> I remember from my own childhood years how the news of the Crystal Palace reached over into Germany, how, in remote provincial towns, pictures of it were hung on the walls of bourgeois rooms. All that we imagined from old fairy tales of princesses in glass caskets, of queens and elves who live in crystal houses, seemed to us to be embodied in it.[2]

THE poetic associations of glass inspired architects to execute designs that depended on the expressive qualities of the material. At the end of the nineteenth century, this manifested itself in a greater appreciation of the diverse

4

5

properties of glass and the design of a number of botanical glasshouses which adopted a more explicitly structural approach. By the twentieth century, exponents of glass, such as the writer Paul Scheerbart (1863–1915) and the architect Bruno Taut (1880–1938) and later the designer and engineer Richard Buckminster Fuller (1895–1983), were spellbound by the futuristic possibilities of transparency and structural expression.

ONE of the most prominent examples of expressed structural ironwork in the nineteenth century is the Great Palm House at Schönbrunn Castle, Vienna (1880–2), the summer residence of the imperial court. It was designed by the court architect Franz von Sengenschmid in collaboration with the structural engineer Sigmund Wagner. Von Sengenschmid toured the glasshouses of Europe before he began. His design eliminated the traditional masonry back wall and solid roof found in most European buildings and devised a new form more closely related to English glasshouses, like the Palm House at Kew. Though Alphonse Balat's grand glass-rotunda winter-garden for Leopold II was constructed with an exposed structure at Laeken in 1876 and there were 'exo-structures' in Munich and Frankfurt, nothing had been expressed so blatantly as in the Palm House at Schönbrunn. The mainly wrought-iron structure, with interior columns, arches and brackets, encloses a central space for palms with a temperate house in one wing and a tropical house in the other.

A COMPLEX of glasshouses built in 1905–7 at the Royal Botanical Garden at Dahlem in Berlin, which was later to attract Scheerbart and Taut's attention, was a complete departure from the more typical decorative nineteenth-century conservatories.[3] It was designed by Alfred Koerner of the Royal Building Office. There were several glass chambers providing different climates and in the centre the Great Palm House, 61 metres long, 30 metres wide and a dramatic 26 metres high. The structural designer and builder was Heinrich Müller-Breslau who devised the three-hinged arched-girder construction. According to Kohlmaier

4–5 The Great Palm House,
Schönbrunn, Vienna,
Franz von Segenschmid
and Sigmund Wagner,
1882.
6 Interior of the Great
Palm House,
Schönbrunn.

and Von Sartory, the style was a break from monumental architecture with base, pilasters and cornices, and followed the pure structural function of a chamber for plants, the result was a prototype for German Expressionism.[4] The architect and the director of the garden, who both made inspection trips to Holland, Belgium and Russia, were impressed by the glasshouses in the Imperial Gardens of St Petersburg because they dealt with a similar severe climate. They concluded that the majority of condensation problems came from structural elements protruding through the glass skin, particularly iron glazing bars. These Koerner designed in American pitch pine, which is very resistant to deterioration, with condensation channels cut into the side similar to those in the Crystal Palace. He devised a method of suspending them below the structure to reduce the thermal bridging. It resulted in a dramatic exposed structure.

PERHAPS more exciting to Scheerbart, because of its translucency, was the Subtropical House also designed by Koerner at Dahlem and built just after the Great Palm House also at Dahlem. Devoid of decoration, it resembles a church with its nave, side aisles and even an apse. It is difficult to believe that it came from the same architect's hand, though Koerner explained that the basilica form was rational, accommodating both tall and low plants.[5] Built in 1909, the structural expression of exposed bolts and rivets is in the Jugendstil tradition popular in Central Europe at that time.

THE inverted slope of the roof of the Palmarium at the Casino in Pau, with its view of the snow-covered Pyrenees, created a dynamic environment that would certainly have appealed to the glass Expressionists. The winter-garden and casino, completed in 1900, were designed by the architect Emile Bertrand in 1896 and built on an elliptical ring of sixteen cast-iron columns surrounded by a curvilinear glass vault with delicate structural framing, successfully combining a masonry theatre with glass and iron.

BETWEEN 1910 and 1920 Paul Scheerbart wrote extravagant and fantastic tales that would be considered science fiction today – he was the German Expressionists' Jules Verne. Taut, who was greatly influenced by his Utopian

phantasmagoria, described him as the 'only poet in architecture'. Scheerbart had a fanatical love for glass architecture, and his moral views about it are idealistic and full of joy:

Colourful glass destroys hate
Without a glass palace life is a burden
Only colour-happiness with glass culture
Light permeates everything and is alive in crystal
Glass brings us the new era; brick culture is a burden
Bricks pass away; coloured glass endures[6]

SCHEERBART awoke the lofty dreams of young architects of the Expressionist period with his ideas of glass architecture: light, crystal clear, colourful, mobile structures floating and soaring to change the European citizen by releasing him from his brick box into a new light.

TECHNICALLY, Scheerbart's glass visions were practical and, in retrospect, prophetic. He understood the problems of heat loss, heat gain and condensation, but suggested that several skins of glass, combined with air-conditioning machinery, could provide a successful environment: 'Glass is also useful in the tropics. There, one requires only three-ply or four-ply glass walls and a few sheltering walls of white canvas. Cooling units can easily be installed in the walls. Air is a poor conductor of heat.'[7] Scheerbart saw the familiar glass conservatory expanding in size until it became detached from the dwelling, and isolated within the garden. The new citizen would then leave his masonry house and move into a world of coloured double-glass walls held in reinforced concrete frames, with ceramic floors, glass furniture, glass-fibre cloth and glass lamps.

IN 1914, the same year as Bruno Taut built his famous Glass House at the Werkbund Exhibition in Cologne, Scheerbart's text 'Glasarchitektur' was printed in *Der Sturm*. Excerpts from this prophetic work capture the spirit that stirred young architects of the *Gläserne Kette* (Glass Chain group), who were looking for some salvation during the trying months before the First World War.[8] *Der Sturm* provided the communicative link between architects, artists and writers embroiled in the unreal but Utopian world of Expressionism. Scheerbart was one of their prophets:

6

7 Plan of Great Palm
 House complex,
 Royal Botanic Gardens,
 Dahlem, Berlin, designed
 by Alfred Koerner,
 1905–7.
8 Great Palm House,
 Dahlem.
9 Interior of the Great
 Palm House under
 construction.
10 Great Palm House,
 Dahlem.
11 Section of the Great
 Palm House, Dahlem.
 Hot-water pipes were
 hung under the roof
 structure and radiators
 heated the vaults below.
12 Subtropical House,
 Dahlem, Alfred Koerner,
 1908–9.
13 Longitudinal section of
 the Great Palm House,
 Dahlem, showing
 tropical plants.

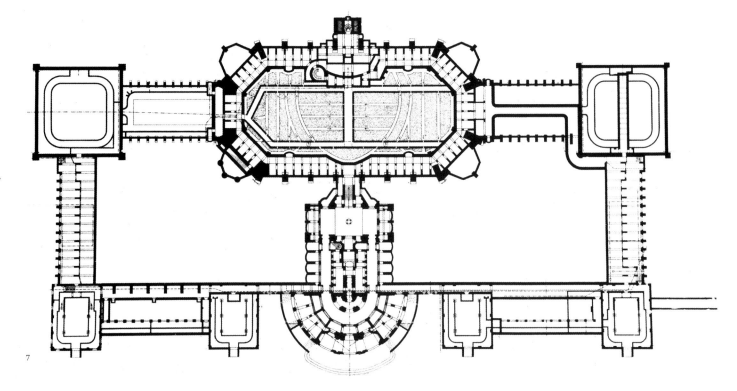

7

8

9

10

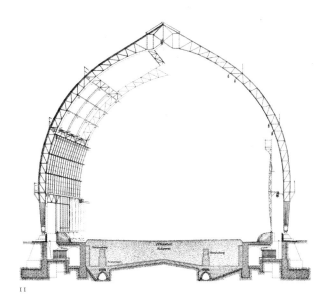

11

12

13

14

We live for the most part within enclosed spaces. These form the environment from which our culture grows. Our culture is in a sense a product of our architecture. If we wish to raise our culture to a higher level, we are forced for better or for worse to transform our architecture. And this will be possible only if we remove the enclosed quality from the spaces within which we live. This can be done only through the introduction of glass architecture that lets the sunlight and the light of the moon and stars into our rooms not merely through a few windows, but simultaneously through the greatest possible number of walls that are made entirely of glass-coloured glass. The new environment that we shall thereby create must bring with it a new culture.[9]

SCHEERBART predicted accurately the light-zoning restrictions that shaped most of New York City's wedding-cake skyscrapers.

No doubt a terrace formation is necessary in taller glass buildings and with several storeys, since otherwise the glass surfaces could not reach the free light-conducting air, to which they aspire …

This terrace formation of the storeys will of course quickly replace the dreary frontal architecture of brick houses.[10]

It was the steam railway that produced the brick metropolis culture of today from which we all suffer. Glass architecture will come only when the metropolis in our sense of the word has been done away with. Even if we cannot for the present assume that our sense organs will evolve further from today to tomorrow, we shall nevertheless be justified in supposing that to begin with we may attain that which is accessible to us – to wit, that part of the spectrum which we are able to perceive with our eyes, those miracles of colour which we are capable of taking in. The only thing that can help us to do this is glass architecture, which must transform our whole life – the environment in which we live.[11]

IN an article about *Glasarchitektur*, Adolf Behne, Secretary of the Work Council for Art, an arch-propagandist of the Modern Movement and a colleague of Taut, demonstrates the faith shared by the *Gläserne Kette* in Scheerbart's vision:

15, 16 Exterior and interior of
the Glass House at the
Werkbund Exhibition,
Cologne, Bruno Taut,
1914. It was a concrete
lamellar structure 'to
demonstrate the use
of glass in all its varied
aesthetic charm.'

15

*The idea of a glass architecture is perfectly simple and
is to be understood just as Scheerbart presents it … in
the light of gayest optimism. It is not the crazy caprice
of a poet that glass architecture will bring a new
culture. IT IS A FACT! New social welfare
organizations, hospitals, inventions or technical
innovations and improvements – these will not bring
about our new culture … but glass architecture will.
Glass architecture is going to eliminate all harshness
from the Europeans and replace it with tenderness,
beauty and candour.*[12]

ARCHITECT Bruno Taut was the most ardent
proponent and interpreter of Scheerbart's
message. Besides designing some of the best
German multiple housing, he was a prominent
figure during the Expressionist period after the
war. In 1919 he published *Die Stadtkrone*, a treatise on town planning emphasizing residential
layouts on the lines of garden cities with the
Stadtkrone as public buildings visible to all
around, full of idealistic glass imagery. His
Alpine Architektur, a Utopian project consisting of
thirty drawings published in 1919, was divided
into six sections: the crystal house; architecture
of the mountains; the alpine structure; earthcrust
architecture; star architecture; and cathedral
star. The fantastic drawings are of imaginary
glass projects, nestled between and crowning
the mountains of southern Europe with crystal-
domed buildings on the Riviera. As Scheerbart
was the sage and prophet, Taut was the disciple
attempting to bring the dream into
reality. Taut's Glass House, at the Werkbund
Exhibition in Cologne, made a lasting impression on his colleagues. Built to demonstrate the
new uses of glass, it was 'proof of the new art of
architecture'; Taut described his pavilion as:

*The lightest possible concrete structure, destined
to demonstrate the use of glass in all its varied
aesthetic charm, the variegated shining glass prisms
of its glass envelopments, its glass ceilings, glass
floors, glass tiles, and the cascade, lit up from beneath,
and a giant kaleidoscope, which was intended to
illustrate by its illumination at night all that glass
might achieve towards the heightening of intensity
in our lives.*[13]

16

17 Two-mile diameter
tensegrity dome over
Manhattan,
Richard Buckminster
Fuller, 1950s.

THE GLASSHOUSE

IN 1920 Taut found a new medium for expression in the periodical *Stadtbaukunst Alter und Neuer Zeit* (Urban Architecture Ancient and Modern). He ran a series called *Frühlicht* (Early Light) from 1920 to 1922, in which he could carry on the Expressionist spirit, publishing articles by his favourite architects and his friends. There were two issues of *Frühlicht*, the first being discontinued with an apologetic letter from the publisher explaining that Taut had used too much freedom in airing the younger architects' radical views.

PERHAPS the most exciting theoretical project for Taut was the House of Heaven, a huge all-embracing sacred structure in which all the arts merge into one. The House of Heaven was conceived as a temple of the *Zeitgeist* that united the views of the *Glaserne Kette* members. Just as Walter Gropius saw painters and sculptors under the arm of great art and architecture, so too did Taut, designing the cathedral of the future as a truly twentieth-century structure in which all arts worked together, perhaps modelled on the great Gothic cathedrals. Between the inner and outer glass skins is the lighting. It will be switched on inwards and outwards, changing from lighting the proceedings in the room, to creating an effect outside. Both inside and outside will be lit through richly coloured glass walls. If one approaches by night from the air, it appears from far off like a star. And it sounds like a bell. To build the roofs, prisms of coloured glass will be electrolytically joined, and for the walls, the prisms will be poured. In a very stable structure the glass prisms of the roof could also be poured as one. Roofs and walls will echo the crystals of the outer structure in a subdued manner, like bas-reliefs, crisp and stylish, and in their glittering richness they will absorb the deepest colours of the sparkling glass windows. In fact they are not glass windows, since walls and roof are all bright and colourful. The windows will therefore be like colourful carpets, darker and even more colourful than the walls and roof. All the forms climb, struggle and grow upwards, pulled on by the roof star. Steep and harsh, weak and delicate in the manifold flux of form, the colours are deep and glowing, mysteriously luminous, each arm of the star being one of the colours of the rainbow.

THE verticals of the columns bind the whole together. Flashing and sparkling, the sun catches the glittering colours, the grey day speaks earnestly through them, and the moon and stars twinkle their light through the coloured glass like little silver bells.[14]

TO sum up Taut's exuberant attitude at this time, the introductory page in the first *Frühlicht* entitled 'Down with Seriousism' proclaims: 'In the distance shines our tomorrow. Hurray, three times hurray for our kingdom without force! Hurray for the transparent, the clear! Hurray for purity! Hurray for crystal! Hurray and again hurray for the fluid, the graceful, the angular, the sparkling, the flashing, the light – Hurray for everlasting architecture!'

THE trend in the mid-twentieth century has been for buildings to become increasingly sophisticated structurally, but with regressive skins, having rather naive hermetically sealed enclosures and requiring machines to convert large quantities of energy to maintain desired conditions. Few of these buildings would have pleased Scheerbart. Perhaps Frank Lloyd Wright's Wayfarer's Chapel above the Pacific at Palos Verdes, California, built in 1951, or Peter Behrens's glasshouse above the Seine in Paris of 1925, would have met his ideal. Most certainly he and Taut would have been thrilled by Peter Grund's steel and glass church and the architecture of Bruce Goff. Goff infilled the hard coal masonry walls with large glass cullets in the Ford House at Aurora, Illinois, 1949, and the Price Studio in Bartlesville, Oklahoma, 1957. Exotic glass furniture in the Price's house fits Scheerbart's description. This design for a musician, made from aluminium structure, transparent plastic and aluminium globes, fulfils Scheerbart's prediction of building with plastics: 'and one is going to try to invent materials that can compete with glass. I am referred to materials that are as elastic as rubber but also transparent.'[15]

RICHARD Buckminster Fuller's proposal for a two-mile diameter tensegrity dome over the island of Manhattan in the 1950s was daring and would have excited Scheerbart and the nineteenth-century visionary Loudon, who foresaw vast Gardens of Adonis covered with glass. Inside these glazed spaces, building as we know

17

it would be superfluous. Grand dimensions were fundamental to the Gardens of Adonis, for it must be presented as a sky vault, like Buckminster Fuller's United States Pavilion of 1967 at Montreal, where activity focuses on displays, with little comprehension of the enclosing background.

FOR many years Fuller had been an advocate of economic enclosures developed from his studies of geometry. He reasoned that the repetition of building elements, like the stick, the joint and the skin, took advantage of mass-production and mass-marketing because within the shell varied levels, partitioning, equipment and climate determine the potential activity that could take place inside a personalized house within a house. His ardour, like Scheerbart's prophetic musings, was summed up in an interview about the United States Pavilion at Montreal's Expo '67: 'From the inside there will be uninterrupted visual contact with the exterior world. The sun and moon will shine in the landscape, and the sky will be completely visible, but the unpleasant effects of climate, heat, dust, bugs,

glare etc will be modulated by the skin to provide a Garden of Eden interior.'[16]

FULLER's pavilion has a spherical diameter of 250 feet and is 200 feet high, covering about an acre. Like Loudon's Birmingham dome each level had a different temperature within the space, the warmest being at the top. Mechanical failures thwarted Fuller's Garden of Eden. The original intention was to create a skin that could react dynamically to exterior forces in order to modulate the interior climate. Fuller was not asking a great deal from his skin, merely shading. A solar-activated motor was mounted over the centre hub of three interior hexagonal frames that formed the skin's structure. As the sun moved across the sky and struck each of the six hundred motors, it would close silvered triangular roller blinds, shading the building during the day. At night a switch closed them all, reducing radiation heat loss and some conduction. Fuller's dome followed Bruno Taut's maxim, that exhibitions in Europe be banned and be replaced by demonstrations of architecture and its potential. The pavilion for the

18 Glasshouse over the Seine at the International Exposition of Decorative Arts, Peter Behrens, 1925.

18

Werkbund Exhibition was one of the few attempts in the twentieth century to develop a building's integument to be as advanced as its structure.

IN recent years an increasing concern for the efficient use of energy has resulted in an architecture in which design and fabric are often determined by climatic control techniques. Two very different botanical glasshouses that exemplify this approach are the Princess of Wales Conservatory, Kew, opened in 1987, and the Lucille Halsell Conservatory in San Antonio, Texas, completed in 1987. Situated on opposite sides of the world they have contrasting climates to contend with and are glazed accordingly. The Princess of Wales Conservatory responds to its temperate, British climate by maximizing on glazing. Before starting work on the building in 1977, Gordon Wilson, the project manager and project architect, carried out extensive research into the form it should take, visiting glasshouses in Europe and North America. This led him to conceive of the Princess of Wales Conservatory

as an idealized south-facing glazed hill. Forming a series of adjoining houses, it accommodates a number of habitats as diverse as the Namib Desert and the tropical cloud forest. Unlike many botanical gardens in temperate climates, however, the tropical plants are able to follow their natural cycle without a recourse to a dormant winter phase. There is no need for artificial lighting, and air circulation and ventilation are, in the main, by natural means. The rising ground of the hill enables small plants to 'see over' those in front of them in order to receive winter sun. A near vertical south wall of glass allows a low winter sun to be admitted efficiently while reflecting some of the heat from the higher summer sun. Wilson devised the series of accumulated pyramids to be stepped and staggered in form, as the site did not allow the 'south-facing' hill to extend very far east to west. Several clerestory-like gables facing south open up to let sun further into the building.

FOR a glasshouse located in the hot, dry climate of southern Texas, it is as necessary to limit the area of glazing as it is to maximize it at Kew. At

19 United States Pavilion, Expo '67, Montreal, Richard Buckminster Fuller.

19

20

21

22

20 Site plan of the Lucille
Halsell Conservatory,
San Antonio, Emilio
Ambasz, 1987.
21 Section of one of the
individual glasshouses
that make up the Lucille
Halsell Conservatory.
22 Exterior view of the
Lucille Halsell
Conservatory.

San Antonio, Emilio Ambasz confined glass to the roofs of the individual glasshouses grouped around the courtyard, which, with their separate microcosms, make up the Lucille Halsell Conservatory. Dug out of the soil, the glasshouses are cooled and protected by the earth. The complex as a whole is also sheltered within the landscape by earth berms. Each of the major spaces is a concrete dish that floats independently in the unstable clay soil with the superstructure of the glass roof springing from the ring beam rim.

BOTH conservatories succeed in extending beyond their utilitarian objectives. At Kew, enlightened research into a form that would best serve a botanical garden's concern for economy of energy produced an impressive pyramidal configuration. In the Lucille Halsell Conservatory, Emilio Ambasz combines off-the peg components, such as the space-frame, glazing with opening lights, and forms devised for optimal ventilation and shading with pragmatic and in-situ concrete foundations and berming. Nevertheless, the effect is as poetic as any of the Expressionists' projects. Viewed from a distance the roofs of the glasshouses appear as crystalline peaks, floating without any visible bases. The magic is prolonged with the visitor's advance. On entering the complex the courtyard appears as an oasis with its palm trees, flowers and free-form lily pool, amid the parched Texas landscape.

THE change in focus towards environmental issues in the late twentieth century has made the design challenge to develop a sophisticated enclosing skin, which was initially highlighted in the 1960s by James Marston Fitch, all the more pressing for the twenty-first century.[17] Ideally the crystalline skin, the interface with the outside world, should be able to perform lunal and climatic transformations: to be opaque or transparent, closed or open, to seal or to breath, to insulate or to transpire. Then *the glasshouse* will be as harmonious in its relationship with natural forces as the plants it shelters, for it is these forces of natural selection that, through the millenniums, have made plants transform and adapt.

23 Princess of Wales
   Conservatory, Royal
   Botanic Gardens, Kew,
   Gordon Wilson, 1987.
24, 25 Interior view of the
   Princess of Wales
   Conservatory.

25

EXPRESSIONISTS AND BEYOND

I

1 Colurnella, *De Re Rustica* (on Agriculture and Trees), translated by Harold Boyd (London, 1940), 51, III, book XI, vol III, p 161.

2 John Claudius Loudon, 'Roman Gardens', *An Encyclopaedia of Gardening* (London, 1835, pp 24–5.

3 *Ibid.*

4 *The Diaries of John Evelyn* (Everyman, 1907), 20 September 1700, vol II, p 363.

5 Kenneth Lemmon, *The Golden Age of Plant Hunters* (London, 1968), p 10.

6 Saloman De Caus, *Hortus Palatinus* (Frankfurt, 1620).

7 Kenneth Lemmon, *The Golden Age of Plant Hunters*.

8 Stephen Hales, *Vegetable Staticks or an Account of Some Statical Experiments on the Sap in Vegetables* (1727).

9 Steven Otto made this observation in informal conservation with the author.

10 Lemmon, *The Golden Age of Plant Hunters*, p 16.

II

1 Walter Nicol, *The Gardener's Kalendar* (Edinburgh, 1810).

2 Kenneth Lemmon, *The Golden Age of Plant Hunters* (London, 1968).

3 *Transactions of the Horticultural Society of London*, II, 1871, pp 171–7.

4 John Claudius Loudon, *Remarks on the Construction of Hot-Houses* (London, 1817).

5 *Ibid.*

6 Charles Rohault de Fleury, *Dessin pour un Jardin des Plantes au Musée National d'Histoire Naturelle* (Paris, 1856).

7 Nicholas Pevsner, *South Devon*, The Buildings of England (London, 1952), p 51.

8 Stephan Koppelkamm, *Glasshouses and Wintergardens of the Nineteenth Century* (Granada, London, 1987), p 21.

III

1 *The Diaries of John Evelyn* (Everyman, 1907), 7 August 1685, vol II, p 234.

2 The Florentine liquid thermometer, introduced to Robert Boyle in 1661, was only formally disclosed to the Royal Society by Robert Hooke in 1694.

3 John Claudius Loudon, *An Encyclopaedia of Gardening* (London, 1835).

4 John Claudius Loudon, *Remarks on the Construction of Hot-Houses* (London, 1817).

5 John Claudius Loudon, *A Short Treatise on Several improvements recently made in Hot-Houses* (Edinburgh, 1805).

6 *Transactions of the Horticultural Society of London*: II, 1817; IV, 1822; V, 1824; VI, 1826; VII, 1829; and second series I, 1825.

7 *The Gardener's Magazine and Register of Rural and Domestic Improvements*, 1831, part II, p 177.

IV

1 John Claudius Loudon, *An Encyclopaedia of Gardening* (London, 1822).

2 *Ibid* pp 337–9.

3 *Ibid.*

4 *Transactions of the Royal Horticultural Society of London*.

5 John Claudius Loudon, 'Artificial Rain', *Science of Gardening, An Encyclopaedia of Gardening* (London, 1822), no 701, book II (London, 1822), in which he quotes from *Transactions of the Horticultural Society of London*, vol III, p 15.

V

1 Walter Benjamin, *Paris Capital of the Nineteenth Century* (Berne, 1835, and reprinted *Perspecta 12*).

2 See Kerry Downes, *Hawksmoor* (London, 1959), p 64.

3 Brent Elliot and Andrew Payne, *Victorian Flower Gardens* (London, Weidenfeld & Nicholson, 1988).

4 Illustrated in Bradley's New *Improvements of Planting and Gardening* (London, 1718).

5 Jeffry Wyatt dropped the 't' and added the 'ville' to his name in 1824 to mark his renovation of Windsor Castle. He was knighted in 1828 according to Edward Diestelkamp.

6 Edward Diestelkamp, 'Palaces of Light', *Country Life*, 11 November 1993.

7 'The Garden', *The Task and Selected other Poems*, ed James Sambrook (Longmann, London/New York, 1994), line 566, p 130.

8 See H and J A Repton, *Fragments on the Theory and Practice of Landscape Gardening* (London, 1816).

9 See G F Chadwick, *The Works of Sir Joseph Paxton* (London, The Architectural Press, 1961), pp 79–80.

10 D T Fish, *Cassell's Popular Gardening* (4 vols, London, 1884–6), vol III, p 46.

11 Stephan Koppelkamm, *Glasshouses and Wintergardens of the Nineteenth Century* (New York, Rizzoli, 1981), p 40.

12 For a description of stylistic change in conservatories see Brent Elliot and Andrew Payne, *Victorian Flower Gardens* (London, Wiedenfeld & Nicolson, 1988).

13 Georg Kohlmaier and Barna von Sartory, *Houses of Glass: A Nineteenth Century Building Type* (Cambridge, MIT Press, 1986), p 370.

14 *Ibid* p 333.

15 Karl Ludwig von Zanth, *La Wilhelma, villa mauresque de sa Majesté le roi Guillaume de Wurtenberg* (Paris, 1855).

16 Kohlmaier and Von Sartory, *Houses of Glass*, p 277.

17 *Ibid* p 258.

18 Marcus Binney, 'The Mystery of the "style Jules Verne"', *Country Life Annual*, 1970.

19 Eliot and Payne, *Victorian Flower Gardens*.

NOTES

VI

1 See Charles McIntosh, *The Book of the Garden* (Edinburgh, 1853).
2 Weeks & Co; Ormson & Co; W H Lascelles & Co; Messenger & Co; Boulton & Paul; Halliday & Co; Mackenzie and Moncur; and Handyside & Company.
3 See Richard Sheppard, *Cast-Iron in Building* (London, 1945).

VII

1 Loudon's designs for the Birmingham Horticultural Society were published in *The Gardener's Magazine*, August 1832, pp 407–28.
2 Horace Jones's music hall unfortunately suffered a fire in which several people panicked and were killed. It was rebuilt and used as the temporary St Thomas's Hospital. The Surrey Zoological Gardens are now completely built over.
3 Drawing in Westminster Library, 'Marylebone Road', signed by Burton and dated 1842.
4 Burton had previously been associated with Joseph Paxton; his office had prepared the working drawings for the Great Conservatory at Chatsworth. No doubt this led Burton to suggesting the ridge and furrow for Regent's Park.
5 Documented in Westminster Reference Library London.
6 Edward Diestelkamp is the expert on Turner and has written exhaustively on his works particularly that at Kew. See Diestelkamp, 'The Design and Building of the Palm House, Royal Botanic Garden, Kew', *Journal of Garden History*, vol 2, no 3, pp 233–72. See also 'Richard Turner and his glasshouses', *Glasra*, 5 (1981).
7 H R Hitchcock, *Early Victorian Architecture in Britain* (London, 1954), p 515.
8 George F Chadwick, *The Works of Sir Joseph Paxton* (London, Architectural Press, 1961), p 78.
9 Peter Ferriday, *The Architectural Review*, February 1957.
10 *Kew Bulletin*, vol 26, 3.

11 Hector Horeau also received a runner-up prize in the Paris Halles competition and was designer of the winter-garden at Lyons.
12 Great Exhibition of 1851, official illustrated catalogue.
13 First published in 1940 (Cambridge, Mass, 1963).
14 Two main glass pavilions and only one lean-to arm were built in 1833.
15 See G F Chadwick, *The Work of Sir Joseph Paxton*, London, 1961, p 93.
16 Georg Kohlmaier and Barna von Sartory, *Houses of Glass, A Nineteenth-Century Building Type* (Cambridge, MIT Press, 1986), p 161.
17 *Ibid* p 189.
18 *Ibid* p 336, and Koppelkamm, *Glasshouses and Wintergardens of the Nineteenth Century* (London, Granda Publishing Ltd, 1981), p 34.
19 Kohlmaier, *Houses of Glass*, pp 379–81.
20 *Ibid* pp 386–8.
21 *Ibid* p 388.
22 *Ibid* p 281.
23 According to the Mrs Loudon (ed), *Encyclopaedia of Gardening* (London, 1850), p 94.
24 W Bridges Adams, *Westminster and Quarterly Review*, April 1850.
25 See Kohlmaier, *Houses of Glass*, p 356.
26 The Norfolk Island Pine is found in New Zealand and is similar to the monkey-puzzle popular in Victorian England.
27 See Chadwick, *The Works of Sir Joseph Paxton*, p 139.
28 *Ibid* p 47.
29 A more detailed description of the palace and its history can be found in a dissertation, Graham T Smith, 'The Kibble Palace' (University of Strathclyde, 1971).
30 In 1905, a glass People's Palace was built for that purpose.
31 See Kohlmaier, *Houses of Glass*, pp 195–7.
32 *Ibid* pp 238–244.
33 *Ibid* p 267.
34 *Ibid* p 177.
35 *The Gardener's Chronicle*, 7 April 1877.

VIII

1 *Minutes and Proceedings of the Institution of Civil Engineers*, 1849–50, p 166.
2 Georg Kohlmaier and Barna von Sartory, *Houses of Glass, A Nineteenth-Century Building Type* (Cambridge, MIT Press, 1986), p 303.
3 W Bridges Adams, *Westminster and Foreign Quarterly Review*.
4 See George F Chadwick, *The Works of Sir Joseph Paxton* (London, Architectural Press, 1961), chapter on the Great Exhibition, for an excellent detailed account.
5 W Bridges Adams, 'The Industrial Exhibition of 1851', *Westminster and Foreign Quarterly Review*, April–July 1850, p 91.
6 *Illustrated London News*, 6 July 1850, vol 17, p 13.
7 Chadwick, *The Works of Sir Joseph Paxton*, pp 107–9.
8 A construction similar to the Crystal Palace was built at Oxford station. The Science Museum, London, has one of the Oxford bays.
9 A cigarette falling into a similar gap between the floor boards at Sydenham was suggested as the cause of its fire.
10 W Bridges Adams, *Westminster and Foreign Quarterly Review*, April 1850, p 91.
11 Joseph Paxton, 'What is to become of the Crystal Palace?' (1851).
12 See Chadwick, *The Works of Sir Joseph Paxton*, the chapter on the Sydenham Crystal Palace, for an account of this episode.
13 A pictorial history is to be found in Patrick Beaver, *The Crystal Palace* (London, 1970).
14 A more specific description can be found in Chadwick, *The Works of Sir Joseph Paxton*, p 148.
15 See Chadwick, *The Works of Sir Joseph Paxton*, p 156.

16 Paxton was elected MP for Coventry in 1854.

17 Paxton's letter to the editor of the *Illustrated London News*, 5 July 1851, p 11.

18 An illustration of the Victoria Way appeared in *Country Life*, 9 December 1965.

19 Chadwick, *The Works of Sir Joseph Paxton*, p 157.

20 H R Hitchcock, *Early Victorian Architecture in Britain* (London, 1954).

21 *Illustrated London News*, 5 March 1859.

22 John Ruskin, *The Stones of Venice*, vol 1, appendix 17, p 456.

IX

1 Walter Benjamin, *Paris, Capital of the Nineteenth Century* (Berne, 1835, and reprinted *Perspecta* 12).

2 W Bridges Adams, *Westminster and Foreign Quarterly Review*.

3 See Christopher Hobhouse, *1851 and the Crystal Palace* (London, 1837) or John McKean, *The Crystal Palace*, AID (London, Phaidon, 1991).

4 See Susan Buck-Morss, *The Dialectics of Seeing* (Cambridge, MIT Press, 1991).

5 *Ibid* p 89.

X

1 Susan Buck-Morss, *The Dialectics of Seeing* (Cambridge, MIT Press, 1991).

2 *Ibid* p 85.

3 See *Glassarchitektur* (Leipzig, 1914) for an account of the gardens by Scheerbart.

4 Georg Kohlmaier and Barna von Sartory, Houses of Glass: A Nineteenth Century Building Type (Cambridge, MIT Press, 1986) p 190.

5 *Ibid* p 199 for quote from Koerner, *Die Bauten des Königlichen Botanischen Gartens in Dahlem* (Berlin, 1910).

6 Translated by the author from Paul Scheerbart, *Glasarchitektur* (Leipzig, 1914). The statements were incised into Taut's Glass House of 1914 at the Werkbund Exhibition in Cologne.

7 Paul Scheerbart, 'The Architect's Congress', *Frülicht*, 1, p 26.

8 The *Glasernekette* or Glass Chain was an exchange of circular letters, Utopian sketches and essays instituted by Taut and Adolf Behne that linked the group together.

9 Dennis Sharp (ed), 'Das Milieu und sein Einfhuss auf die Entwicklung der Kultur', *Paul Scheerbart's Glass World*, chapter 1 (London, 1972), p 41.

10 'Terraces', chapter 62, *Ibid* p 62.

11 'The Transformation of the World's Surface', chapter 102, *Ibid* p 71.

12 Published in *Wiederkehr der Kunst*, 1919.

13 Bruno Taut, *Modern Architecture* (London, 1929).

14 From *Frülicht*, translated by James Read.

15 Paul Scheerbart, *Glasarchitektur*.

16 *Architectural Forum*, 1967.

17 Letter of 2 September 1965 from James Marston Fitch to Bruce Graham, partner in Skidmore Owings and Merrill, architects of the John Hancock Building, Chicago. This was written as a result of a debate about skin versus structure held at the Cranbrook Conference, in Michigan, during June 1965, which was attended by the author.

A

ABERCROMBIE, J *The Hot-House Gardener …*
London, 1789.

ADAMS, M and Godwin, E *Artistic
Conservatories,* London, 1880.

ADANSON, M *Familles des Plantes,* 2 vols,
Paris, 1763.

AMES, W *Prince Albert and Victorian Taste,*
London, 1967.

ANDERSON, J *A Description of a Patent
Hot-House …* London, 1803.

AUGER, B *The Architect and the Computer,*
London and New York, 1972.

B

BANHAM, P R *Theory and Design in the
First Machine Age,* London and
New York, 1960.

BANHAM, P R *The Architecture of the
Well-Tempered Environment,*
London and New York, 1969.

BASKERVILLE, T *Account of Oxford,* 1690.

BEAN, W J *The Royal Botanic Gardens, Kew,*
London, 1908.

BEAVER, P *The Crystal Palace,* London, 1970.

BENJAMIN, W *Paris, Capital of the Nineteenth
Century,* Berne, 1935 (reprinted
Perspecta 12).

BINNEY, M 'The Mystery of the "style Julies
Verne"', *Country Life Annual,* 1970.

BLUNT, W *The Compleat Naturalist,*
London, 1971.

BOUDON, F and Loyer, F *Hector Horeau,
Architecte de la transparence,* Directions
de l'Architecture, Paris.

BRADLEY, R *The Keeping of Exotics,*
London, 1718.

BRADLEY, R *New Improvements of Planning
and Gardening both Philosophical and
Practical, explaining the Motion of the
Sap and Generation of Plants,*
London, 1718.

BRADLEY, R *A Philosophical Account of the
Works of Nature … to which is added an
Account of the State of Gardening, as it is
now in Great Britain and other Parts of
Europe,* London, 1721.

BUCKLEY, F *Old London Glasshouses,*
London, 1915.

BUCK-MORSS, *The Dialectics of Seeing,*
Boston, 1991.

Builder 38, 1848; 18, 31, 1852.

C

CANHAM, A E *Air-Supported Plastic
Structures, Materials and Design Factor,*
Reading, 1967.

CASSON, H *An Introduction to Victorian
Architecture,* London, 1948.

CHADWICK, G F *The Works of Sir Joseph
Paxton,* London, 1961.

Civil Engineer and Architectural Journal, V, 1851.

COBBETT, W *The English Gardener,*
London, 1829.

COLLINS, P *Changing Ideals in Modern
Architecture,* London, 1965.

COMMELEYN, I *Nederlantze Hesperides,*
Amsterdam, 1676.

CONRADS, V and Sperlich, H *Fantastic
Architecture,* London and
New York, 1963.

Crystal Gardens Preservation Society,
Victoria, 1977.

D

DALE, A *Fashionable Brighton,*
Newcastle upon Tyne, 1947.

DAVIES, J *The Victorian Kitchen Garden Room,*
London, 1986.

DE CAUS, S *Hortus Platinus,* Frankfurt, 1620.

DE LA COURT VAN DE VOORT, P *Lanhuren
Lusthaven, Plantagien,* Leyden, 1737.

DESMOND, R (ed) *Kew Bulletin,* vol 26, 3,
1972.

DICKSON, J *The English Garden Room,*
London, 1986.

DIESTELKAMP, E 'The Design and Building
of the Palm House, Royal Botanic
Garden, Kew', *Journal of Garden
History,* vol 2, no 3, pp 233–72.

DIESTELKAMP, E 'Richard Turner and his
glasshouses', *Glasra,* 5 (1981).

DIESTELKAMP, E 'Palaces of Art', *Country
Life,* November 1993.

DINGWALL, R and Lawton, B *The Climatron.*
date?

DOWNES, C *The Building for the Great
Exhibition,* London, 1852.

DOWNES, K *Hawksmoor,* London, 1959.

DREWITT, F *The Romance of the Apothecaries
Garden at Chelsea,* London, 1928.

BIBLIOGRAPHY

E

ELLIOT, B and Payne, A *Victorian Flower
Gardens,* London, 1988.

EVELYN, J *Kalendarium Hortense or, The
Gardener's almanac directing what he is
to do monthly throughout the year. And
what fruits and flowers are in prime,*
London, 1666.

EVELYN, J *The Diary of John Evelyn,* (vol II,
Everyman, 1907).

EXPOSITION UNIVERSELLE, *Rapport
Général,* vol I, Paris 1891.

F

FAIRCHILD, T *The City Gardener,*
London, 1722.

FISH, D *Cassell's Popular Gardening,* 4 vols,
London, 1884–6.

FLETCHER, H *The Story of the Royal
Horticultural Society,* London, 1969.

FLETCHER, H and Brown, R *The Royal
Botanic Gardens, Edinburgh,*
Edinburgh, 1970.

Florist, XI, 1855.

G

Garden, IV, 1872; IV, 1875.

Gardener's Chronicle 1850; 1860; 1877; 1880;
1885; 1886; 1896.

Gardener's Journal. Dates?

Gardener's Magazine, 1832.

GERETSEGGER, H and Peintner, M
Otto Wagner 1841–1918, London
and New York, 1970.

GIBSON, J *A Short Account of Several Gardens
near London,* 1691.

GIEDION, S *Space, Time and Architecture,*
Cambridge, Mass, 1963.

GLOAG, J, *A History of Cast-Iron in
Architecture.* Date?

GLOAG, J, *Mr Loudon's England,*
London, 1970.

GLOAG, J, *Victorian Taste,* London, 1962.

GORSE, P A *Wandering through the
Conservatories at Kew.* Date?

GROEN, J van der *Der Nederlantsten Hevenir,*
Amsterdam, 1669.

H

HALES, S, *Vegetable Staticks or an Account of
some Statical Experiments on the Sap
in Vegetables,* London 1727.

HESSE, H *Neue Garten-Lust,* Leipzig, 1696,
1714, 1734.

HIBBERD, S *The Floral World and Garden
Guide,* London, 1871.

HIBBERD, S *The Amateur's Greenhouse and
Conservatory,* London, 1873.

HITCHCOCK, H R *Early Victorian Architecture
in Britain,* London, 1954.

HITCHCOCK, H R *Architecture:
Nineteenth and Twentieth Centuries,*
London, 1971.

HITCHINGS & CO, *Greenhouse Heating
and Ventilating Apparatus,*
New York, 1889.

HOBHOUSE, C *1851 and the Crystal Palace,*
London, 1937.

Household Words, London, 1850

HYMANS, E and MacQuitty, W *Great
Botanical Gardens of the World,*
London, 1969.

I

Illustrated London News, VIII, 1848; XI, XII,
1850; VII, 1851; VIII,1852; 1853;VII,
1854; III, 1859.

INSTITUTE of Horticultural Engineering,
Annual Report, Wageningen,
Holland, 1965.

INSTITUTE of Civil Engineers, *Minutes and
Proceedings,* 9, 10, 1849–50; 19, 1851.

J

JACKSON, A *London's Termini,*
London, 1969.

JONES, P P *Napoleon, An intimate Account
of the Years of Supremacy 1800–14,*
San Francisco, 1992.

K

KERR, R *The Gentleman's House; or how to
plan English Residences from the
Parsonage to the Palace,* London, 1864.

KNIGHT, C *Cyclopaedia of London,*
London, 1843.

KOHLMAIER, G and Von Sartoy, B *Houses of
Glass, A Nineteenth-Century Building
Type,* Boston, 1986.

KOPPELKAMM, S *Glasshouse and
Wintergardens of the Nineteenth Century,*
New York, 1981.

L

LANGFORD, T *Plain and Full Instructions to
raise all sorts of Fruit-Trees that prosper in
England with directions about making
plantaions and for making liquors of the
several sorts of fruit,* London, 1681.

LANGLEY, B *The Principles of Gardening,* 1728.

LEMMON, K *The Covered Garden,* London,
1962.

LEMMON, K *The Golden Age of Plant Hunters,*
London, 1968.

LIGHTHOLER, T *The Gentleman and Farmer's
Architect,* London, 1762.

LINDEBOOM, G *Boerhaave, the Man and his
Work,* Leiden, 1968.

LINNAEUS, C, *Hortus Uppsaliensis,* Uppsala,
1748.

LONDON and Wise, *The Retired Gardener,*
London, 1706.

LOUDON, J C *A Short Treatise on Several
improvements recently made in Hot-
Houses; by which from four-fifths to nine-
tenths of the fuel commonly used will be
saved; time, labour and risk, greatly
lessened; and several other advantages
produced. And which are applicable to
Hot-Houses already erected, or to the
Construction of New Hot-Houses,*
Edinburgh, 1805.

LOUDON, J C *Remarks on the Construction
of Hot-Houses, Pointing out the most
advantageous forms, naterials and
contrivances to be used in their
construction; also, a review of the various
methods of building them in foreign
countries as well as in England,*
London, 1817.

LOUDON, J C *Sketches of Curvilinear Hot-Houses; With a Description of the Various Purposes in Horticultural and General Architecture, to which a solid Iron Sash Bar (lately invented) is applicable,* London, 1818.

LOUDON, J C *A comparative View of the common and curvilinear Mode of roofing Hot-Houses,* London, 1818.

LOUDON, J C *An Encyclopaedia of Gardening; Comprising the Theory and Practice of Horticulture, Floriculture, Arboriculture, and Landscape Gardening. Including all the Latest Improvements; A General History of Gardening in all Countries; and a Statistical View of its Present State, with suggestions for its Future Progress in the British Isles,* London, 1822.

LOUDON, J C *The Different Modes of Cultivating the Pine Apple, from its first Introduction in Europe to the Improvements of T. A. Knight, Esq,* London, 1822.

LOUDON, J C *The Green-House Companion, Comprising a General Course of Green-House and Conservatory Practice throughout the Year; A Natural Arrangement of all the Green-House Plants in Cultivation with a Descriptive Catalogue of the most desirable to form a collection, their proper soils, modes of propagation, management, and references to Botanical works in which they are figured. Also the proper treatment of Flowers in Rooms, and Bulbs in Water Glasses,* London, 1824.

LOUDON, J C *Illustrations of Landscape Gardening and Garden Architecture; or, A Collection of Designs, Original and executed for Laying out Country Residences, of every degree of extent, from the cottage and Farm to the National Palace and Public Park or Garden; Kitchen Gardens, Flower Gardens, Cemetries, &c; In different styles, by different artists of different periods and countries. Accompanied by Letter press descriptions in English, French and German,* London, 1830–33.

LOUDON, J C *An Encyclopaedia of Cottage, Farm and Villa Architecture and Furniture; Containing Numerous Designs for Dwellings, from the Villa to the Cottage and the Farm, including Farm Houses, Farmeries, and other Agricultural Buildings; Country Inns, Public Houses, and Parochial Schools: With the Requisite Fittings-up, Fixtures, and Furniture; and Appropriate Offices, Gardens, and Garden Scenery; Each Design Accompanied by Analytical and Critical Remarks,* London, 1832–3.

LOUDON, J C *The Suburban Gardener & Villa Companion; Comprising the choice of a suburban villa residence, or of a situation on which to form one; the arrangement and furnishing of the house; and the laying out, planting and general management of the garden and grounds,* London, 1838.

LOUDON, J C *The Derby Arboretum: Containing a catalogue of the trees and shrubs included in it; a description of the grounds and directions for their management; a copy of the address delivered when it was presented to the Town Council of Derby; by its founder, Joseph Strutt, Esq. And an account of the ceremonies which took place when it was opened to the public, on September 16, 1840,* London, 1840.

LOUDON, Mrs (ed) *Encyclopeaedia of Gardening,* London, 1850.

LODDIGES, Conrad and Sons, *The Botanical Cabinet,* I, 1817.

LORD and Burnham, *Some Greenhouses We have Built,* New York, 1929.

M

MACFARLANE, W *Catalogue of Cast-Iron Manufactures,* 6th ed, II, Glasgow, 1882.

MARKHAM, V *Paxton and the Bachelor Duke,* London, 1935.

MARREY, B and Monnet, J *La grande histoire des Serres and des Jardins d'Hiver France,* Paris, 1900.

MARSTON, P *The Book of the Conservatory,* London, 1992.

MATHESON, E *Works in Iron,* London, 1873.

MCCRACKEN, E *The Palm House and Botanic Garden, Belfast,* Belfast, 1971.

MCDONALD, C *Gardeners' Dictionary,* II, 1807.

MCGRATH, R and Frost, A *Glass in Architecture,* London, 1937.

McINTOSH, C *The Greenhouse, Hot-House & Stove,* London, 1838.

McINTOSH, C *The Book of the Garden,* Edinburgh, 1853.

McKEAN, J *The Crystal Palace,* London, 1994.

MESSENGER & Co, *Artistic Conservatories,* London, 1880.

MIGNOT, C *Architecture of the Nineteenth Century,* Fribourg, 1983.

MILLER, P *The Gardener's Dictionary,* London, 1731.

MOORE, D *Botanical & Horticultural Tours,* London, 1860.

MUSGRAVE, C *The Royal Pavilion,* Brighton, 1951.

N

NICOL, W *The Gardener's Kalender,* Edinbugh, 1810.

O

VAN OOSTEN, H *The Dutch Gardener,* London, 1703.

O'BRAIN, P *Joseph Banks,* 1993.

P

Perspecta, vol 1, New Haven, Conn, 1952.
PAXTON, J *What is to become of the Crystal Palace?* London, 1851.
PEVSNER, N *Pioneers of Modern Design,* London, 1960.
PEVSNER, N *South Devon: The Buildings of England,* London, 1952.
PLATT, H *The Garden of Eden,* London, 1654.
Punch, London, 1851.

R

REPTON, H *Sketches and Hints on Landscape Gardening,* London, 1794.
REPTON, H *Observations on the Theory and Practice of Landscape Gardening; including some remarks on Grecian and Gothic Architecture,* London, 1803.
REPTON, H *Designs for the Pavilion at Brighton,* London, 1808.
REPTON, H and J A *Fragments on the Theory and Practice of Landscape Gardening; including some remarks on Grecian and Gothic Architecture,* London, 1816.
Revue Générale de l' Architecture et des Travaux Publiques, Paris, 1849.
ROBINSON, W *The Garden,* London, 1872.
ROHAULT DE FLEURY, C *Dessin Pour un Jardin des Plantes au Musée National d'Histoire Naturelle,* Paris, 1856.
ROWAN, A *Garden Buildings,* London, 1968.
ROWLEY, W *The Garden under Glass,* 1914.
RUSKIN, J *The Stones of Venice,* London, 1851–3.

S

SAUNDERS, A *Regent's Park,* London, 1969.
SCHEERBART, P *Glasarchitektur,* Leipzig, 1914.
SHARP, D (ed), *Paul Scheerbart's Glass World,* London, 1972.
SHAW, C, *London's Market-Gardens,* London, 1880.
SHAW, J, *Forcing Houses ...* Whitby, 1794.
SHEPPERD, R, *Cast-Iron in Building,* London, 1945.
SIMO, M L, *Loudon and the Landscape: From Country Seat to Metropolis,* New Haven and London, 1988.
SMITH, G T, *The Kibble Palace,* dissertation for University of Strathclyde, Glasgow, 1971.
SWEET, R, *Hot-House & Greenhouse Manual,* London, 1825.
SWITZER, S *The Practical Fruit Gardener,* London, 1724.

T

TAUT, B *Alpine Architecture,* Leipzig, 1919.
TAUT, B (ed) *Frühlicht,* Magdeburg, 1920.
TAUT, B *Modern Architecture,* London, 1929.
TAYLOR, G *Some Nineteeth-Century Gardeners,* London, 1951.
TEXIER, E *Tableau de Paris,* Paris, 1853.
THORNBURY, G W *Old and New London,* 1873–8.
THOMPSON, J *A Practical Treatise on the Construction of Stoves and other Horticultural Buildings,* London, 1838.
TOD, G *Plans, Elevations and Sections of Hot-Houses, Greenhouses ... an Aquarium, Conservatories etc, including a Hot-House and Greenhouse in Her Majesty's Gardens at Frogmore,* London, 1812.
Transactions of the Horticultural Society, II,1817; IV, 1822; V, 1824; VI, 1826; VII, 1829; second series, I, 1835.
TRESIDDER, J and Cliff, S *Living under Glass,* New York, 1986.

V

VEITCH, J *Hortus Vechii,* London, 1906.

W

WEBBER, R, *The Early Horticulturists,* Newton Abbot, 1968.
WEBBER, R *Covent Garden,* London, 1969.
Westminster and Foreign Quarterly Review, I, 1850.
WOODS, M and Swatz Warren, A *Living under Glass,* New York, 1986.
WRIGHT, W *Greenhouses, their Construction and Equipment,* London, 1917.

Z

ZANTH, K L von, La *Wilhelma, villa mauresque de sa Majesté le voi Guilliame de Wurtenberg, exécuté d'après les plans et sous la direction de L. de Zanth,* Paris, 1855.

AKG, London p94 fig 42, p174 fig 98, p218 fig 8, p219 fig 12.

Arcaid: Martine Hamilton-Knight/Arcaid p78 fig 7, fig 8, fig 9; Richard Bryant/Arcaid p82 fig 16; p101 fig 57; p146/6 fig 33; p150 fig 39; p226 fig 23, fig 24; p227 fig 25.

© Ashmolean Museum, Oxford p17 fig 22

Courtesy of Emilio Ambasz p215 fig 3, p225 fig 20,21,22.

© Bibliothèque centrale MNHN, Paris p154 fig 50.

© Bibliothèque Nationale de France, Paris p206 fig 12, p210 fig 20, 21, 22.

Botanical Garden, University of Copenhagen p156 fig 54, 55, 56, 57.

Botanischer Garten und Botanisches Museum Berlin-Dahlem, Ikonothek – Photo M Heilmeyer 1994 p157 fig 59, p218 fig 9, p219 fig 10, 13.

British Library, London/Bridgeman Art Library, London p63 fig 15.

Canadian National Exhibition Archives p202 fig 4, 5

Gerard J Moudry, retired Chief Horticulturist, Dept of Recreation and Parks, City of Baltimore, Maryland, USA, p161 fig 68.

Collection de l'Académie d'Architecture, Paris p7; p168

fig 83, p169 fig 84, fig 85.

© Country Life Picture Library p60 fig 8, p91 fig 36, p118 fig 5.

Devonshire Collection, Chatsworth. Reproduced by permission of the Chatsworth Settlement Trustees p65 fig 19, p89 fig 32.

Ecole Nationale Supérieure des Beaux-Arts, Paris p161 fig 67

Edifice/Lewis p140 fig 23

Royal Botanic Garden Edinburgh p57 fig 3, p151 fig 42, 43.

Emap Construction: p190 fig 24

Eno Collection Miriam and Ira D Wallach Division of Art, Prints and Photographs, The New York Public Library, Astor, Lenox and Tilden Foundations p25 fig 38.

E T Archive p2.

Mary Evans Picture Library p44 fig 4

Mark Fiennes p27 fig 40.

John Feltwell/Garden Matters p104 fig 61, p105 fig 64, p164 fig 75,76,77.

The Garden Picture Library: The Garden Picture Library/John Riley, p79 fig 10, The Garden Picture Library/John Bethell p80 fig 13, The Garden Picture Library/Brigitte Thomas p89 fig 31, The Garden Picture Library/Joanne Pavia p128 fig 30.

Liz Garnett p18 fig 23, p64 fig 17, 18, p152 fig 47, p155 fig 53.

Robert Muir Gibb p67 fig 25.

Sophia Gibb p137 fig 16.

Giraudon/Bridgeman Art Library p9 fig 3

Guildhall Library, Corporation of London p193 fig 29, 30

Guildhall Library, Corporation

of London/Bridgeman Art Library, London p186 fig 18, p191 fig 25.

Kunsthalle Hamburg p157 fig 58.

John Hewitt p48 fig 12, p98 fig 50.

Keith Hewitt, Photographer p36 fig 16, p77 fig 6.

Angelo Hornak, Photographic Library p86 fig 25.

INBEL p109 fig 71, fig 72

INDEX/Cantarelli p17 fig 20, p126 fig 27; INDEX p 17 fig 21.

Meg Jullien p134 fig 9.

Anthony King/Medimage p20 fig 28, p80 fig 14, p102 fig 58, p103 fig 59, fig 60, p106 fig 66, p107 fig 67, 68, p111 fig 79, p117 fig 3, p125 fig 22, p127 fig 28, p 127 fig 29 p169 fig 86.

Landeshauptstadt Hannover p106 fig 65

R Lautman/Monticello p26 fig 39.

London Borough of Lambeth Archive Department p135 fig 12.

Maidstone Museum and Art Gallery, Kent/Bridgeman Art Library, London p189 fig 23.

Tony Mott p216 fig 4.

Musée des Beaux-Arts, Pau/Bridgeman Art Library, London p76 fig 5.

Nationalmuseum Stockholm p11 fig 8.

Natural History Museum/Bridgeman p13 fig 12.

Photo courtesy of the New York Botanical Garden, Bronx, NY p162 fig 69, p162 fig 71, 72.

Novosti p160 fig 64, 65.

Österreichische Nationalbibliothek, Vienna p159 fig 62, 63.

Courtesy of the Royal Ontario Museum, Toronto, Canada p203 fig 6.

Hugh Palmer p22 fig 31, 32, p29 fig 30, p41 fig 25,26,27, p65 fig 20, p73 fig 33, p79 fig 11, p81 fig 15, p83 fig 19, p87 fig 27, p96 fig 47, p132 fig 5.

Photothèque des Musées de la Ville de Paris p24 fig 35, p166

fig 78,79.

© Photo RMN p30 fig 4, p31 fig 5.

Pilkington Archive. Reproduced with permission of Pilkington plc p23 fig 34.

Private Collection/Bridgeman Art Library, London p14 fig 13.

Rheinisches Bildarchiv p172 fig 93, 94.

Royal Botanical Gardens, Kew/Bridgeman Art Library, London p10 fig 5.

Royal Horticultural Society, Lindley Library p32 fig 6, p62 fig 14, p68 fig 26.

The British Architectural Library, RIBA, London p 55 fig 28, p84 fig 21, p85 fig 22, 23, 24, p87 fig 28, p90 fig 33.

Glyn Satterley p84 fig 20, p131 fig 3, p151 fig 44, p170 fig 87, 88, p174 fig 100.

Fritz von der Schulenberg/The Interior Archive p91 fig 35

Harry Smith Horticultural Collection p86 fig 26, p133 fig 8.

The Friends of Sefton Park Palm House p 129 fig 32.

With permission of Sheffield City Council Recreation Department p134 fig 10.

The Slide File: Tim Hannan/The Slide File p139 fig 20; George Munday/The Slide File p140 fig 22, p141 fig 25.

Stadtmuseum Munich p206 fig 11.

Stapleton Collection, London p177 fig 3.

Stapleton Collection/Bridgeman Art Library, London p186/7 fig 17, p188 fig 20.

Rupert Truman: front cover, p43 fig 3, p75 fig 3, p144 fig 29, p145 fig 30.

Courtesy of the Board of Trustees of the V&A Museum, London, p5, p13 fig 11.

Victoria & Albert Museum, London/Bridgeman Art Library, London p21 fig 29, p178 fig 4, p180 fig 7.

Viennaslide/Harald Jahn p158 fig 60, p159 fig 61.

Collection Roger-Viollet p141 fig 26, p212 fig 24, p220 fig 14.

Bildarchiv der Landeshauptstadt, Wiesbaden p171 fig 89.

Yale Centre for British Art, Yale University Art Gallery, Gift of Yale University Gallery Associates and Charles Scribners & Co p194 fig 31.

PHOTOGRAPHIC CREDITS

ACKNOWLEGEMENTS
For Neeva Gayle

THIS new edition carries with it two sets of acknowledgements formulated many years apart. FIRSTLY my thanks must go to David Jenkins, Phaidon's discerning architectural editor, who was instrumental in commissioning this edition based on the original that had been in print for some seventeen years. He has been an invaluable guide along the way. At Phaidon, editor Helen Castle accepted the daunting task of ensuring continuity and rigour in the text and Sophia Gibb took up the marathon challenge of finding new exciting colour photographs of the extant glasshouses.

THE original edition published in 1974 could be considered a seminal work. I am indebted to others who have subsequently carried on with their own research, articles and books, particularly Georg Kohlmaier and Barna von Sartory, Stefan Koppelkamm, May Woods and Arete Swartz Warren, and Edward Diestelkamp. Brent Elliott, garden historian, glasshouse author and

librarian at the Royal Horticultural Society's Lindley Library was very helpful in offering his research and articles for my review. Here in Canada, architectural historian Stephen Otto provided valuable sources and Dr Eric Hood did a rigorous edit of the text for which I am most grateful. On a more practical level, my wife and I made several trips to London where we were graciously sheltered by our friends Anthony and Nancy Whyatt. IN the early 1970s, many individuals and organizations contributed to my original study. The students at the University of Cambridge that built my experimental glasshouse included Clare Frankl, Brenda and Robert Vale, Jean-Paul Porchon, Dan O'Neil, Murdah and Michael Goulden, who later wrote a paper on early glasshouses and helped me in my research. Allan Baird and Richard Winterton produced a beautiful historic brochure which indicated to me that this material could be a book. Graham Smith, former student in the Department of Architecture, University of Strathclyde, gave me excellent information on the Kibble Palace. THE University of Cambridge helped finance our glasshouse experiment and Professor Sir Leslie Martin and my fellow teachers at the Department of Architecture provided a Brancusi Travel Fellowship.

I AM particularly indebted to the directors of many botanical gardens for their information. They include those at: Belgian Botanical Gardens, Meise; Hamburg Botanic Gardens; Jardin des Plantes, Paris; Longwood Gardens, Brandywine, Pennsylvania; Milwaukee County Botanic Gardens; and Missouri Botanic Gardens, St Louis. I am also most grateful to: Aidan Brady, Director of the National Botanic Gardens, Glasnevin, Dublin; Gilbert Daniels, Director of the Hunt Botanical Library, Pittsburgh; Professor T Eckardt, Director of the Berlin-Dahlem Botanic Gardens; and H J Van Hattum, Director of the Leiden University Botanic Gardens. Director John Gilmore and his staff at the Cambridge Botanic Garden were most helpful and gave me free run of their rare books; and R Desmond, formerly librarian at the Royal Botanic Gardens, Kew, generously forwarded many of his valuable references to me and advised on the section about Richard Turner.

GARDEN author Miles Hadfield sent me important references and advised on the original manuscript, as did Professor G F Chadwick. Professor Reyner Banham provided the initial inspiration by suggesting that perhaps the nineteenth-century horticultural environment could be as interesting as nineteenth-century architecture.

MANY London Libraries have been of assistance: British Museum; Chiswick District Library; Guildhall Library and Art Gallery; London Borough of Lambeth, Minet Library; Rare Prints Library of the Greater London Council; and Westminster City Libraries. Other sources have also proved invaluable. They include: Bibliothèque Nationale, Paris; Leiden University Library Map Department; Historic American Building Survey; University Cambridge Library; and Department of Architecture and Fine Arts, Cambridge.

THE Danish architects Ib and Jorgen Rasmussen gave me initial ideas and photographs. The Belgium Embassy in London organized a visit to the Royal Garden at Laeken. SEVERAL companies contributed information and assistance: Pilkington Brothers Ltd, Howard Cross of Lord and Burnham and Michael Hope of Critall-Hope. For the original edition I am indebted to the staff at the Department of Architecture, Cambridge, and particularly Christine Albut who struggled through my rough notes and Frank Lipsius for editing the original text.

Tottenham, Ontario
January 1996

PHAIDON PRESS LTD
Regent's Wharf
All Saints Street
London N1 9PA

PHAIDON PRESS INC.
180 Varick Street
New York, NY 10014

www.phaidon.com

First published 1996
Reprinted in paperback 2005
© 1996 Phaidon Press Limited

Text © John Hix

ISBN 0 7148 4525 6

A CIP catalogue record for this book is available from the British Library.

Library of Congress Cataloging In Publication Data available.

Printed in Hong Kong